Intelligent Assistant Systems: Concepts, Techniques and Technologies

Table of Contents

Preface vi

Section I:
Foundations

Chapter I
Interaction Scenarios for Information Extraction 1
Gunter Grieser, Technical University Darmstadt, Germany
Steffen Lange, University of Applied Sciences Darmstadt,
Germany

Chapter II
Assistance and Induction: The Therapy Planning Case 15
Klaus Jantke, Research Institute for Information Technologies,
Germany
Nataliya Lamonova, Hokkaido University, Japan

Chapter III
Wrapper Induction Programs as Information Extraction
Assistants 35
    Klaus Jantke, Research Institute for Information Technologies,
       Germany
    Carsten Müller, SAP AG, Germany

Chapter IV
Modeling Confidence for Assistant Systems 64
    Roland H. Kaschek, Massey University, New Zealand

Chapter V
Intelligent Support for Building Knowledge Bases for
Natural Language Processing 86
    Son Bao Pham, University of New South Wales, Australia
    Achim Hoffmann, University of New South Wales, Australia

Chapter VI
Formalization of User Preferences, Obligations and Rights 114
    Klaus-Dieter Schewe, Massey University, New Zealand
    Bernhard Thalheim, Christian Albrechts University Kiel,
       Germany
    Alexei Tretiakov, Massey University, New Zealand

Section II:
The Memetics Approach to Assistance

Chapter VII
Building Intelligent Multimodal Assistants Based on Logic
Programming in the Meme Media Architecture 145
    Kimihito Ito, Hokkaido University, Japan

Chapter VIII
From Planning Tools to Intelligent Assistants: Meme Media and
Logic Programming Technologies 169
    Nataliya Lamonova, Hokkaido University, Japan
    Kimihito Ito, Hokkaido University, Japan
    Yuzuru Tanaka, Hokkaido University, Japan

Chapter IX
Memetic Approach to the Location-Based Ad Hoc Federation
of Intelligent Resources 182
  Yuzuru Tanaka, Hokkaido University, Japan

Section III:
Applications

Chapter X
From E-Learning Tools to Assistants by Learner Modelling
and Adaptive Behavior 212
  Klaus Jantke, Research Institute for Information Technologies,
    Germany
  Christoph Igel, Universität des Saarlandes, Germany
  Roberta Sturm, Universität des Saarlandes, Germany

Chapter XI
Mathematics in Virtual Knowledge Spaces: User Adaptation
by Intelligent Assistants 232
  Sabina Jeschke, Berlin University of Technology, Germany
  Thomas Richter, Berlin University of Technology, Germany

Chapter XII
Building a Virtual Trainer for an Immersive Haptic Virtual
Reality Environment 264
  Alexander Krumpholz, CSIRO ICT Centre, Australia

Glossary 280

About the Authors 315

Index 321

Preface*

Intelligent Assistant Systems

Information is becoming the raw material of modern society. That "difference that makes a difference" (Bateson, 1979) is the driving force of modern service industry. Our information spaces have been technologized and their size as well as their complexity increased. Access to information spaces and the capability to use them effectively and efficiently has become a key economical success factor. An information dilemma has been diagnosed (Kuhlen, 1999). The alternatives are (1) to search the information spaces oneself and spend an increasing amount of time for satisfying one's information needs; and (2) to delegate the searching task to an information assistant the performance of which is time-consuming to control and the effectiveness of which is hard to assess. The first choice dominates currently. However, using such an information assistant must be the ultimate goal, as one cannot reasonably expect that technologization will stop or even be undone. In fact technologizing of the world has a long history. It is inextricably connected with technologizing the word, (Ong, 1996, p. 101), as "(s)poken words are always modifications of a total situation which is more than verbal. They never occur alone, in a context simply of words." Technologization has significantly restructured human consciousness Ong (1996). What we are witnessing right now should be understood as the latest step in the process of technologizing the word. That process began with the invention of script (about 3200-3100 BCE), and was followed by the invention of letters (about 1500 BCE), and print (1540 CE) (Ifrah, 2000, pp. 3-25).[1] The latest step is the automation of uttering and understanding words and text in which we here include calculation and computation. This sums up the capability of verbally controlling processes of all kinds. Enzensberger (1970) reports the analogy that El Lissitsky drew in 1923 between language use and modes of transportation and, in particular, vehicles. He related articulated language to upright gait; writing to the wheel; and the printing press to animal powered carts. El Lissitzky did not suggest analogies in language use for automobiles and airplanes. One is tempted to suggest that computers correspond to automobiles, and the Web to airplanes. Would it be venturing too far to relate intelligent assistants to space crafts?

With this book, we contribute to the genesis of a particular kind of software systems, that is, intelligent assistant systems. Most of the chapters in this book, in fact, focus on what we call "assistance." Currently there is no consensus regarding what exactly "assistance" means and what an assistant system is. Actually, we aim at bringing into existence such consensus. Several chapters in this book suggest preliminary answers to the question, "what is assistance?" This book furthermore demonstrates that assistant systems will become reality, as the technology for implementing intelligent assistant systems is available and the problems that require assistance for their solution are "out there." The chapters in this book are quality assured versions of topics that were presented at a workshop that was held in March 2005. The acceptance rate was below 50%. A variety of issues regarding intelligent assistant systems are addressed such as their scope, purpose, architecture, implementation, deployment, their theoretical background, and use.

The issue underlying this book will not go away soon. Rather, the fact that assistance in the last 30 years has continuously been dealt with seems to suggest that it is used by the various authors because of a need to address a deep-rooted worrying issue. That issue is the role that is played by computers and humans respectively during their interaction. Several authors of the chapters in this book suggest that "intelligent assistant systems" will soon become reality. The technology developed so far and the approaches discussed in this issue show that this suggestion is realistic. A number of advanced general approaches to computer-based technologization of words and text were proposed in the past but were not heavily used in application systems, a point being made in Sowa (2002). We expect that this will not happen to intelligent assistant systems. They will make their way to mass systems, firstly due to aspects of the genesis and evolution of computers, and secondly due to being limited to relatively well-understood domains. The main point regarding the first issue is that since computers were invented in the fifth decade of the 20th century and came into wide-spread use in the sixth and seventh decade of that century they continued to become ever more powerful, so that solutions of practical problems became feasible that were not feasible only a short time before that. It was as early as at the end of the eighth decade of the 20th century that Winograd (1979), relying on a study of the U.S. Department of Defense, wrote that computers "are not primarily used for solving well-structured mathematical problems or data processing, but instead are components in complex systems. … Many computer scientists spend the majority of their time dealing with embedded computer systems such as message systems and text editing and formatting systems." By about 1975 the task focus of computers had changed from computation to communication (Hevner & Berndt, 2000).

With the dominant use of computing technology today being for business application, (Hevner & Berndt, 2000, p. 13), a significant increase took place in the number of individuals who are directly affected by computers and are engaged in using them. They also use computers in an increasing number of domains and tasks. The complexity of problems, for the solution of which computers are key components, continues to increase. The traditional approaches of using computers turn out to be ineffective for these problems of higher complexity. On the one hand, these approaches require the human problem solver to at the same time maintain a good understanding of the overall solution architecture as well as the solution detail. Many humans experience difficulties meeting this requirement. On the other hand, the approach fails to let computers work out the problems and their solutions, as humans often under the applying resource restrictions cannot understand and validate these solutions.

The Oxford English Dictionary Online defines "complex" as "(c)onsisting of parts or elements not simply co-ordinated, but some of them involved in various degrees of subordination; complicated, involved, intricate; not easily analyzed or disentangled." A related but more operationalized definition was given by Victor Basili (see Banker, Datar, Kemerer, & Zweig, 1993). He defined the term "complexity of a system" as the resources needed to successfully use that system. If we consider a problem as a system the main components of which are a current state C, a future state F, and an actor A who wants to transform C into F given the boundary conditions B, then problem complexity can be understood as a particular instance of system[2] complexity, that is, as the resources required to transform C into F. That definition can be looked at from a quantitative point of view. Then problem complexity can, for example, be understood in terms of the number of points being used to score a problem. This approach is similar to the one taken in the Function Point methodology (see Garmus & Herron, 1996). Rather than from this standpoint problem complexity can be considered qualitatively. Then problem complexity can be understood in terms of the kind of resources needed for solving the problem at hand. New levels of problem complexity then ask for new kinds of resources or for new ways of using known ones. In terms of computer applications we think that new resources and new ways to use old resources can best be understood as what could be called "the interlocutor metaphor" or "role" that a computer system plays in an interaction with a human.

The concept of interlocutor metaphor can be discussed in at least two different ways. Firstly, it can be related to other high-level views of computer applications that make up a conceptual framework for understanding such applications. Secondly, the various interlocutor metaphors can be discussed. We follow a top-down approach and first list those views at computer applications that jointly seem to capture most of their diversity:

- **Functionality**, that is, the operations the application provides that together constitute its behavior.

- **Quantity**, that is, the number of computer applications the computer user has to or may consider using to achieve his/her goals while interacting with an application at hand.

- **Quality**, that is, the computer application's fitness for stated and implied needs. In particular:

  1. **Behavior metaphor**, that is, a qualification of the application A that makes its behaviour intelligible, such as *mechanical* (behaviour explanation in terms of the structure of A), *intelligent* (behaviour explanation in terms of the reasoning capabilities of A), *intentional* (behaviour explanation in terms of the affection to objects in the environment of A), *social* (behaviour explanation in terms of A being part of a community of interacting entities), *mobile* (behaviour explanation in terms of A's capability to change the location within the space in which it resides), and *adaptive* (behaviour explanation in terms of A's capability to adapt to its environment)[3].

  2. **Interlocutor metaphor**, that is, a qualification of the kind of interlocutor as which the application communicates such as *tool*, *collaborator*, *peer*, or *master* in the 1:1 human-computer-interaction. Also for the communication with software components a qualification of the kind of interlocutor such as *client*, *server*, *broker*, *proxy*, and so forth. For a more elaborated list of such interlocutor metaphors see, for example, Buschmann, Meunier, Rohnert, Sommerlad, and Stal (1999).

3. **Interface metaphor**, that is, a qualification of the way of using the application's interface such as *direct manipulation*, *document*, and *dialog*. See, for example, Satzinger, Jackson, and Burd (2004) for an introduction.

4. **Interaction type**, that is, a qualification of the type of human-computer-interaction that the application implements, such as batch, transformational, or reactive.

5. **Interaction sense**, that is, the key human senses that the application appeals to.

The interlocutor metaphors for 1:1 human-computer-interaction were taken from human cooperative labor organization. The generalness of computers enables them to embody many different interlocutor metaphors and thus to appear as qualitatively different resources. Computers can therefore be used for solving problems of quite different complexity. The mentioned interlocutor metaphors for one-on-one human-computer-interaction are discussed in more detail below.

- **master – tool**, that is, in this relationship the master is superior to the tool and the latter has no or only little latitude in performing the tasks allocated to him/her. The success criterion applied to that relationship is that the tool exactly carries out what it is instructed to. Successful use of a tool depends on the master's capabilities of, first, to structure problem solving procedures into steps that can be carried out by the tools at hand and, second, to handle the tools appropriately. A currently employed version of this relationship is the chain of command in the military all over the world.

- **master – collaborator**, that is, in this relationship the collaborator has a relatively large latitude regarding what tasks to perform and how to do them. However, the master is superior. The success criterion applied to this relationship is that the master achieves the goals. For that, the collaborator appropriately contributes capabilities to the problem the master tries to solve. Successful use of a collaborator depends on capability to learn about and to adapt to the master's way of conceptualizing and solving problems as well as the master's ability to use the collaborators capabilities and to delegate tasks, that is, let the collaborator do what the collaborator is good at. A currently employed version of this relationship is the relationship between an enlightened manager[4] and the manager's subordinates.

- **peer – peer**, that is, in this relationship partners interact with each other and neither of them has power over the other one or dominates him/her. They cooperate according to their individual goals for tasks and in a way that appears advisable to them. Successfully employing this relationship means perpetuating it and depends on the capability to find peers that are willing to achieve compatible goals and to engage in communication processes that stimulate the ongoing process of goal achievement. A currently employed version of this relationship is the relationship between friends.

These three relationships between interlocutors cause five different roles in 1:1 relationships to exist in which computerized systems can interact with humans. The role of collaborator has two obvious specializations, that is, agent (one might consider the notorious 007 as an archetype of it), and assistant (an archetype of which might be Sherlock Holmes' well-known companion Dr. Watson). In this book we mainly discuss aspects of the assistant role occupied by a computer in the master—collaborator relationship. We forecast that the trend will continue towards more computers becoming more powerful and used more in everyday life and that more complex applications are dealt with. We therefore anticipate that "computers in the role of collaborator as well as in the role of "peer" will continue to attract attention.

The analysis regarding the increasing complexity of problems that have to be solved is not entirely novel. It is actually quite old. Engelbart (1962) writes, for example, "Man's population and gross product are increasing at a considerable rate, but the complexity of his problems grows still faster, and the urgency with which solutions must be found becomes steadily greater in response to the increased rate of activity and the increasingly global nature of that activity. Augmenting man's intellect … would warrant full pursuit by an enlightened society if there could be shown a reasonable approach and some plausible benefits."[5] Engelbart even used a particular instance of the interlocutor metaphor. He called the resource that he was asking for "clerk." There are at least two respects, however, in which we differ in our approach from Engelbart's and comparable ones. We do not aim at creating a particular artefact that would be capable of aiding a human user in all contexts, situations, and conditions. Rather, we aim at domain dependent aids. We furthermore concede that "agent," "assistant," and "clerk" are unlikely to be the only reasonable instantiations of the interlocutor metaphor that can be employed in solving complex problems.

We follow Winograd (1972) in conceiving assistants as systems that understand what they do and that are capable of answering respective questions. In the same spirit, Robertson, Newell, and Ramakrishna (cited after Sondheimer & Relles, 1982, p. 106) write, "One does not wield an intelligent assistant, one tells it what one wants. Intelligent assistants figure out what is necessary and do it themselves, without bothering you about it. They tell you the results and explain to you what you need to know." From an architectural view that spirit suggests that assistants contain a domain model, a user model, and a situation model that combines the state of affairs of these two models as far as these are relevant for the task at hand. We do not aim at conceiving assistant systems as a particular kind of information system, as the latter from a functional view are understood as "technologically implemented medium for the purpose of recording, storing, and disseminating linguistic expressions as well as for the supporting of inference making" (Hirschheim, Klein, & Lyytinen, 1995, p. 11). In this definition and for this preface, a medium is a device or an individual that intermediates between two parties. For several modern assistant systems that would be a too narrow definition, since it presupposes a human being is one of the communicators and the communication —a verbal one. To cover these modern systems one must conceive assistant systems as embedded systems, that is, as systems that are embedded in other systems and store, record, exchange, and process signals. If one matches the master-assistant communication against Shannon's communication model (Shannon, 1993) then one finds that certain encoding or decoding steps may be superfluous. Additional to this more technical point one finds that the assumption of a deliberate choice of messages does not necessarily apply to the input that is fed into an assistant system. Rather, such input may result from a master activity that is independent of the assistant. Consider for example a power-steering or a breaking-assistant. The master's activity (steering or breaking respectively) occurs as a natural problem solving behavior and sensors derive the assistant system's input from this behavior. Furthermore, the technical problem of Shannon's communication theory (i.e., the reconstruction of a message that was chosen at a particular point in space at a different point in space at a later time) is not the technical problem of an assistance theory. The technical problem of assistance theory is firstly to identify the master's state of affairs, intent, and activities; and secondly the identification of those responses to a master's activity that are likely to aid the master in it's the current course of action as well as a qualification of the identified responses according to their suitability of being provided to the master.[6]

With respect to those cases in which a human is presupposed to verbally communicate with the assistant, we, however, can stick to understanding the assistant as an information system. The kind of linguistic expressions that the assistant system is then supposed to handle successfully depends on the purpose of that system, so do the particular inferences that could be made. According to our understanding of assistant systems as highly capable, adaptive, cooperative, domain specific problem solving aid—the mentioned linguistic expressions must enable an assistant to autonomously find solutions for problems the master needs a solution for but does not want to or cannot deal with. The assistant's capabilities must be such that they can be tailored towards an as smooth as possible interaction with the master. A promising approach to that was suggested by Maes (1994). It is based on a three-valued logic ("yes," "maybe," and "no" being the truth-values). The assistant would obtain a confidence value with respect to its current suggestion to the master. The assistant would then match this confidence value with one of the truth values and would use for that respective master-definable confidence threshold values. Further action to be taken would then depend in the obvious way on the resulting truth value.

Intelligent assistant systems are knowledge media, which, according to Tanaka (2003, p. 11), are defined as media to "externalize some of our knowledge as intellectual resources and to distribute them among people."[7] Until now the archetype of knowledge media is the book. Tanaka, (2003, pp. 30–31) provides interesting details regarding the history of books. While books are very effective in disseminating knowledge, they are less effective with respect to operationalizing (i.e., putting knowledge to action) and reusing it, as the book is a passive medium. Tanaka points out that each knowledge medium additionally to the knowledge represented in it is equipped with an access method. The computer is an active knowledge medium. The access methods that can be used with respect to the knowledge stored in a computer can thus be more effective and efficient than the ones that can be used with respect to a book. Also, parts of the knowledge stored in a computer can be stored in "active form," that is, as a program that actually can be executed. Consequently the computer has the potential to substitute the book as the number one knowledge medium. For that to be achieved, however, the computer's powers must be harnessed and suitable end-user interfaces provided. These interfaces would enable modification and reuse of the stored knowledge with high-level end-user-proof operations. This is what Tanaka and his collaborators have aimed at and achieved with the implementation of the meme media. These media are highly relevant for assistance theory, as they seem to have the potential for effective reuse of existing knowledge.

Assuming two systems interacting with each other, Liebermann and Selker (2000, p. 618) define the context of an interaction step as any aspect of that system interaction which is not explicit in that step. With this definition, obviously adaptive knowledge media such as assistant systems have to be context sensitive because adaptation means changes carried out though no respective explicit command; only an incomplete or syntactically invalid one was issued. As Liebermann and Selker (2000, p. 623) note, computer applications always include an application model, a user model, and a task model. Traditionally these models have been only implicit in the application's code. Liebermann and Selker (2003, p. 623) argue that better suited "for contextual computing are systems that represent a system model explicitly and try to detect and correct differences between the user's system model and what the system actually can do." Winograd's 1972 request that intelligent assistant systems should understand what they are doing seems to suggest that an intelligent assistant has an explicit and dynamic model of itself.

If one tries to identify computerized systems that implement the interlocutor metaphors mentioned above then one easily identifies tools, such as case-tools, text-processors, compilers, and so forth, as implementing the master-slave relationship. Regarding assistant systems the situation appears to be more difficult, however. The references (Boy, 1991; Burke, Hammond, & Young, 1997; Kaiser, Feller, & Popovich, 1988; Maes, 1994; Marcus, 1982; O'Connor, 2000; Winograd, 1972) show that assistants were constructed as an example for programming/software development and software project planning; e-mail processing; meeting scheduling; retrieving bibliographic information, piloting aircraft, and browsing (selecting new cars, choosing a rental video, finding an apartment, selecting a restaurant, and configuring home audio systems). There are several assistant systems in modern cars, for example, for steering, breaking, and accelerating. As an aid in the rather well understood area of software component installation, intelligent assistants have found a quite widespread use. In this book we bring some new examples. Of course there are not only success stories. Realizing intelligent automated assistance is quite difficult for domains that are not well understood such as everyday office work. To illustrate this Liebermann and Selker (2000) use the example of Microsoft's Word that has the capability of after a "." replace the first nonblank character by its capital-case version (i.e., replace "r" by "R").[8] Word often, even after a user has undone that correction, recorrects, and uses the capital character. It would not be too hard to stop Word from doing that. However, the vendor would have to see this as a sensible feature. Microsoft Inc., for example, has acknowledged difficulties with their office assistant by making it easier to switch on or off. They also have changed the default for this assistant from switched-on to switched-off in the more recent versions of Word.

According to the Oxford English Dictionary Online, an assistant is "one who is present, a bystander; one who takes part in an assembly. Usually in *pl.*," or "one who gives help to a person, or aids in the execution of a purpose; a helper, an auxiliary; a promoter; *also*, a means of help, an aid." This book is supposed to promote the genesis of assistant systems as everyday-life gear. According to our analysis so far, assistant systems are interactive, user-adaptive problem solving aids that understand what they do, accept goals being set as input rather than instructions or deduce such goals, and, once these goals are identified, aim at solving them independently from their user. Assistant systems that interact with humans will often incorporate a question answering component as well as an explanation component. We assume that intelligence can improve effectiveness and efficiency of assistants. We thus anticipate assistants to be intelligent. For us that means that available information is exploited as effectively as possible for aiding the master in achieving the goals. It is characteristic for assistance (of information systems) (Boy, 1991) that (1) the responsibility remains with the master; (2) the master may ask or cause the assistant to execute a task whenever the master whishes so or it becomes necessary; and (3) the assistant may be proactive such that it is ready for upcoming tasks if the respective preparation does not interfere with the current activities.

Agent systems[9] are similar to assistant systems. We distinguish these from each other in such way that agents are systems that have an operational mode in which they are not necessarily interactive, adaptive, or even accessible. Again querying the Oxford English Dictionary Online results in the following the word "agent" may be applied for referring to persons or things. The most important of the replied explanations are (1) "One who (or that which) acts or exerts power, as distinguished from the *patient*, and also from the *instrument*"; (2) "He who operates in a particular direction, who produces an effect. … The efficient cause"; (3) "Any natural force acting upon matter, any substance the presence of which produces phenomena, whether *physical* as electricity, *chemical* as actinism, oxygen, *medicinal* as chloroform, and so forth"; (4) "One who does the *actual work* of anything, as distinguished from the instigator or employer; hence, one who acts for another, a deputy, steward, factor, substitute, representative, or emissary. (In this sense the word has numerous specific applications in Commerce, Politics, Law, and so forth, flowing directly from the general meaning.)" These explanations seem to be consistent with our belief that agents are different from tools as agents act on their own in achieving complex user goals while tools require successive instruction to carry out relatively simple tasks. It also appears to be justified to distinguish agents from assistants. Agents often do their job without much or any interaction with the user. Assistants typically would do their job in close interaction with the user, observe what he or she is doing and propose aid that is likely to be acceptable for the user.

Book Outline

The topics in this book are grouped into three sections. Within each section, the material is listed in the alphabetical order with respect to the author names. The topics in the first section deal with various kinds of foundational problems that are relevant for intelligent assistant systems. The topics in the second section are devoted to the exploration of the use of meme media technologies for intelligent assistant systems. Finally, the topics in the third section focus on using intelligent assistant systems.

Foundational problems that are relevant for intelligent assistant systems seem quite naturally to be connected to the information that such an assistant needs to acquire and use for being an effective and efficient problem solving aid to its master. These processes of information acquisition and utilization seem quite naturally to be related to reasoning about subjects that are relevant for intelligent assistant systems. As intelligent assistant systems are supposed to learn and draw inferences from available data, respective contributions need to explore processes of information acquisition and utilization as well as the structure of the involved subjects. Formalization of these processes and structures is the final aim, as that is the foundation on which intelligent assistant systems effectively can be developed. The Foundations chapter has six topics which in the sequel are briefly abstracted.

The chapter of Gunter Grieser and Steffen Lange deals with the question of how the interaction between humans (in the role of master) and computers (in the role of assistant) may be designed such that both partners are enabled to bring in their respective strengths. In the context of Information Extraction from semistructured documents, several scenarios of interaction are identified and analyzed with respect to their adequacy for cooperative problem solving. The theoretical considerations are illustrated by a particular interaction approach called consistency queries.

Learning aptitude is a must for intelligent assistant systems. The chapter by Klaus Jantke and Nataliya Lamonova focuses on this capability and considers a specific form of learning, that is, planning in complex and dynamic environments. Plans are hypotheses about how to solve a problem. Inductive learning in this topic is identified as a crucial task of an intelligent assistant system. In the area of therapy plan generation, inductive learning plays a particularly important role. Therapy planning must include reasoning about the conditions of plan-executability in the future. Estimates of several future parameter values are driving the inductive planning process. Obviously, aiding problem solving in other domains may benefit from this work.

The chapter by Klaus Jantke and Carsten Müller addresses the human use of search engines and in particular their still often unsatisfactory quality and the resulting negative usage experience. Currently, search engines are tools that are not easy to wield and that are far from assisting their human users. Wrappers are extraction procedures for extracting information on demand. Typed wrappers employing in a sophisticated way information extraction technology have characteristics of intelligent assistants. The chapter stresses the dichotomy of internal mechanisms and external assistance behavior. Jantke and Müller contribute to the discussion about the functionality and quality of a computerized system that establishes intelligent assistance. They also discuss the potentials and risks of a long-term trend of substituting tools by assistants.

Roland H. Kaschek, in his chapter considers the problem of assistance such that it can be separated into two parts, that is the assistant's generation of best guesses of what to propose to the master, and the assessment of these best guesses according to their suitability of being proposed to the master. He proposes using a calculus of confidence in judgments for reasoning about models of the master. Models in his approach are understood as sets of judgments. While he initially considers judgments only individually, he later on provides concepts for combining judgments (i.e., conjunction of judgments and conditional judgment). The calculus proposed allows then to calculate the confidence in combined judgments. The chapter's recommendation is then finally to propose to the master those best-guesses that score highest with respect to confidence.

Son Bao Pham and Achim Hoffman consider the problem of assisting human experts in developing knowledge bases for a number of natural language processing tasks. The techniques they propose are embedded into the knowledge acquisition framework KAFTIE. It has been designed earlier for building knowledge bases for natural language processing. KAFTIE includes an intelligent assistant, the rule suggestion module. This module assists the expert (in the role of the master) by suggesting new rules in order to address incorrect behavior of the knowledge base at hand. Initial experiments with the new rule suggestion module are reported. They suggest that the cooperation between the expert and the assistant may lead to the development time for the knowledge being reduced and the knowledge base to be more compact.

In their chapter, Klaus-Dieter Schewe, Bernhard Thalheim, and Alexei Tretiakov aim firstly at formalizing user preferences, obligations and rights in the context of Web information systems and secondly at indicating how this formalization can be used to reason about a specification of a Web information system. Storyboarding is used for specifying Web information systems and the resulting storyboards are represented by an algebraic expression in a Kleene algebra with tests. User preferences are then formalized using the equational theory of these algebras. This enables sophisticated propositional reasoning that can be applied to WIS personalization. Obligations and rights give rise to a propositional deontic logic that, for example, could be applied with respect to problems of security or safety.

The second section is concerned with employing Tanaka's meme media technology for assistant systems. This technology is not genuinely associated with assistance. However, its potential of significantly increasing effectiveness and efficiency of reusing knowledge artifacts together with computers being active media may actually prove to be key parts in assistant creation, maintenance, and use.

Kimihito Ito introduces a software architecture for building intelligent multimodal assistants. This architecture includes three basic components: a meme media system, an inference system, and an interface assistant system. This embodied assistant makes multimodal presentations available to users. The author's experimental implementation of the architecture is reported. This experimental implementation shows how character agents are defined in a simple declarative manner using logic programming on meme media objects.

Nataliya Lamonova, Kimihito Ito, and Yuzuru Tanaka introduce an approach for creating Web-application capable of operating in complex environments. The approach shows how Meme Media technologies combined with other technologies can be used for solving several kinds of problems related to Therapy Planning in clinical trials. The combined us of logic programming and fuzzy logic for creating Web applications is also introduced in this chapter.

Yuzuru Tanaka focuses on reusing of resources found in the Web. At least two parameters of such reuse task can be identified, that is the scope of search and the required interoperability of the resources. Both of these parameters may change during a reuse attempt in an unpredictable way. Intelligent assistant systems for such reuse tasks must aid the master in performing ad hoc federation of resources. This chapter deals with using meme media technologies for ad hoc federation of intelligent resources over the Web. It proposes the Wiki piazza architecture that works as a repository and lookup service, and combines this service with a location reference service to propose a way of restricting the scope of discovery using location-dependent contexts.

The third section deals with human learning. Learning is an activity undertaken for being prepared to master anticipated tasks. If carried out successfully it thus is highly beneficial for the involved individuals as well as their social groups. Learning itself, however, is a time-consuming and difficult process. Improving effectiveness and efficiency of learning processes is therefore a challenge. A drawback of many approaches that aim at improving learning based on computer technology is that they do not provide an effective learning environment but deteriorate and more or less restrict themselves to content delivery. This certainly ignores most of the complexities in technology supported learning. The topics in this chapter are briefly summarized in what follows.

Klaus Jantke, Christoph Igel, and Roberta Sturm set out with the observation that humans need assistance in learning. Learning belongs to the more complex activities undertaken by humans, as it deeply connected to the complexities of the learner. These authors argue that tools that support human learning tend to be complex themselves and be limited in effect. They propose steps toward assistance in e-learning and systematically illustrate these steps by means of the authors' e-learning projects and systems eBuT and DaMiT. These steps are summarized in a process model proposed to the e-learning community.

Sabina Jeschke and Thomas Richter are concerned with the problem of the increasing speed with which new scientific knowledge is created. They argue that the traditional "learning on supply" does no longer apply and that learners should be guided towards efficient self-controlled learning. They recommend applying new media and technology for achieving a respective turning point in the educational system and discuss four areas of the application of these media and technologies: the presentation of mathematical content; intelligent lexicon toolkits that learn from natural language texts: homework training courses that are able to break up assignments into elementary subproblems as needed by the learner; and virtual laboratories that are able to provide courses that adapt to the errors of the learner and are rich enough to be used in research problems.

Alexander Krumpholz focuses on a particular aspect of the important problem of acquiring physical capabilities (rather than mental ones). He describes the virtual trainer that was developed for CSIRO's temporal bone dissection simulator. This simulation software runs on an immersive haptic virtual reality environment. The prototype system uses a task model based on a finite state machine to describe the procedure and interactive landmarks to trace the user's action in relation to vital structures. This gives the user an activity related feedback. A virtual trainer of product quality needs to take note of the research on intelligent tutoring systems for tailoring feedback for the students and maximize their knowledge and skill acquisition. Various features for such a system are described in the chapter.

Roland H. Kaschek
Massey University, New Zealand

References

Ahituv, N., & Neumann, S. (1990). *Principles of information systems fore management*. Dubuque, IA: Wm. C. Brown Publishers.

Banker, R., Datar, S., Kemerer, C., & Zweig, D. (1993). Software complexity and maintenance costs. *Communications of the ACM, 36*(11), 81–94.

Barstow, D., Shrobe, H., & Sandewall, E. (Eds.). (1984). *Interactive programming environments*. New York: McGraw-Hill.

Bateson, G. (1979). *Mind and nature: A necessary unity*. New York: Dutton.

Boy, G. (1991). *Intelligent assistant systems*. Academic Press.

Burke, D., Hammond, K., & Young, B. (1997). The FindMe approach to assisted browsing. *IEEE Expert, 12*(4), 32–40.

Buschmann, F., Meunier, R., Rohnert, H., Sommerlad, P., & Stal, M. (1999). *Pattern-oriented software architecture: A system of patterns*. Chichester: John Wiley & Sons.

Engelbart, D. (1962). *Augmenting human intellect: A conceptual framework*. Excerpt from Summary Report AF0SR-3223 under contract AF 49(638)-1024, SRI Project 3578 for Air Force Office of Scientific Research,

Menlo Park, California. Reprinted as (Wardrip-Fruin, N., Montfort, N., 2003, pp. 95–108).

Engelbart, D., & English, W. (1968). A research centre for augmenting human intellect. In *Proceedings of AFIPS Fall Joint Computer Conference, 33, Part 1* (pp. 395–410). (Reprinted as C. Wardrip-Fruin, N., Montfort, N., 2003, pp. 233–246).

Enzensberger, H. (1970, November-December). Constituents of a theory of the media. *New Left Review, 64,* 13–36. Reprinted as (Wardrip-Fruin, N. and Montfort N., 2003, pp. 261–275).

Garmus, D., & Herron, D. (1996). *Measuring the software process: A practical guide to functional measurements.* Upper Saddle River: Prentice Hall.

Haase, K. (1997). Do agents need understanding? *IEEE Expert, 12*(4), 4–6.

Häuble, G., & Trifts, V. (2000). Consumer decision making in online shopping environments: The effects of interactive decision aids. *Marketing Science, 19*(1), 4–21.

Hevner, A., & Berndt, D. (2000). Eras of business computing. *Advances in Computers,* (52, Chapter 1). Academic Press.

Hirschheim, R., Klein, H., & Lyytinen, K. (1995). *Information systems and data modeling: Conceptual and philosophical foundations.* Cambridge: Cambridge University Press.

Ifrah, G. (2000). *The universal history of numbers III: The computer and the information revolution.* London: The Harvill Press.

Kaiser, G., Feller, P., & Popovich, S. (1988). Intelligent assistance for software development and maintenance. *IEEE Software, 5*(3), 40–49.

Kuhlen, R. (1999) (In German). *The consequences of information assistants.* Frankfurt: Suhrkamp Verlag.

Liebermann, H., & Selker, T. (2000). Out of context: Computer systems that adapt to, and learn from context. *IBM Systems Journal, 39*(3/4), 617–632.

Maes, P. (1994). Agents that reduce work and information overload. *Communications of the ACM, 37*(7), 31–40, 146.

Marcus, R. (1982, March-April). User assistance in bibliographic retrieval networks through a computer intermediary. *IEEE Transactions on Systems, Man, and Cybernetics,* 116–133.

O'Connor, R. (2000). *An architecture for an intelligent assistant system for use in software project planning*. Doctoral thesis, City University of London.

Ong, W. (1996). *Orality and literacy: The technologizing of the word*. London: Routledge.

Sandheimer, N., & Relles, N. (1982). Human factors and user–assistance in interactive computing systems: An introduction. *IEEE Transactions on Systems, Man, and Cybernetics, 12*(2), 102–107.

Satzinger, J., Jackson, R., & Burd, S. (2004). *Systems analysis and design in a changing world* (3rd ed.). Thomson Course Technology.

Shannon, C.E. (1993). A mathematical theory of communication. In N.J.A. Sloane & A.D. Wyner (Eds.), *Claude Elwood Shannon, collected topics* (pp. 5–83). New York: IEEE Press.

Sowa, J. (2002). Architectures for intelligent systems. *IBM Systems Journal, 41*(3), 331–349.

Tanaka, Y. (2003). *Meme media and meme media market architectures: Knowledge media for editing, distributing, and managing intellectual resources*. IEEE Press, John Wiley & Sons.

Wardrip-Fruin, N., & Montfort, N. (2003). *The new media reader*. Cambridge: The MIT Press.

Winograd, T. (1973, November). Breaking the complexity barrier (again). In *Proceedings of the ACM SIGPLA – SIGIR Interface Meeting on Programming Languages – Information Retrieval* (pp. 13–30). Reprinted as chapter 1 of (Barstow, Shrobe, & Sandewall, 1984).

Winograd, T. (1979). Beyond programming languages. *Communications of the ACM, 22*(7), 391–401. Reprinted as chapter 25 of Barstow et al. (1984).

Endnotes

[1] See, furthermore http://www.gutenberg.de/erfindu2.htm (In German) for different figures that seem to be suggested by latest research.

[2] For an accessible introduction to systems theory see Chapter 4 of Ahituv and Neumann (1990).

[3] The metaphors "mechanical" and "intentional" are adapted versions of Daniel Dennett's "mechanistic" and "intentional" stances. See, for more detail, for example, Haase (1997).

[4] The rate of this kind of manager in the set of all managers is apparently rather small.

[5] It may be instructive to also take note of Engelbart and English (1968).

[6] A very similar view is taken in Liebermann and Selker (2000, p. 620).

[7] Please note that I use the term "knowledge representation" as a metaphorical expression. I do not really believe that knowledge can be represented. Rather I think that Shannon's communication model applies to human communication. According to this model humans select messages but send and receive only signals. Human communication has a chance of working out fine if these signals then can be decoded and a suitable message be re-constructed. In my view the term "knowledge" refers to a reification of the capability of systems to respond to external stimuli differently when they occur at different times or repeatedly.

[8] Obviously the "." is taken as an indicator for the end of sentences. That this is not the only use of the symbol causes the problem.

[9] Note that the term (software) agent is used in a number of different ways. Tanaka (2003) discusses three meanings of the word. O'Connor (2000, p. 38) says that among "the agent community there is no commonly agreed definition" of the term.

[*] I am thankful for the suggestions made by Barry Jackson, Klaus P. Jantke, Nadav Katz, and Bernhard Thalheim.

Acknowledgments

A number of colleagues have contributed to this book. This is the place to thank all of you! Without your efforts this book would not exist. The first ones to mention are those who served on our editorial office and who cared for the required reviews being provided: Gunter Grieser (Technical University of Darmstadt), Klaus P. Jantke (FIT-Leipzig), Roland Kaschek, Kinshuk, Klaus-Dieter Schewe (all from Massey University), Yuzuru Tanaka (Hokkaido University), and Bernhard Thalheim (Christian-Albrechts-Universität Kiel). Further colleagues helped us make a good book with the reviews they prepared. They areThomas Roth-Berghofer, Aleksander Binemann-Zdanowicz, Steve Corich, Gill Dobbie, Gunar Fiedler, Sabine Graf, Tiong Goh, Annika Hinze, Alexander Kuckelberg, Taiyu Lin, Martin Memmel, Peggy Schmidt, Jose Maria Turull-Torres, Michael Verhaart, Gerald Weber, Yuejun Zhang, and Xiafong Zhou.

Roland H. Kaschek
Palmerston North, New Zealand
September 2006

Section I

Foundations

Chapter I

Interaction Scenarios for Information Extraction

Gunter Grieser, Technical University Darmstadt, Germany

Steffen Lange, University of Applied Sciences Darmstadt, Germany

Abstract

This chapter deals with the question of how the interaction between humans and computers may be designed to enable both partners to bring in their respective strengths. In the context of information extraction from semi-structured documents, several scenarios of interaction are identified and analyzed with respect to their adequacy for cooperative problem solving. The theoretical considerations are illustrated by a particular interaction approach called consistency queries. The chapter aims to initiate a discussion concerning the design and investigation of interaction scenarios which enable humans and machines to collaboratively solve problems.

Motivation

Today, computers help humans nearly everywhere. In most cases, however, they serve as a tool to support humans rather than seriously assisting them. It is time for a shift from tools to assistants.

When humans and computers are working together, one has to distinguish different motivations for their cooperation. The first motivation may be efficiency. For a human, it is much better to give tasks to the computer in that the user is now freed of it. Or alternatively, the task can be solved much faster by a computer.

More interesting is the second motivation: necessity. Cooperation of humans and computers cannot be avoided if none of them alone could succeed. Clearly, such cooperation needs some kind of interaction—the largest benefit can be achieved if both are treated as partners solving a problem together.

In this chapter, we are interested in how interaction scenarios are composed such that the *overall performance* is optimized. Both partners, human and computer, have to bring in their strengths, and both have to take care of the weaknesses and the needs of the other. The overall task should be divided into subtasks which are—in order to optimize the general performance—assigned to the partner who is best suited to solve them. Current interaction scenarios mainly focus on the needs of the human and often ignore that the human has to provide relevant input to enable the machine solving its subtasks efficiently. How do existing scenarios meet the needs of the machines? How can they be changed such that the machine receives the relevant input, and how to enable the user to provide it? These are the questions we are interested in.

The overall performance is influenced by the abilities of both players, including their ability to provide the respective partner the relevant information. There are two extremes: one is that the human user alone is solving the overall task, which one would not call cooperation. The other extreme is that the computer is solving the problem autonomously, which it rarely achieves and again, is not cooperation. If both partners are really working together in order to solve a problem, relevant information has to be exchanged and therefore a certain level of interaction is necessary. For example, in the scenario discussed in the next section, a special type of interaction is inevitable.

In this chapter, the aspects discussed so far are illustrated by means of a case study. In our case study we focus on information extraction from semi-structured documents—a relevant problem when accessing and processing information available over the World Wide Web. Variants of cooperation scenarios for collaboratively solving the task of information extraction are discussed. Here, we study the two aspects of efficiency and necessity of cooperation. We present an interaction scenario which takes the needs of both, the machine and the user, into account and abstract it afterwards to the general model of so-called consistency queries. A short discussion concludes the chapter.

The Problem of Information Extraction

Most of the content available on the Internet is assumed to be consumed by humans. For this purpose, it is wrapped in syntax like HTML, resulting in particular semi-structured documents to be interpreted and visualized by browsers. Colors, fonts, pictures, and all the other tricks from the toolboxes are used to guarantee that the visualizations are attractive for humans and support the humans in easily accessing the relevant content.

However, finding the corresponding content in the semi-structured documents is not that easy, even for machines. Even worse, more and more content providers now try to wrap their content in a way such that it can be easily accessed by humans but not by machines.

The pictures in Figure 1 showing a page from eBay listing certain products may serve as illustration.

Everyone expects tools (or even assistants) to support them when searching, accessing, and processing particular information. Hence, it would be of great importance and a great challenge if machines could provide appropriate assistance in this task.

While the general task of information extraction (IE) is to locate specific pieces of text in arbitrary structured documents, we focus here on the so-called wrapper approach which relies on the semi-structuredness of the given documents. Wrappers are special programs which are applied to documents and extract information out of it.

For example, you might expect a wrapper that extracts the following information for each product from the eBay page displayed in Figure 1: the name of the product, the current price, and the time remaining until the end of the auction.

Figure 1. A document from eBay and its visualization

As mentioned above documents prepared for the Internet have to be interpreted by browsers and therefore do need to contain syntactic expressions which are controlling its interpretation including its visual appearance and its interactive behavior. The relevant information is embedded into those syntactic expressions. Wrappers can exploit such syntactic structures.

Although experienced programmers are able to create such wrapper programs, this is a rather time consuming and error-prone task. It is highly desirable to have a system that assists the user in the process of creating or finding appropriate wrappers. In the following, we want to discuss different approaches of how humans and machines can solve this task cooperatively.

Variants of Interaction Scenarios

In this section, we discuss several approaches to the design of interaction scenarios for systems supporting the user in finding appropriate wrappers. These approaches are systematically analyzed along the following dimensions:

- the kind of user/system interaction required,
- the assumption about the capabilities of the user, and
- the assumptions about the capabilities of the system.

The general task is as follows. A user visits some document d. After a bit of reflection the user knows which information I the user is interested in. In the eBay example above these are the displayed products, their prices, and the remaining times. To get this information in a machine readable form—being of importance if, for instance, it forms the input of further information processing tasks—the user needs a wrapper that given the document d extracts exactly the required information I.

There are different possibilities for how a system may assist the user to obtain the corresponding wrapper.

In the simplest scenario, one may consider the system as a kind of database that allows the user to access a pool of existing wrappers, say a pool containing the wrappers W_1, W_2, ..., and W_n.

- **Approach 1:** The system displays the pool of all wrappers. The user selects one wrapper, say W_i, from the pool and causes the system to apply W_i to the document d on hand.

In this scenario the user is fully responsible to pick up an appropriate wrapper. This approach assumes that the user has sufficient knowledge about all the wrappers available and their capabilities.

Clearly this approach requires neither any kind of sophisticated interaction between the user and the system nor any particular capabilities of the system. The most exciting part of the job has to be done by the user.

In the next approach, the system acts more like an assistant. It rather proposes solutions, thereby exploiting the information requested from and provided by the user.

- **Approach 2:** The system selects a wrapper W_i from the pool and applies W_i to the document on hand. Moreover, the system displays the information extracted to the user. In the case that this is exactly what the user wants, the user agrees with the choice of the system. Otherwise, the user causes the system to select another wrapper.

By reducing the responsibilities of the user, Approach 2 necessarily results in a session that consists of a series of user/system interactions. Since the system illustrates the behavior of the proposed solution instead of confronting the user with the proposed solution itself, that is, the wrapper W_i actually selected, even a nonspecialist has the chance to evaluate the quality of the proposed solution. Note that a wrapper is appropriate for the desired information extraction task if it extracts exactly the information I from the document d.

There are several possibilities to improve Approach 2. Along the one dimension, one may refine the selection strategy of the system. Along the other dimension, one may exploit the capabilities of the user to illustrate her expectations in a more transparent way.

- **Approach 3:** In case the wrappers selected in previous steps, say $W_{i,1}$, $W_{i,2}$, ..., and $W_{i,k}$, do not meet the user's expectations, in the next step the system selects a wrapper $W_{i,k+1}$, that behaves on the current document d differently than $W_{i,1}$, $W_{i,2}$..., and $W_{i,k}$, respectively.

Compared to Approach 2, Approach 3 does not require any new feature of the system—what is stressed here is the idea to exploit the standard capabilities of the system in a more reasonable way.[1]

The next approach places more responsibility on the user side.

- **Approach 4:** In case the wrapper W_i selected does not meet the user's expectations, the user refines her response by providing more information:
  o The user marks one (or all) information piece(s) that are erroneously extracted, when applying W_i to d.
  o The user provides one (or all) additional information piece(s) that are erroneously *not* extracted, when applying W_i to d.

Apart from Approach 1, all other approaches faced so far require that the user and the system combine their capabilities in order to solve the problem on hand. Although less interaction as in Approach 2 will already do, the capabilities of the user can be exploited in a more stringent way. As one result, if the required wrapper belongs to the managed pool of wrappers it can be found much faster.

But what happens if the managed pool does not contain a suitable wrapper? In this case, a completely different approach has to be chosen.

In the extreme case—similarly to Approach 1—the user may solve the problem autonomously, that is, the user has to create an appropriate wrapper.

- **Approach 1':** As before, the system displays the pool of all wrappers. If the user determines that none of the wrappers in the pool is suited, the user creates a new wrapper, say W_j, and causes the system to include W_j in the pool as well as to apply W_j to the document d.

However the creation of a new wrapper is a rather time-consuming process and, even for specialists, this process is quite susceptible to errors. To overcome these peculiarities, another type of system is required. Now a kind of "machine intelligence" has to be implemented, since the system is responsible for the creative part, that is, the creation of a new wrapper. This results in the following approach:

- **Approach 2':** If it turns out—maybe as a result of the interaction between the user and the system—that none of the wrappers in the pool is suited, the system creates a new wrapper W_j and applies W_j to the document d. Moreover the system displays the information extracted to the user. In case this is exactly what the user wants, the user agrees with the choice of the system. Otherwise, the user causes the system to create another wrapper.

The situation described in Approach 2' differs remarkably from the one underlying Approach 2. The pool of available wrappers is always finite, while there are infinitely many different wrappers that can potentially be created. In the first case, the number of wrappers in the pool managed by the system gives a lower bound on the overall number of user/system interactions. In the second case, there is no such bound. No matter which kind of "machine intelligence" is implemented in the system, there is some need for an appropriate user/system interaction. Without any appropriate feedback, the system has no chance to navigate appropriately in the infinite search space.

In the next section—based on Approach 2'—a particularly tailored user/system interaction scenario is exemplified. This scenario is designed in such a way that:

- The system obtains sufficiently valuable information to be successful in creating a suited wrapper.
- The "machine intelligence" implemented in the system exploits the information presented as much as possible, therewith trying to minimize the number of interactions.
- Even a nonspecialist is able to provide the information required.

The LExIKON Approach: Consistency Queries

In the last section we discussed a couple of interaction scenarios imaginable for IE. The most sophisticated interaction scenario was based in the idea that users and machines cooperatively create wrappers. In fact, a lot of wrapper induction systems based on machine learning techniques exist. In this section, we first want to present the author's implementation named LExIKON. In the second part, we discuss a general scenario—called consistency queries (Grieser, Jantke & Lange, 2002)—of interaction for creating wrappers.

The LExIKON Interaction Scenario

For the sake of this chapter, a short presentation of the LExIKON interaction scenario shall suffice. For more details about LExIKON, the reader is referred to Grieser, Jantke, Lange, and Thomas (2000), Grieser and Lange (2001), and Lange, Grieser, and Jantke (2003).

In the LExIKON system, a user is providing documents and, by pointing to information pieces of interest in a document under inspection, exemplifying what the user is interested in. Coming back to the eBay example one may imagine that the user points to the name, the price, and the remaining time for a particular product, say the book by Rusell and Norvig.

This data is fed into a learning engine. This engine is performing an inductive program synthesis task which generates wrappers. Naturally, the wrapper generated by the learning engine is hypothetical, since it originates from few examples only and may be the subject of further revisions in subsequent steps.

As discussed, the users should not be confronted with the technicalities of the created wrapper. Instead, the hypothetical result of the LExIKON learning engine is communicated to the user by illustrating the power of the learnt wrapper on the underlying document. Instead of showing the current wrapper (written in some cumbersome programming language named AEFS; see Lange, Grieser, & Jantke, 2003), the user is shown what the wrapper is extracting from the current document. The user receives a list of all information pieces that are extracted from the underlying document.

As the current wrapper is generated on the basis of very limited information, it might happen that the wrapper is not doing what the user expects. In these cases, the user provides an example that illustrates what is missing in the extraction results of the system or an example that illustrates what has been extracted erroneously.

When the user is satisfied with the result achieved on a sample document, she may proceed on to another document or, alternatively, interrupt the learning process and adopt the generated wrapper, at least for a certain time. Learning may be continued later.

The general scenario of the LExIKON system's human-machine interaction is surveyed in Figure 2. Naturally, in the LExIKON implementation there are more options to communicate with the system. However, these are not of interest here.

Consistency Queries

The interaction scenario used in LExIKON as well as many other wrapper induction environments like Baumgartner, Flesca, and Gottlob (2001), Chidlovskii, Ragetli, and de Rijke (2000), Knoblock, Lerman, Minton, and Muslea (2000), Kushmerick (2000), and Lerman, Minton, and Knoblock (2003) can be abstracted and modelled in formal terms.

A query learner constitutes the core component of an adaptive system for IE.

Figure 2. The LExIKON interaction scenario

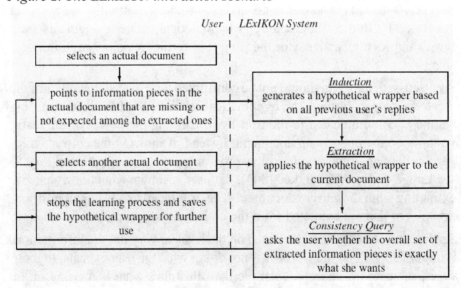

Depending on the overall history of the interaction between the system and the user, the query learner generates a wrapper that is stored in the system. The system interacts with the user by asking consistency queries. Via consistency queries, the system provides the user information about the behavior of the stored wrapper in a user-friendly way. It presents exactly the information pieces (subsequently called data, for short) that the most recent wrapper outputs when it is applied to the most recent document. The user answers a consistency query either by indicating that, focussing on the most recent document, the stored wrapper meets the user's expectations or by providing a counter-example that witnesses the weakness of the wrapper.

More formally speaking, the interaction between the system and the user takes place in accordance with the following rules.

Initially, the system starts with a default wrapper h_0 which does not extract any data from any document. Furthermore, the user selects an initial document d and presents d to the system.

The system applies the most recently stored wrapper h_i to the current document x_i, where $x_0 = d$. Let $F(h_i, x_i)$ be the set of data that has have been extracted from x_i by the wrapper h_i.[2] Now, the consistency query $q_i = (x_i, F(h_i, x_i))$ is presented to the user for evaluation.

Depending on whether or not $F(h_i, x_i)$ is correct (i.e., $F(h_i, x_i)$ contains only interesting data) and complete (i.e., $F(h_i, x_i)$ contains all interesting data), the user is going to answer the consistency query q_i. If her expectations are met, the user signals that the wrapper h_i is accepted for the current document x_i. In addition, the user may select another document d' which is subject to further interrogation and returns the accepting reply $r_i = d'$. Otherwise, the user selects either a data item n_i which was erroneously extracted from x_i (i.e., a negative example) or a data item p_i which is of interest in x_i and which was not extracted (i.e., a positive example). As a result, the user returns the rejecting reply $r_i = (n_i, -)$ or $r_i = (p_i, +)$.

Now, the system stores and analyses the user's response. Based on all previous interactions, the last consistency query q_i, and the corresponding reply r_i, the query learner generates the wrapper h_{i+1} that is stored as its new hypothesis. Afterwards, the process continues as described above.

Next, for the interaction between the system and the user to be a reasonable one both the user and the query learner have to fulfil certain requirements.

A query learner M is said to be *open-minded* if for all users U, all wrappers f, and all interaction sequences $IS = ((q_i, r_i))_{i \in N}$ between M and U with respect to f there are infinitely many $i \in N$ such that r_i is an accepting reply. Intuitively this means that an open-minded query learner does not get stuck in a single document. Conversely, if M is not open-minded, it might happen that the user does not get the opportunity to inform the system adequately about her expectations.

On the other hand, a query learner can only be successful in a case when the user illustrates her intentions on various different documents. Consequently, a user U is said to be *co-operative* if for all open-minded query learners M, for all wrappers f, all interaction sequences $IS = ((q_i, r_i))_{i \in N}$ between M and U with respect to f, and all $x \in N$ there is an accepting reply r_i with $r_i = x$.

Let us now consider the implications of this model. For formal verification, the reader is directed to Grieser, Jantke, and Lange (2002). Moreover, note that the successfulness of the overall approach is based on the assumption that the user truthfully provides information pieces correctly reflecting her intention which is supposed to be stable over time.

First, the interaction is doomed to failure if the involved players (query learner and user) do not meet the imposed fairness constraints (i.e., open-mindedness and cooperativeness).

Second, IE by consistency queries is situated quite far below in a larger hierarchy of identification types well studied before (e.g., Jantke & Beick, 1981). That means that IE as focussed here is quite ambitious and doomed to fail in situations where other more theoretical learning approaches still work. However, the cases in which it works are very well understood by means of theoretical insights.

Next, one can ask about different types of query learners. It turns out that it is always possible that the learner works in a *consistent* manner and can return *fully defined* wrappers that work on every document potentially given. Both properties are known to hardly be achievable in other machine learning scenarios. Further key insights refer to the strength of other properties which might be desirable from a practical point of view. Can IE as focussed here always work incrementally by taking wrappers developed before and just presenting a few new samples? Can a query learner decide when the work is done? It turns out that all these desirable properties turn out to be restrictions and cannot always be guaranteed.

Finally, since the user is only willing (perhaps, even only capable) to process implicit information about the learning progress made, the following effect occurs: although two different query learners may generate completely different sequences of hypotheses, the resulting interaction sequences may be identical, and therefore the user cannot distinguish both learners.

Conclusion

Often, intuition and reality do not coincide. For example, one can prove in the model of consistency queries the following counter-intuitive fact (Grieser, Jantke, & Lange, 2002): The Approaches 2 and 3 discussed do not make difference. Formally, one can always replace a query learner which expects counterexamples (i.e., data erroneously extracted or data not extracted) as replies by a learner which simply needs binary feedback: either the wrapper works correctly or not for the given document. This means, from the necessity point of view there is no need for a more involved scenario. However, if we take efficiency into account, both scenarios differ. Effects like this must be studied in detail.

This chapter aims to initiate a discussion concerning the design and investigation of interaction scenarios which enable humans and machines to collaboratively solve problems.

References

Baumgartner, R. Flesca, S., & Gottlob, G. (2001). Visual Web information extraction with Lixto. In *Proceedings of the 27th International Conference on Very Large Data Bases* (pp. 119–128). Roma, Italy.

Chidlovskii, B., Ragetli, J., & de Rijke, M. (2000). Wrapper generation via grammar induction. In *Proceedings of the 11th European Conference on Machine Learning* (pp. 96–108). LNAI 1810. Stanford, USA.

Grieser, G., Jantke, K.P., & Lange, S. (2002). Consistency queries in information extraction. In *Proceedings of the 13th International Conference on Algorithmic Learning Theory* (pp. 173–187). LNAI 2533. Lübeck, Germany.

Grieser, G., Jantke, K.P., Lange, S., & Thomas, B. (2000). A unifying approach to HTML wrapper representation and learning. In *Proceedings of the 3rd International Conference on Discovery Science* (pp. 50–64). LNAI 1967. Kyoto, Japan.

Grieser, G., & Lange, S. (2001). Learning approaches to wrapper induction. In *Proceedings of the 14th International FLAIRS Conference* (pp. 249–253). Key West, FL.

Jantke, K.P., & Beick, H.R. (1981). Combining postulates of naturalness in inductive inference. *Elektronische Informationsverarbeitung und Kybernetik, 17*(8/9), 465–484.

Knoblock, C., Lerman, K, Minton, S., & Muslea, I. (2000). Accurately and reliably extracting data from the Web. *Data Engineering Bulletin, 23*(4), 33–41.

Kushmerick, N. (2000). Wrapper induction: Efficiency and expressiveness. *Artificial Intelligence, 118*(1-2), 15–68.

Lange, S., Grieser, G., & Jantke, K.P. (2003). Advanced elementary formal systems. *Theoretical Computer Science, 298*, 51–70.

Lerman, K., Minton, S., & Knoblock, C. (2003). Wrapper maintenance: A machine learning approach. *Journal of Artificial Intelligence Research, 18*, 149–181.

Endnotes

[1]   Note that it has to be generally assumed that every wrapper W_i in the managed pool—given any document d as input—reaches a well-defined final stage.

[2]   Here, it has to be demanded that the wrapper hi is defined on input x_i. Otherwise, the interaction between the system and the user will definitely crash. Consider the corresponding discussion concerning Approach 3.

Chapter II

Assistance and Induction:
The Therapy Planning Case

Klaus Jantke,
Research Institute for Information Technologies Leipzig, Germany

Nataliya Lamonova,
Hokkaido University, Japan

Abstract

Software systems on their way from tools to assistants have to be equipped with learnability. This does apply in complex problem solving environments, in particular. Planning in complex and dynamic environments is learning. Plans are hypotheses proposed for execution. How is the system's assistance to the human user related to the system's ability to understand the user's needs and desires? Inductive learning is identified as a crucial task of an intelligent computer assistant. In the area of therapy plan generation, inductive learning plays a particularly important role. Therapy actions planned have to be based on reasoning about executability conditions in the future. Estimates of several future parameter values are driving the inductive planning process. The issue of induction is only one among a variety of assistance features. The present approach has to be seen as a contribution to a larger concerted endeavor towards intelligent systems' assistance.

From Planning Tools to Planning Assistants

"It is difficult to predict, especially the future" is attributed to Niels Bohr in the one or in the other formulation. The words quite naturally call forth ideas about the complexity of the natural sciences and of physics, in particular. Beyond it, these words may nicely serve as a motto for all work on planning in complex, dynamic environments.

By their very nature, *plans* are intended to specify actions to be performed *in the future*. If the environment in which plans are to be executed is not trivial, executability of particular actions cannot be guaranteed under all circumstances at planning time.

Consequently, the generation of plans that are likely to be executable requires reasoning about the future. This is a quite ambitious task.

Advanced computerized planning tools support the human user in thinking about the future—they are reasoning instruments. The present chapter addresses the step from planning tools to planning assistants. Planning assistants relieve their human partners from some of the difficult tasks of pondering about the future.

We should not expect planning assistants to transform unsolvable problems into solvable ones. If the future is difficult to foresee, this does apply to planning assistants as well. It would be a misconception to expect planning assistants to forecast executability conditions which cannot be determined on the basis of incomplete and vague information available in dynamic environments. Instead, we expect them to deal with the high complexity of reasoning based on only incomplete information.

Humans have severe difficulties in reasoning based on incomplete information, because human thinking is usually strongly biased. Humans unconsciously take a large amount of facts for granted. It is rather difficult to find the borderline between justified belief and unjustified wishes.

In a recent report to the European Commission, Bibel, Andler, da Costa, Küppers, and Pearson (2004), the authors stress the point that humans have a tendency towards thinking in local terms and thus are unable to oversee various consequences of their actions (pp. 52, 53). The ultimate recommendation derived in this report reads as follows:

System-based assistants could compensate this local human nature with globally oriented advice based on global aspects of the respective situation. (p. 71)

Planning assistants may outperform humans in "thinking" in an unbiased way. One of their main tasks is induction in cold blood.

Planning in Dynamic Environments: The Domain

Unbiased induction offered as the core competence of computer assistants is the main topic of the present chapter. This topic may be discussed in any area where humans and their computerized assistants deal with the preparation of future activities. For the present investigation, the authors have chosen a case study in medical therapy planning inspired by earlier work in Dötsch, Ito, and Jantke (2005) which has its roots in even much earlier work on therapy plan generation for complex process control installations (Arnold, 1996; Arnold & Jantke, 1997). The present work is intended to complement a publication of this chapter's second author (Lamonova, Ito, & Tanaka, 2006) where technologies for a general planning approach are introduced and discussed in much more detail.

The technologies focused in the present chapter are just the technologies for the assistants' logical reasoning about the future.

For a systematic treatment, we need to recall the basic peculiarities of the underlying domain as done before in Arnold (1996) and Dötsch et al. (2005), for example The first mentioned book deals with therapy plan generation for complex processes like those in chemical installations whereas the second publication is directed towards medical therapy. The issue of induction seems to be almost the same in both cases.

Reasoning when a human's health or a complex technological installation is in trouble is complicated by a number of peculiarities classified into three groups as follows:

1. fundamental peculiarities characterizing dynamics and complexity,
2. domain-specific dynamics, and
3. derived, but essential peculiarities.

For every class of peculiarities, we are giving a few instances drawn from Dötsch et al. (2005) to illustrate the type of difficulties we are facing and trying to attack, supported by an intelligent computer system's assistance.

1. **Fundamental peculiarities:**
    - Several target parameters cannot be controlled directly. For instance, a human's blood pressure can only be controlled through a number of indirect medications.
    - There are several process parameters of which one cannot regularly access current values. Repeated tests, though possible in principle, may by physically exhausting and mentally unacceptable to human patients.
    - The execution of some actions may depend on external resources, the availability of which may be locally undecidable. This is particularly true for actions which depend on environmental details like communication channels, transportation facilities, and administrational customs.

2. **Domain-specific dynamics:**
    - Certain constraints underlying the executability of actions need to be satisfied throughout the whole execution period of some action. For instance, some medication may necessarily require the absence of fever.
    - The execution of actions is time consuming. The amount of time necessary to complete some actions cannot be estimated, in general. Usually, so-called time-outs serve as an upper time limit for executing actions.
    - Usually, there are alternative actions. Those actions may have advantages and disadvantages; there might be no clearly preferred decision.

3. **Derived peculiarities:**
    - So far, the human body is only insufficiently understood. There are far too many process parameters to be taken into account. Data has to be dropped and, thus, all information is incomplete by nature.
    - The state of the human body changes even in case no actions at all are executed. There is no assumption of persistency.

- There are many interacting processes, and even if a current plan is perfect, it may fail by an unexpectable interaction with some other process. For instance, a schedule of surgery may be perfect, but break down if some doctor falls ill. It may also surprisingly turn out that some therapy treatment is more exhausting for a patient than initially expected.

These characteristics surveyed have to be taken into account when subsequently developing the authors' approach toward system assistance in medical therapy planning.

So-called wicked problems are those that are believed to call for more than just tool support—for intelligent systems' assistance. Wicked problems are those problems the understanding of a solution of which is very likely to be changed as soon as problem solving starts. Are problems of planning in complex, dynamic environments forming a class of wicked problems in this sense? At a first glance, this seems not to be the case. What a successful therapy is does not change over medical treatment.

But a closer look reveals that planning under the circumstances summarized do indeed face the typical difficulties of wicked problems. You start problem solving and arrive at some (partial) solution which is truly satisfying. But as time goes by, the previously satisfying solution turns out to be unfeasible. In planning, this is not only caused by a changing and, perhaps, deeper problem understanding of the human user or by a drift in the user's intentions, but by a change of the problem itself. The absence of persistence seems to be the core reason that makes planning in complex, dynamic environments wicked.

It is the authors' strong belief that planning needs systems' assistance. The present chapter can only provide some particular contribution towards future generations of planning assistants.

Types of Assistance in Dynamic Plan Generation

According to the peculiarities of the domain sketched in the preceding chapter, therapy planning, plan execution, plan monitoring, and plan revision constitute some rather complex network of reasoning and acting in dependence on and in response to each other. Therapy plan generation is central and has been in the focus of Arnold (1996) and Arnold and Jantke (1997).

Figure 1. Therapy plan generation in a knowledge processing infrastructure

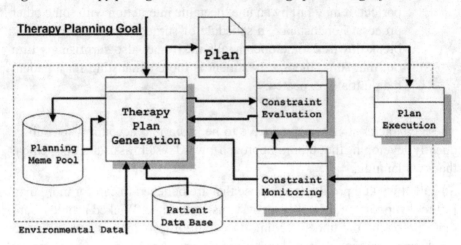

The connections and interactions in such a knowledge representation and processing architecture may be even more complex than depicted. There are, for instance, recent approaches (Nebel, 2004) where the patient data base is dynamically—and hypothetically—updated based on contextual ontologies. The authors of the present chapter are aware of the fact that their system architecture of choice displayed in Figure 1 is just one among several alternatives.

In the system architecture underlying the present work, potentially every reasoning and acting part can be automated. A full medical therapy assistant would be capable of *planning*, of *constraint* evaluation, of *plan execution*, and of *constraint monitoring*. For good reasons that are more social or legal in nature, an automation of plan execution seems currently not very likely. Note that this is a fundamental difference from therapy planning for industrial installations (Arnold, 1996).

The core task to be automated is clearly the therapy plan generation in response to given goals of therapy. Plans are complex objects assembled upon a usually large repository of available actions. Which particular actions may be employed does depend not only on the goal and on the other planning actions invoked so far, but on a variety of constraints that has to be checked at planning time. It is difficult to imagine automated plan generation where constraint evaluation is done by hand. Consequently, a minimal assistant's functionality in medical therapy plan generation does cover the two essential tasks of *therapy plan generation* and *constraint evaluation* indicated in Figure 2.

The underlying databases are also indicated by a light gray shading as these, naturally, have to be available in electronic form.

Assistants for medical therapy plan generation as sketched in Figure 2 generate plans which are then handed out to human users for execution.

It is left to the human user to take care of executability and, if necessary, to return plans for revision.

Derived from the underlying architecture and functionality, there is a linear hierarchy of types or degrees of assistance:

- A minimal assistant for therapy plan generation does perform therapy plan generation over a given meme pool of planning knowledge and with respect to particular patient data. Plan generation does include constraint evaluation.

- An extended assistant for therapy plan generation extends a minimal assistant's service by constraint monitoring for plans that are not yet completely executed. If constraints are violated, it alerts the human user to plan revision.

- A complete assistant for therapy plan generation completes an extended assistant's service. If constraints are violated, plan revision is done autonomously.

Figure 2. Minimal functionality of an intelligent planning assistant

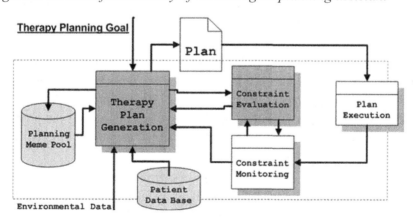

As already said, a further completion of the assistant's work by enclosing execution tasks into its duties seems not to be an appropriate target of research and development, at least for the time being.

The planning assistant's core reasoning processes are plan assembly from available planning knowledge in the given meme pool and logical reasoning about the applicability of therapy actions under given information about the patient's status and the current environmental conditions.

These two key reasoning processes are deeply dovetailed. In approaches like Lamonova et al. (2006), for example, part of the logical reasoning is located in the logic programming technology.

The present research aims at a separate investigation of the logical reasoning process with emphasis on the study of planning assistants of a varying logical reasoning competence.

Inductive Reasoning as Intelligent Assistance

Medical therapy planning knowledge (see Dötsch et al., 2005; Lamonova et al., 2006 for more technical details) residing in the meme pool contains actions that are hierarchically structured and may call further actions. Whether or not an action may be executed depends on conditions which have to be satisfied at execution time.

The key problem of planning in complex dynamic environments is that the values of process parameters at execution time are not known at planning time. Even worse, the exact execution time is usually unknown. For every process parameter, there is usually known some history represented in the patient data record.

Figure 3 is illustrating a few effects of process parameter forecasting. There are variables x and y where history values of x are indicated by crosses x whereas values of y are given by plus marks +. Certain history values are known at planning time t_0. For illustration, we are discussing the problem whether or not the constraint $x > y$ may be valid at execution time which is estimated to range between t_1 and t_2.

The first forecast in the upper right diagram seems to say that the validity of $x > y$ is guaranteed. In contrast, the last diagram suggests that the constraint

Figure 3. At planning time forecasting process parameter values at execution time

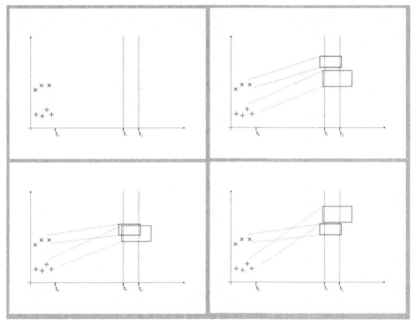

must be violated for sure. The second forecast displayed in the lower left diagram admits of the constraint's truth as well as of its falsity.

Humans engaged in planning need support or, better, assistance in forecasting. The authors suggest to use a neural network apparatus as a forecasting tool, that is, to base the intelligent planning assistants' reasoning about the validity of actions constraints on certain artificial neural network functionalities.

Nowadays wavelet **neural networks** are widely used to perform different tasks in information processing including the forecast of non-linear signals of various natures. The combination of wavelet theory and neural networks has lead to the development of **wavelet networks**. Wavelet networks are feed-forward neural networks using wavelets as activation function.

A proposed structure for a wavelet neural network is shown in Figure 4.

An advantage of this type of neural network consists in the following. Wavelet activation functions are localized in both space and time, which allows it to process time-dependent or not spatially uniform signals of different natures.

Figure 4. Structure of a wavelet neural network

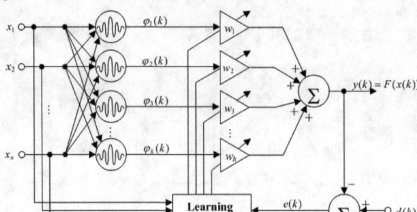

For a vector input $x(k) = (x_1(k), x_2(k),...,x_n(k))^T \in R^n$ to this system, the following output is obtained:

$$F(x(k)) = y(k) = \sum_{i=1}^{n} w_i \varphi(d_i(x(k) - t_i)) = w^T \varphi(d(x(k) - t)), \quad w_i, d_i, t_i \in R^n, \quad (1)$$

where $\varphi(\bullet)$ - mother wavelet function,

$d = (d_1, d_2,..., d_n)$ - parameter vector of wavelet's stretching,

$t = (t_1, t_2,..., t_n)$ - parameter vector of a shift of wavelet,

w^T - vector of adjusted synaptic weights,

h - number of neurons in the hidden layer.

As a mother wavelet, one can use families of such wavelets including Haar, Daubechies, Mayer, POLYWOG-wavlets (POLYnomials WindOwed with Gaussian types of functions), RASP-wavelets (RAtional functions with Second-order Poles) and many others.

As a **learning algorithm** for such a neural network, we propose one that relies on the algorithm for a wavelet neural network on the basis of a sliding window.

$$\begin{cases} w_j(k+1) = w_j(k) + \varphi^{-1}(k+1)(d_j(k+1) - w_j^T(k)\varphi(k+1))\varphi(k+1), \\ \gamma(k+1) = \gamma(k) + \|\varphi(k+1)\|^2 - \|\varphi(k-s+2)\|^2, \end{cases} \qquad (2)$$

where w - adjusted synaptic weights,

d - trained signal,

k - discrete time,

s - length of a sliding window.

The proposed structure for a wavelet neural network has both computing simplicity and the possibility to work with time-dependent processes, a relevant property which has been verified (Bodyanskiy & Vynokurova, 2003; Vynokurova, Lamonova, & Shilo, 2004). Thus, it is appropriate to build on it the assistant's internal reasoning about future medical conditions of therapy planning actions' executability.

Wavelet networks have been used in classification and identification problems with some success. The strength of wavelet networks lies in their capabilities of catching essential features in 'frequency-rich' signals.

Recall that the reasoning process about the validity of action constraints has two subsequent components:

- forecasting the values of process parameters, and
- evaluating constrains over hypothesized values.

The first process component brings in uncertainty, whereas the second brings in arbitrariness trough modality[1] as illustrated in Figure 3. There is a rather deep interference of both processes. Consequently, there is some need for more experimental evaluation and for deeper investigation into the trade-offs of tuning parameters of the one and of the other reasoning process.

For the purpose of the present chapter, introducing medical therapy planning as a case of the transformation from tools to intelligent assistants, this chapter is intended to illuminate the sophistication and the complexity of reasoning establishing system's assistance.

An intelligent assistant performs reasoning processes which are usually far beyond human comprehension. A certain part of the reasoning results can

Figure 5. Hypothetic knowledge (in dark grey) in medical therapy plan generation

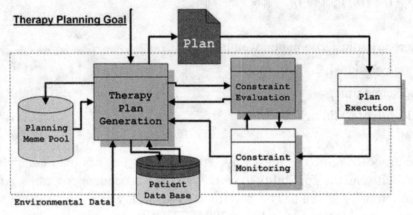

never be communicated to human users. For illustration, a medical therapy plan may contain some particular action of which another alternative has been discarded. When asked, the system may explain the reason for discarding an action by informing the user that the action's constraints are (guessed to be) violated. For demonstrating this, the system may visualize the knowledge about the value pattern over time. Explaining the derivation of (1) estimating the execution time interval and (2) the related process parameter values is usually unacceptable.

The authors' approach sketched in the preceding part of this chapter is slightly changing our perspective at therapy plan generation illustrated in Figures 1 and 2. Related discussions may be found already in Arnold (1996).

It turns out that not only the generated therapy plan is hypothetic in nature. The patient database does also contain hypothetic data written into the database during plan generation. Basically, those data are histories of patient record parameters extended ahead of planning time into the future of plan execution time, though the latter one is also vague and uncertain.

Theoretically, an exact forecast would provide an ideal basis. But one may not count on exact predictions in complex and dynamic environments. Which properties are desirable as substitutes of absolute correctness? This is a question for an intelligent assistant's reasoning skills.

The authors are going to approach the problem in small steps. Figure 6 shall serve as an illustration.

When parameter forecasting is a key task among others of an intelligent planning assistant's duties, it takes place over time. Later forecasts are usually based on more data and may be revised according to the earlier forecasts' precision. Consequently, later forecasts will usually differ from earlier ones, hopefully being more precise.

Figure 6 is visualizing predictions of some process parameter values for some variable y given by green plus marks $+$. There is another process parameter x indicated in red which is assumed to be constant, for simplicity. As in Figure 3, the constraint under consideration is $x > y$. Parameter forecasting is visualized at three subsequent time points of planning named t_0, t_0' 0 and t_0''.

The property advocated here is monotonicity of forecasting. There is no need for predictions as sharp as possible. Instead, a moderate monotonicity seems to be highly desirable. Monotonicity means that the range of a parameter's value predicted is shrinking over time finally approaching the parameter's true value.

In the illustration provided in Figure 6, the monotonicity property appears as the inclusion of a later forecast's predicted areas in those of earlier fore-

Figure 6. Monotonic predictions at subsequent points t_0, t_0' 0 and t_0'' of planning time

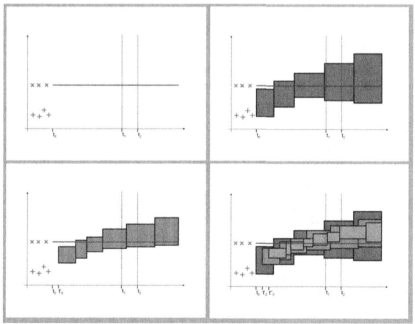

casts. The lower rightmost diagram shows the overlay of three subsequent predictions.

Whether or not some planning assistant's reasoning about future parameter values enjoys the property of monotonicity has an important impact on the appearance of the system's assistance. In addition, this appearance depends, naturally, on the underlying logic of constraints and its interference with forecasting. For simplicity, we assume an elementary modal logic, where constraints are only considered invalid, if there is no point in time and no possible combination of parameter values from their predicted range satisfying the formula in classical arithmetics.

Under such a logical approach, monotonic forecasting implies that whenever constraints[2] are found invalid and actions, therefore, are discarded, there never occurs the necessity to take those actions into account again. This simplifies planning a lot. Intuitively, in dependence on the implemented logic and the implemented forecasting, intelligent assistants may or may not appear, say, serious, that is, discarding therapy actions only in those cases where they really have to be discarded forever.

The Peculiarities of Intelligent Assistance

This section is intended to summarize the authors' contribution. The focus of the present chapter is not so much on technologies, but on the question of what intelligent systems' assistance is and how to introduce assistants. From the case study of the present publication, the authors' key hypothesis is *Intelligent Systems' Assistance needs Induction and Induction makes Assistance.*

The argument may be kept short: The service provided by a computerized assistant is of particular value if it goes beyond the limits of the human partner's imagination. This involves learning about the human's wishes, needs, preferences and so on, but also learning about environmental and domain conditions. In the case of a complex and dynamic application domain, learning never ends. Induction is truly substantial.

To say it more technically, intelligent assistants have to induce hypotheses. Hypothesizing of a computer cooperating with a human has several implications.

- The offered assistance may be based on incorrect or incomplete hypotheses.

- Hypotheses may change over time and so may change the assistance offered.

- The way hypotheses are constructed may be beyond human comprehension.

- Hypotheses may be difficult to communicate resp. to understand by a human such that it may be reasonable to keep them hidden to the human partner.

Understanding these implications is important to direct future research and development. It is practically important to human users who would like to draw benefit from cooperation with an intelligent computerized assistant. One needs to understand the partner, even if it is only a machine. Perhaps the most important point is that these implications are crucial to all social, commercial, and political processes when performing the transformation from computerized tools to computerized assistants.

The implications may be paraphrased quite drastically as follows:

- The reasoning process of an intelligent assistant is beyond the comprehension of the average human cooperation partners. It does not make sense to explain how reasoning results have been achieved and why alternatives are ruled out.

All these points can easily be found in the domain of medical therapy planning. The only exception is the problem of communicating the hypotheses. The key hypotheses are therapy plans, and those are obviously communicated. But this, however, is only the first impression. A closer look reveals that in every hypothesis are hidden pieces of information like, for instance, the expected execution time of every atomic action. In dependence on the logics in use, there may be (hidden) annotations to the action constraints informing the planner about modalities of the constraint's hypothesized validity.

In contrast to other approaches (Nebel, 2004), the present case study deals with hypothesizing about the domain, only. The assistant's reasoning is getting even more involved if hypothesizing refers to the system's knowledge about the human cooperation partner as well.

Related Work and Cooperation

For intelligent computer assistance in medical therapy planning, a considerable number of contributions from different areas have to be brought together. The authors decided to get engaged in a comprehensive endeavor of meme media applications to medical therapy planning. This idea has been first laid out in Dötsch et al. (2005).

Ideas of memetics and meme media are fundamental to a more comprehensive understanding of the overall approach. Relevant fundamentals can be found in Tanaka (2003), where the interested reader is directed to further readings.

The authors are aware of the fact that they might not directly contribute to meme media technologies. Cooperation is highly desirable and Lamonova et al. (2006) may be seen as an indicator of such a successful cooperation.

Research in mathematical logics is also far beyond the authors' intention. They are aware of the need of using reasoning mechanisms which are known to be sound. Logical knowledge is, so to call, imported and one may easily think of a logical calculus as being plugged into the present approach—plug and plan.

Applications in any area, especially in the wide fields of medical domains, require an intense cooperation with domain experts. Future work in the area will require to set up such a cooperation.

There is a side effect to be taken into account. As discussed in Dötsch et al. (2005), the usage of any memetic plan generation approach will ultimately result in some evolution of domain knowledge as soon as the approach is implemented and used under practically relevant conditions. Knowledge evolution is posing a variety of questions not yet completely understood (Jantke, 2004).

Bringing the knowledge evolution perspective of memetics in contact with the current intelligent systems' assistance issue leads to exciting question that may be approached from a more technological or from a more philosophical point. When intelligent computerized assistants are getting active in a world of meme media evolution, do they gain knowledge by themselves? Working for some time in the area, do those assistants know more than their human partners?

Last but not least, it is necessary to carefully distinguish inductive approaches to planning from those that are deductive. Since the pioneering development of STRIPS (Fikes & Nilsson, 1971), AI planning has been dominated by approaches that are deductive in spirit (Hertzberg, 1989). These logical approaches are bringing with them a concept of plan executability—when a plan has been generated on a logically sound basis, it is executable. This is a wonderful assumption for research chapters and for playing with theorem provers. Unfortunately, it has to be abandoned in a world where information is vague and incomplete and, even worse, persistence cannot be assumed. Under those circumstances, appropriate planning approaches are more inductive than deductive (Arnold & Jantke, 1997).

It is the authors' strong believe that this phenomenon closely relates to the issue of intelligent systems' assistance. You may expect a theorem prover to be inerrable, but you never expect this of your human cooperation partners. This does extend to intelligent computer assistants. Part of their strength is based on their ability to learn, including the generation of hypotheses which may be revised over time (Jain, Osherson, Royer, & Sharma, 1999). Assistance in planning encloses inductive plan generation.

Summary and Conclusion

The present chapter has a rather narrow focus within the wide area of planning in complex dynamic environments: *the transformation from planning tools to planning assistants*. The urgent need for such a paradigmatic shift has been clearly identified (Bibel et al., 2004). The intended contribution of the authors' present work is:

- to clarify what does establish intelligent system's assistance, and
- to exemplify how to gradually perform the transformation into assistants.

There are open questions and extensions of the research presented galore. One is the relationship between initial assumptions about an IT system's functionality and architecture. From the authors' underlying system architecture depicted in Figure 1 there has been derived a certain hierarchy of assistance (see Chapter III). This hierarchy is strictly linear. Are there more complex and, perhaps, more flexible architectures of plan generation from which one may derive a variety of ways to transform planning tools into planning assistants? It may be enlightening to study more systematically the relationship between basic assumptions about functionalities and architectures, in general, and their impact on the variants and degrees of derivable intelligent systems' assistance.

A manifold of further problems relate to the modularity of functionalities and architectures. In infrastructures like the one depicted in Figure 1, one may easily think about "plugging off" some component and substituting it by another one "plugged in." Do we consider the databases as external resources or as an assistant's knowledge? One might argue that a planning meme pool is clearly an external source. But an assistant might also have particular meme objects that have turned to be successful in "his earlier life." What about the logics involved? As discussed in Chapter IV, there may be different logics invoked. A logic determines which constraints are considered valid under which circumstances. Hence, using different logics that interfere with forecasting will lead to the generation of different plans or, at least, to alternatives being generated in a different order. Assistants relying on different logics have "different ways of thinking."

Another crucial parameter is the formal language for plan representation. This language is determining the space of therapy plans that may be potentially generated. The space of hypotheses is specifying "an assistant's imaginativeness."

Computer assistants in cooperation with humans are doing work the humans are not willing or not able to do suitably well by themselves. The crux of those intelligent systems' assistance is that the computer assistants are of a particular value if they are able to work in a way which is partially unexpected or which yields partially unexpected results. When human assistants would show such a behavior, we were calling it creative. A closer look reveals that a computer assistant's "creativity" relies on knowledge representation details and on knowledge processing steps not foreseen by the human partner. As seen in this case study, hiding knowledge representation and processing details to the human user does very much characterize the quality of service a planning assistant is providing. So, does the step from tools to assistants means to introduce creativity into computing machinery?

Acknowledgments

The authors have been inspired by Oksana Arnold's seminal work on planning in complex dynamic environments. Yuzuru Tanaka has coined the term Meme Media. His pioneering work on knowledge media has lead to a novel integration of technologies as reported in Dötsch et al. (2005) and Lamonova et al. (2006). Cooperating with Volker Dötsch and, in particular, with Kimihito Ito, was and still is very enjoyable and fruitful.

References

Arnold, O. (1996). *Die Therapiesteuerungskomponente einer wissensbasier-ten Systemarchitektur für Aufgaben der Prozeßführung*, volume 130 of DISKI. infix.

Arnold, O., & Jantke, K. P. (1997). Inductive program synthesis for therapy plan generation. *New Generation Computing, 15*(1), 27–58.

Bibel, W., Andler, D., da Costa, O., Küppers, G., & Pearson, I. D. (2004, July). *Converging technologies and the natural, social and cultural world* (Special interest group report). European Commission.

Bodyanskiy, Y.V., & Vynokurova, O.A. (2003). Adaptive wavelet neural network predictor. *Problemy Bioniki, 58*, 10–17.

Dean, T.L., & Wellman, M.P. (1991). *Planning and control.* Morgan Kaufmann.

Dötsch, V., Ito, K., & Jantke, K.P. (2005, March 1-5). Human-agent co-operation in accessing and communicating knowledge media: A case in medical therapy planning. In G. Grieser & Y. Tanaka (Eds.), *International Workshop on Intuitive Human Interface for Organizing and Accessing Intellectual Assets* (pp. 68–87). Dagstuhl Castle, Germany. Lecture Notes in Artificial Intelligence, 3359. Springer-Verlag.

Fikes, R.E., & Nilsson, N.J. (1971). STRIPS: A new approach to theorem proving in problem solving. *Artificial Intelligence, 2*, 189–208.

Hertzberg, J. (1989). *Planen. Einführung in die Planerstellungsmethoden der Künstlichen Intelligenz.* BI Wissenschaftsverlag.

Lamonova, N., Ito, K., & Tanaka, Y. (2006). From planning tools to intelligent assistants: Meme media and logic programming technologies. In R. Kaschek (Ed.), *Intelligent assistant systems*. Hershey, PA: Idea Group Publishing.

Jain, S., Osherson, D., Royer, J.S., & Sharma, A. (1999). *Systems that learn*. The MIT Press.

Jantke, K.P. (2005, March 1-5). The biotope issue in meme media implementations. In G. Grieser & Y. Tanaka (Eds.), *International workshop on intuitive human interface for organizing and accessing intellectual assets 2004* (pp. 99–107). Dagstuhl Castle, Germany. Lecture Notes in Artificial Intelligence, 3359. Springer-Verlag.

Nebel, I.T. (2004). *Patient and learner adaptation in technology enhanced learning by induction based on medical context.* (Research Rep. FITL-2004-2). Leipzig: FIT.

Tanaka, Y. (2003). *Meme media and meme market architectures.* IEEE Press and Wiley-Interscience.

Vynokurova, O., Lamonova, N., & Shilo, A. (2004). A wavelet neural network for analysis of the bio-electrical activity of the human brain in the state of a deep hypothermia. In *Proceedings of the 10th International Conference on Theory and Techniques for Information Transmission, Receiving, and Processing* (pp. 309–310). Kharkov, Ukraine.

Wilkins, D.E. (1988). *Practical planning: Extending the classical AI planning paradigm.* Morgan Kaufmann.

Endnotes

[1]   When the knowledge about process parameters in the future may be reasonably represented as possibly overlapping boxes in the time-value space (see Figure 3, especially the lower leftmost case), logical reasoning is getting some touch of modal logics (Arnold, 1996).

[2]   In fact, this is more involved and holds only for classes of "reasonable constraints."

Chapter III

Wrapper Induction Programs as Information Extraction Assistants

Klaus Jantke,
Research Institute for Information Technologies Leipzig, Germany

Carsten Müller,
SAP AG, Germany

Abstract

*These days, **search engines** are useful tools relying on quite elaborated technologies which, albeit their enormous frequency of usage and the sophistication of the technologies invoked, continuously frustrate thousands of users. They are simply tools not easy to wield, but they are far from being assistants to their human users. **Wrappers** are extraction procedures which exploit knowledge of how to wrap information into documents for extracting such information on demand. Wrappers alone are nothing more than highly specialized tools. But the development of wrapper types and information ex-*

traction technologies has paved the road for a transformation of information extraction tools into intelligent assistants. Such a technology transformation program is outlined and discussed in some detail. The chapter stresses the dichotomy of internal mechanisms and external assistance behavior.

It is the authors' general intention to contribute to the discussion about perspectives of intelligent systems' assistance. Which properties, features or "systems' abilities" do establish intelligent assistance beyond the limits of comfortable tools? What are related advantages and drawbacks? What are the potentials and what are the risks of the general trend from tools to assistants? Wrapper induction serves as a representative case study.

Preliminaries on Assistance and Learning

The ability to learn is surely a core feature of intelligence. Computer assistants need, possibly among a large variety of other characteristics, the ability to learn. But **learning theory** is not the theory of intelligent systems' assistance. **Learning theory** provides insights into key problems, approaches and algorithmic solutions toward intelligent systems' assistance. The ability of computer systems to support humans in problem solving, in learning, in entertainment or in other activities is, for sure, a complex one only partially understood so far. This chapter deals with the problem of bringing research in *hard core **machine intelligence*** to applications in *intelligent systems' intelligence.*

Bringing theoretical results to work for the benefit of human users is usually still a long way. Mathematical theorems do not solve any problem in reality. In the best case, they give us some hint how to do so. Even the most elegant, tricky, efficient, or however nice algorithms do not solve problems directly. They have to be embedded into systems, in environments, and have to be invoked in scenarios where system components interact with each other and with their human users appropriately.

The chapter deals with the question of how to exploit results in **algorithmic learning** for a paradigmatic shift from tools to intelligent computer assistants. *What does establish systems' assistance?*

Although the chapter deals with a particular application case study—the connection of the (more academic) **LExIKON** wrapper induction functionality in the (commercially oriented) service architecture of **SAP's TREX** system, the authors' focus is on the transfer from tools to assistants. What makes TREX + LExIKON an intelligent assistant in contrast to the tool TREX?

An answer to those questions for the essence of intelligent systems' assistance will be exemplified. It is worth a discussion of how to generalize.

Introduction and Motivation

Thousands of users' frustration in using contemporary search engines has many reasons. One is an obvious lack of intelligence of these tools. If you search, for instance, the Web for the term "Wrapper Induction," you easily get some ten thousands of hits[1]. This is a completely crazy result because only a few tens of scientists world-wide know and use this terminus technicus. Machine intelligence is missing—there are only more or less comfortable tools available, but not yet any intelligent assistants.

Apart from this phenomenon, the use of search engines can also lead to anger and dissatisfaction due to other reasons. In some cases, for instance, the relevant information is scattered all over the list of results which makes it nearly impossible to find the desired data. The reason for this is that most search engines only use standard **text retrieval** functionalities for their ranking (Baeza-Yates & Ribeiro-Neto, 2000). If the search engines had access to the semantics of the indexed documents, they could adjust their ranking to the users' needs.

Another dilemma is that the result pages often lack useful information concerning the contents of the presented documents. Title and content snippet serve as the only criteria to determine the relevance of the document that is going to be presented. As these features do not necessarily reflect the semantics of the documents, users might be surprised about the content of the selected document.

So how can the search results be improved? Of course, users can influence the search results by setting up their queries in a more precise way. But what kind of assistantship is it that search engines embody if humans have to adapt to machines? Therefore, the question arises whether it is possible to improve the existing functions of search engines. To answer this question it is important to understand the processes beneath. As already said, search engines are based on text retrieval functionalities (Baeza-Yates & Ribeiro-Neto, 2000). The result set which is produced by a certain query consists of all the documents that contain the query terms. The order of this result set is determined by **TF/IDF** values which have been calculated for each document. Within the process of calculation each word of a document is weighted equally. If it was possible to assign more weight to the important phrases in the process of calculation, the users' needs would be met more closely.

The potential of meeting a user's needs or desires is, in the authors' opinion, the crucial advantage of system assistants over tools. Tools are just passively waiting to be wielded by the human user, whereas assistants might offer a higher quality of service.

In this chapter we will present a method that allows search engines to gain access to the semantics of documents. This method is based on the use of **wrappers**, that is, small programs that can extract single text fragments from the document as a whole. However, the generation of wrappers is a quite difficult and error-prone task. For this reason we will present a learning system for wrappers named **LExIKON**. With the help of LExIKON, users can create wrappers by simply selecting the desired phrases in their Web browser.

LExIKON uses inductive inference in the process of generating wrappers. It differs from other learning systems by its two-level learning approach which provides some functionality that may appear to the human user as intelligent assistance. The LExIKON system is trying to learn what the user wants to be able to extract what the user needs.

It was the key intention of research and development into this technology (Grieser, Jantke, & Lange, 2002; Grieser, Jantke, Lange, & Niehoff, 2000; Jantke, 2003a, 2003b, 2003c; Lange, Grieser, & Jantke, 2003; Lange, Jantke, Grieser, & Niehoff, 2000; Stephan & Jantke, 2002) to bring key results from the theory of inductive inference (see Angluin & Smith, 1983, 1992; Gold, 1965, 1967; Jain, Osherson, Royer, & Sharma, 1999 for a general treatment) to proper applications. The mechanisms of **inductive inference** based on recursion theory, formal language theory, and the like are beyond the imagination of the majority of users interested in information extraction from **semistructured documents**. Therefore, the LExIKON assistant is hiding its reasoning to the human user—one of the key distinctions between system assistants and tools.

The chapter is organized as follows. In the section on "Intelligent Assistance in Information Extraction," the LExIKON approach to wrapper induction will be explained in more details. In the following section on "Learning Technologies Meeting Industrial Requirements," a solution will be provided for integrating LExIKON wrappers into standard search engines with particular emphasis on SAP's system TREX. Thereby, the features of the search engines will be improved.

Intelligent Assistance in Information Extraction

Before introducing the LExIKON system, it is, however, important to think about one's expectations when relying on intelligent assistance for help. Of course, there is the hope that processes might be optimized by the help of intelligent assistants. However, the assistants would only be half as useful if they were difficult to operate. In other words they do not only have to provide a benefit but also have to be handled easily. These considerations played a decisive role during the development of LExIKON.

In the following part, deeper insights into the mechanisms of intelligent systems will be provided by taking the LExIKON-System as an example of **intelligent assistance** (Grieser et al., 2000; Grieser, Jantke, Lange, & Thomas, 2000; Lange et al., 2000). LExIKON is an application for generating wrappers, that is, small programs for the extraction of the semantics of documents. The manual generation of these wrappers by hand is a difficult and error-prone task. The user does not only need deeper insights into the markup language of the document but also a basic knowledge of a programming language which is capable of generating wrappers. With the help of LExIKON, the user can create a wrapper only by selecting the desired text fragments of the document in the user's Web browser.

LExIKON generates wrappers according to the principles of inductive inference (Angluin & Smith, 1983, 1992; Gold, 1965, 1967; Jain, Osherson, Royer, & Sharma, 1999; Klette & Wiehagen, 1980). A typical scenario for creating wrappers starts with the selection of a document. Within this document, the user has to mark positive examples, that is, the information the user wants to get extracted. These tasks are usually intuitively understood (Jantke, 2003a) and can be carried out quite simply as there is a graphical user interface which can be used (see Figure 1).

By pressing the "Learning-Button" not displayed in Figure 1 here, the document is transferred to the LExIKON-system, along with the positive examples. Then, a **two-level learning algorithm** is started. During this learning process the system generates two hypotheses. By generating patterns for the extraction, it supposes to know in which kind of information the user is interested. By generating a grammar for the document, it supposes to know how this

Figure 1. The LExIKON system at work

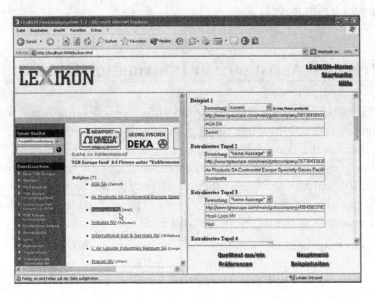

information is embedded in the document. Based on these two hypotheses the system generates an extraction mechanism, namely a wrapper. This wrapper is applied to the document and the results of this extraction process are presented to the user (see "Extrahierte Tupel" in Figure 1). If LExIKON's response does not fit the user's interests, the user can reject some of the extracted examples or mark new positive ones. Afterwards, a new learning process is started.

The system's internal reasoning processes, especially its inductive learning of formal languages and its hypothesizing about suitable information extraction procedures, is hidden to the human user.

AEFS as a Representation Language for Wrappers

For the sake of completeness some information about the generated wrappers will be presented in the sequel. Of course, this information is not needed by the users of the system.

Figure 2. AEFS: An island wrapper of Arity 2

$$\text{extract}(X_1,X_2,Y_0L_1X_1R_1Y_1L_2X_2R_2Y_2) \qquad \leftarrow \qquad l_1(L_1), \text{nc-}r_1(X_1), r_1(R_1),$$
$$\text{nc-}l_2(Y_2),$$
$$l_2(L_2), \text{nc-}r_2(X_2), r_2(R_2).$$

$\text{nc-}r_1(X) \leftarrow \text{not } c\text{-}r_1(X).$	$c\text{-}r_1(XY) \leftarrow c\text{-}r_1(X).$	$c\text{-}r_1(XY) \leftarrow c\text{-}r_1(Y).$
$c\text{-}r_1(X) \leftarrow r_1(X).$		
$\text{nc-}l_2(X) \leftarrow \text{not } c\text{-}l_2(X).$	$c\text{-}l_2(XY) \leftarrow c\text{-}l_2(X).$	$c\text{-}l_2(XY) \leftarrow c\text{-}l_2(Y).$
$c\text{-}l_2(X) \leftarrow l_2(X).$		
$\text{nc-}r_2(X) \leftarrow \text{not } c\text{-}r_2(X).$	$c\text{-}r_2(XY) \leftarrow c\text{-}r_2(X).$	$c\text{-}r_2(XY) \leftarrow c\text{-}r_2(Y)$
$c\text{-}r_2(X) \leftarrow r_2(X).$		

$l_1('<\text{li}>').$

$r_1('; ').$

$r_1(';<\text{i}>').$

$l_2('19').$

$r_2('): <\,=\text{li}>').$

The wrappers which are created by LExIKON belong to the class of Island Wrappers (Thomas, 2000a; Thomas, 2000b). Island wrappers use syntactical information for recognizing the relevant data within documents. More precisely, they assume that there are special text segments called delimiters that mark the beginning and the end of the information in which the user is interested. These text segments belong to a certain language, namely the delimiter language. Extraction algorithms for Island Wrappers look for words within the document that are part of these delimiter languages. In a further step, these algorithms must extract the strings between the words that have been selected.

In order to increase the expressiveness of wrappers, it is also relied on structural constraints. If there is, for example, more than one component to be extracted, wrappers must fulfill the pattern $Y_0L_1X_1R_1Y_1L_2X_2R_2Y_2$. In this pattern, the variables X_1 and X_2 represent the relevant information. L_i and R_i stand for words that belong to the so-called left and right delimiter languages. Y_i represents the rest of the document.

For our purposes, advanced elementary formal systems (AEFS) were introduced as description language for wrappers (Grieser, Jantke, Lange, & Thomas, 2000). The strength of AEFS is twofold, at least. On the one hand, they nicely reflect logical requirements as needed to describe wrapper concepts. On the other hand, they have a well-understood operational semantics within the logic programming paradigm.

An example for a wrapper written in AEFS is presented in Figure 2. The wrapper consists of a head predicate, structural constraints and delimiter languages. The head predicate defines the pattern the extracted tupels have to fulfill, that is, $Y_0 L_1 X_1 R_1 Y_1 L_2 X_2 R_2 Y_2$. Moreover, it indicates which constraints must be strictly followed during the extraction step. After that, the constraints are described. Such a constraint may, for example, contain the order that words of the right delimiter language R_i must not be part of the component X_i. In a third step the delimiter languages are listed. Those wrappers correspond to LR-wrappers that have been introduced by (Kushmerick, 2000). Similiar approaches can be found in (Chidlovskii, 2003; Muslea, I., Minton, S.N., Knoblock, C.A., 2001)

Figure 3. A learning algorithm schema

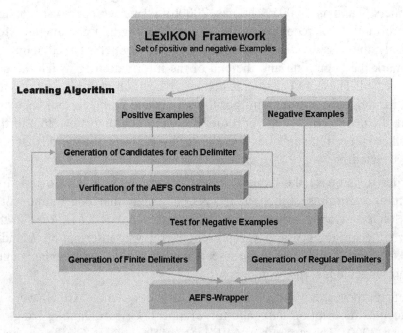

A Learning Algorithm for Wrappers

By providing **learning algorithms** the LExIKON system turns out to be a real assistant to the user. These learning algorithms make it possible to hide the details of the wrapper generation process. The only task that is left to the user is to signal to the system what the relevant text fragments inside the sample document are. Based on these fragments the LExIKON system creates a wrapper. An example of a learning algorithm that generates regular expressions for the delimiter languages is outlined in this subsection. The schema shown in Figure 3 generates a family of learning algorithms by specifying its subroutines.

As already mentioned the user has to provide positive and negative examples to the LExIKON system. In a first step the position of these examples within the document is localized. After that a set of words is created for each delimiter language. In the case that left delimiter languages are involved, the text fragments standing exactly in front of the corresponding components form the relevant elements of these sets. In the case that right delimiter languages are involved, it is the text fragments standing behind the corresponding components that are taken into account. Moreover the text fragments have to meet certain constraints. Before the selection of the words for left delimiter languages it is tested if they can clearly identify the beginning of their corresponding components during an extraction step. For candidates of the right delimiter languages the same procedural idea applies. But in case the end position of the components is relevant. Right delimiters might hit the left delimiters of what follows. As will be seen later, counter examples (negative examples) play a particular role in learning. A necessary requirement for the success of the learning algorithm is that the candidates of the delimiter languages do not appear as delimiters within negative components. If this property can not be fulfilled, the learning algorithm fails. Among all these words, however, only the shortest ones that fulfill these properties are added to the sets of delimiter languages.

The aim of the next step is to find a regular expression for each delimiter language that can express all the words that are included in the initially finite set. The generation of that regular expression takes place as follows. In a first step common substrings of the selected words are directly inserted into this expression. These substrings are determined by means of the "minimal editing distance" algorithm (Hirschberg, 1975). The remaining parts will be integrated either as disjunctive parts, as regular meta-strings or as optional

Figure 4. Two quadruples, first in its source code, and second in tuple format

```
@inproceedings { Jantke/Grieser/Lange2004,
        author = {Jantke, K. P. and Grieser, G. and Lange, S.},
        title = {Adaptation to the Learners' Needs and Desires by Induction and Negotiation of Hypotheses},
        booktitle = {International Conference on Interactive Computer Aided Learning, ICL 2004,
                Sept.\ 29 -- Oct.\ 1, 2004, Villach, Austria},
        editor = {Michael E. Auer and Ursula Auer},
        year = {2004},
        ISBN = {3-89958089-3}
}

(Jantke, K. P. and Grieser, G. and Lange, S.,
  Adaptation to the Learners' Needs and Desires by Induction and Negotiation of Hypotheses,
  International Conference on Interactive Computer Aided Learning, ICL 2004, Sept.\ 29 -- Oct.\ 1, 2004, Villach, Austria,
  2004}


@inProceedings{Lange/Jantke/Grieser/Niehoff2000,
        author = {S.\ Lange and K.P.\ Jantke and G.\ Grieser and W.\ Niehoff},
        title = {{LExIKON} -- {L}ernszenarios f\"ur die {E}xtraktion von {I}nformation aus dem {I}nternet},
        booktitle = {Proc.\ 42nd IWK},
        editor = {},
        year = {2000},
        publisher = {Technische Universit\"at Ilmenau},
        pages = {901--906}
}

(S.\ Lange and K.P.\ Jantke and G.\ Grieser and W.\ Niehoff,
  {LExIKON} -- {L}ernszenarios f\"ur die {E}xtraktion von {I}nformation aus dem {I}nternet},
  Proc.\ 42nd IWK,
  2000}
```

parts. The only regular meta-strings that can be created are '[0-9]+,' '[A-Z]+ and '[a-z]+.' With respect to each delimiter language the above described procedures finally create a regular expression that will be inserted into the wrapper.

For illustration, we briefly discuss some details by means of an example where quadruples have to be extracted from bibliographic data in BibTeX format. This example also shows that the LExIKON technology is not only restricted to documents in the HTML format. It works, on principle, for semistructured documents of any type.

The two bibliographic data sets may be seen as sources in which the user has marked the information he is interested in: the author, the title, the book title, and the year of publication for a particular conference publication. From the user's perspective, some quadruple is presented.

The ultimate goal of the systems' assistance is to generate a wrapper that extracts all those quadruples from any given BibTeX source. In the illustrated case, the user first of all marks the quadruple within the upper source shown in Figure 4. Then he marks a second quadruple within the lower source shouwn in Figure 4.Both are positive examples.

The system's task—as shown in Figure 3—is to form hypothesis for the delimiters surrounding the tupel components according to their position within the document. Let us discuss one of the subtasks in more detail. As long as only the first example is presented by the user, a string like '{' suffices as a left delimiter of the second tuple component, that is, the publication title. Hypothetical delimiter languages are generated and substituted into an AEFS wrapper template. The resulting wrapper extracts the provided example, and it works on a large number of other BibTeX data sets as well. If the user presents the second example, however, AEFS constraints are violated. The mentioned delimiter '{' occurs as a substring of the second tuple component '{LExIKON} – {Lernszenarions f\"ur die {E}xtraktion von {I}nformation aus dem,,, {I}ternet'. To resolve this conflict, the learning algorithm hypothesizes a longer left delimiter for the second component as indicated in Figure 5. To improve readability the delimiters have been underlined and set in bold face in Figure 5.

In the case that the prolongation of the second delimiter is not be possible, other delimiters have to be modified to form a wrapper that works as disired. This means that in the case of n-tuples the learning algorithm simultaneously works on 2 *n hypothetical delimiter languages. Consequently, the search space is huge. Learning algorithms differ with respect to the management of conflict resolution.

Figure 5. Hypothetical delimiters indicated in the source documents

```
@inproceedings ( Jantke/Grieser/Lange2004,
          author = {Jantke, K.P. and Grieser, G. and Lange, S.},
          title = {Adaptation to the Learners' Needs and Desires by Induction and Negotiation of Hypotheses},
          booktitle = {International Conference on Interactive Computer Aided Learning, ICL 2004,
                    Sept \ 29 -- Oct \ 1, 2004, Villach, Austria},
          editor = {Michael E. Auer and Ursula Auer},
          year = {2004},
          ISBN = {3-89958089-3}
)


@InProceedings{Lange/Jantke/Grieser/Niehoff2000,
          author = {S.\ Lange and K.P.\ Jantke and G.\ Grieser and W.\ Niehoff},
          title = {{LExIKON} -- {L}ernszenarios f\"ur die {E}xtraktion von {I}nformation aus dem {I}nternet},
          booktitle = {Proc.\ 42nd IWK},
          editor = {},
          year = {2000},
          publisher = {Technische Universit\"at Ilmenau},
          pages = {901--906}
}
```

Inductive learning algorithms do not rely on human intuition or anything like that. Instead, they do string processing and return what is algorithmically determined. The left delimiters in the illustrated case are finally set to 'hor = {', '0 {', '{', and 'ar = {' (see Figure 5).

There are different instantiations of the learning algorithm schema of Figure 3. In the most simple variant, finite sets of delimiters are collected. Concerning the technology integration, there are strategies for forming regular terms for summarizing and, thus, generalizing finite delimiter sets. In the technology integration of LExIKON and TREX reported below, such a generation of regular terms has been implemented.

With regard to the dozens of design decisions and implementation decisions, one more problem will be exemplified: the usage of negative examples. Though it is known that negative examples may play a crucial role in inductive learning (Angluin & Smith, 1983), we do not really exploit the information provided by counter examples. They are only used to check whether or not the delimiters that have been generated so far are already long enough. If this is not the case, the process of delimiter generation can be started again.

Learning Technologies Meeting Industrial Requirements

As has been mentioned before wrappers are powerful tools to get access to information that is inaccessible for other applications. This leads us to the question for which kind of application information extraction is useful. In a further step the problem must be solved how the respective applications can be connected to LExIKON. In this section we will illustrate how LExIKON wrappers can be integrated into SAP Solutions. This will be achieved with the help of the search engine **SAP TREX**. Thus, we can on the one hand advance the existing functionalities of TREX and on the other hand add new functionalities to it which can be used by other applications.

SAP TREX is the standard search engine service for all SAP solutions. TREX provides an application- and task-specific integration of efficient and powerful text retrieval and text-mining tools. Furthermore, TREX supports flexible document search, the structuring of extensive electronic document collections by using automatic document classification and the extraction of interesting information from a document corpus (text mining).

TREX can process structured, semi-structured and unstructured documents that are written in nearly 200 file formats. Among those are all known document formats such as PDF, HTML, RTF, and all kinds of MS Office formats. Moreover the documents can be indexed by the help of automatic language detection. The available languages are Chinese (simplified and traditional), Czech, Danish, Dutch, English, Finnish, French, German, Greek, Hebrew, Hungarian, Italian, Japanese, Korean, Norwegian (Bokmal and Nynorsk), Polish, Portuguese, Romanian, Russian, Spanish, Swedish, and Turkish.

In terms of search functionality SAP TREX provides Boolean search, error-tolerant search, linguistic search, phrase search, suggestion of alternative search terms, relevancy ranking of search results, cached HTML document previews with highlighted search terms, and federated search. A special feature of SAP TREX is the attribute search which is characterized by its ability to search particularly fast on large structured data volumes. It supports complex attribute queries, that may also contain range operators such as "less than," "greater than," or "between."

With the help of text mining additional search types are provided. Such types of searches are for example the search for similar documents, the search for related terms, the feature extraction that displays the most characteristic keywords of documents and the automatic summarization. For the classification of the documents, taxonomies can be created. The documents can be added to the taxonomy nodes automatically. This can either happen with the help of query based classification or with the help of example based classification.

By now SAP TREX is used by the following SAP solutions: SAP Enterprise portal, SAP Business Intelligence, SAP Knowledge Warehouse, SAP for Automotive (vehicle management system), mySAP Customer Relationship Management, mySAP Human Resources (SAP expert finder), and mySAP Product Lifecycle Management.

SAP TREX and LExIKON

For standard search engines like SAP TREX the content of documents are flat lists of words whereby HTML tags are left out. All text-retrieval features are based on statistical calculations with respect to these lists of words (Baeza-Yates & Ribeiro-Neto, 2000). However, it is impossible for search engines to find out what the important words in a document are. If search engines could, however, distinguish between less and more important phrases within the

Figure 6. Indexing workflow of TREX in its standard form and enhanced by LExIKON technology

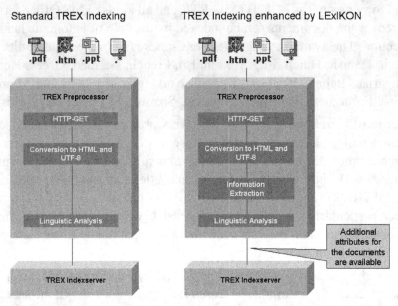

document, users would benefit from this functionality to a great extent. It is exactly this functionality that LExIKON is able to provide to applications.

Before adding a document to an index TREX has to preprocess this document. Preprocessing starts with a HTTP-GET step that has the aim of getting the document from the Web server where it is located. After that a filter step is carried out in order to change the format of the document into HTML and to convert its codepage into UTF-8. Finally, the document has to be analyzed linguistically.

For the integration of LExIKON a fourth step was added to the preprocessing chain (see Figure 6). In this step LExIKON wrappers are applied to the content of the document. The extracted text fragments are added to the document in the form of document attributes. This step is optional and can—if the necessity exists—be activated for a specific index via the user-interface of LExIKON.

Apart from the fact that a new step to the preprocessing chain was added, a second possibility to use wrappers was implemented. TREX provides the functionality to engage in the preprocessing chain with the help of the so-called

Python extension. A Python extension is a small piece of Python code that is executed at a predefined point within the preprocessing chain. For integrating wrapper functionalities into TREX, the user interface of LExIKON offers the possibility to generate Python extensions for wrappers. Moreover the activation of these extensions can automatically be carried out by the user interface. Available types of Python extensions that can be created with the help of the user interface will be presented in the following paragraphs.

Due to LExIKON it is now possible to extract metadata from the document content. Thus, TREX can get information about documents and reuse them to improve its functionalities. One possibility of using the extracted attributes is to influence the ranking of the search results. In the standard case TF/IDF values are computed for each document with regard to the query terms. This calculation is carried out for the content of the document as well as for all of its attributes. By multiplying each value with a weight term and combining all these terms afterwards the document's final TF/IDF value is determined. By considering the extracted attributes and altering their weight the order of the result set can be influenced to approach to the users needs. As a consequence it is possible to obtain a ranking that is based on the documents' semantics.

A nice feature of TREX is the so-called guided search. This means that the original query is extended by an attribute search. Therefore, a list of possible values for each attribute is presented on the result page. Then the user can select one of these attribute values which helps to improve the result set in terms of quality. If, for example, the user looks for mobile phones he will receive a result list containing the mobile phones of all manufacturers'. In addition to that the user will find a list of all manufacturers. Clicking on one manufacturer will then lead to a refinement in the sense that the next result page only contains mobile phones from the selected manufacturer. The attributes that are necessary for the guided navigation can be extracted by LExIKON wrappers.

A similar application would be to use the extracted attributes for classification. As already said, TREX supports the so-called query based classification. This means that administrators can build a taxonomy tree where every node contains a query. During the classification step a document will be added to the left child of a node if it matches the query. Otherwise, it will be added to the right child. These queries can be attribute queries and the attribute values can be extracted by wrappers from the document. This means that—with the help of LExIKON wrappers—an ontology for the documents can be created. (Maehchen A., StaabS., 2001)

However, it is important to note that LExIKON wrappers are not only useful when it comes to the extraction of a document's semantics. It is also possible to extract everything but the semantics. In this respect the field of application reaches from the recognition of advertisement to the recognition of less relevant text fragments. These text fragments can now be excluded from indexing and can thus not falsify the search results any more. This feature was added by using Python extensions.

Moreover, an attribute extraction call was added to the TREX API. In this way, applications using TREX can benefit from LExIKON. An example for a possible application could be a Business Warehouse System that uses wrappers for converting semistructured documents into structured documents. Due to LExIKON it can fill its databases with values that were extracted from semistructured documents located in the Internet.

Before closing this subsection, let us go back to Figure 6 to paraphrase—for the sake of a better understanding—the idea of integrating LExIKON into the SAP TREX environment. As part of its functionality, TREX takes Web

Figure 7. Creating a wrapper for the "object name"

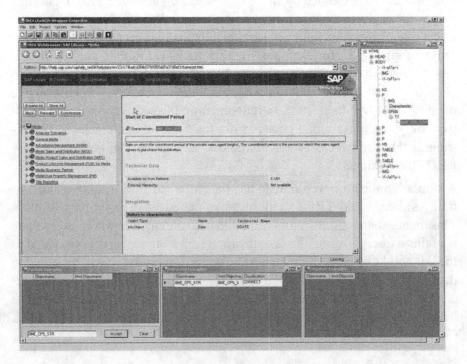

documents and transforms these documents before placing them in its index. The quality of service provided by the system when operating on the index depends very much on what TREX can extract from the information attached to individual documents.

To make the system behave more like an intelligent assistant to its human user, we have designed and implemented an integration of wrapper generation and application into the TREX standard preprocessing workflow. The documents indexed with support of the LExIKON technology have no other outer appearance than those indexed conventionally, but they contain extra information.

Example: SAP Help Portal

We obtained our first results concerning the usage of wrappers for information retrieval from the TREX landscape on SAP Help Portal (http://help. sap.com). The SAP Help Portal is the server where all the documentation of SAP's Solutions is located. On the average 30,000 users visit SAP Help Portal per day; more than 100,000 search requests can be counted.

Originally the documentation of SAP Solutions is either written in MS Word or in a XML editor. Before the files are installed at SAP Help Portal they are transferred into a SAP Knowledge Warehouse system (SAP KW) and categorized in a taxonomy tree. Then they are extracted from there and converted into HTML files. In this format the files are indexed by SAP TREX.

At SAP Help Portal we use LExIKON wrappers for the extraction of metadata in order to improve the search as far as search functionalities and usability are concerned. This will be explained and illustrated subsequently.

The main problem for standard search engines at SAP Help Portal is the creation of an attribute for the title of the document. Without this attribute the document could only be displayed on the result page by the help of its link and content snipped.

The extraction of the title is carried out by LExIKON wrappers. During this process the distinction has to be made between documents which were originally written in MS Word and documents which were originally written in a XML editor. The <title>-tags of word-generated HTML files enclose useful text fragments. In contrast, the <title>-tags of XML-generated HTML files do not contain any information besides the words "SAP Documentation." However, there are <h2>-tags within these documents that enclose useful text fragments. Consequently, two wrappers are necessary for the extraction of the document title.

Moreover, the classification between XML- and Word-generated HTML files is achieved by the help of a third wrapper. This wrapper extracts the *<html>*-tag that contains special attributes depending on the original type of the document.

In the first prototype we used the standard ranking function of SAP TREX. This means that the ranking was only calculated by the TF/IDF values gained from the document content. After a few weeks the users' feedback showed that this kind of ranking does not meet their needs. Due to the statistical calculation of the TF/IDF values short documents are preferred, despite the fact that the users might be mainly interested in long documents.

Moreover, users often search for documents that contain the query terms in their title. Consequently, we decided to add an attribute search, that is, a search for the query terms in the title attribute, in addition to the content search. The attribute search is, of course, weighted much higher than the content search.

However, there are also additional possibilities to improve the search results. XML-generated files, which are only used for describing the SAP Business

Figure 8. The search function of SAP Help Portal

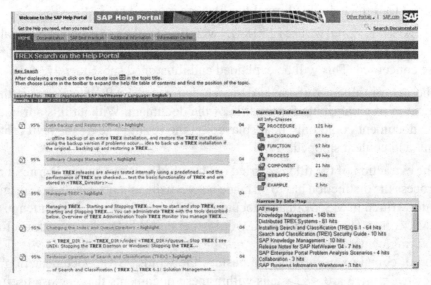

Information Warehouse system (SAP BW) contain, for example, special key words called "object names." These key words represent certain functions or modules of SAP BW and clearly identify a certain document. Most of the queries aiming at this kind of documentation contain such an object name. It is in the users' interest that the corresponding documents are ranked as high as possible. The top ranking of the desired documents is achieved again by an attribute search. The necessary document attribute can only be generated by a wrapper (see Figure 7). By paying close attention to the different needs the ranking could be improved to a great extent.

As already described the taxonomy tree of SAP KW gets lost when the documents are extracted from the system. Only the name of the node ("info-map") the document belongs to is added to the document in the form of metadata. Although the tree can't be rebuilt, it is nevertheless possible to implement a guided navigation regarding the info-maps (see Figure 8). In this respect the wrappers also provide assistance to the users.

Figure 9. A source document before download and conversion

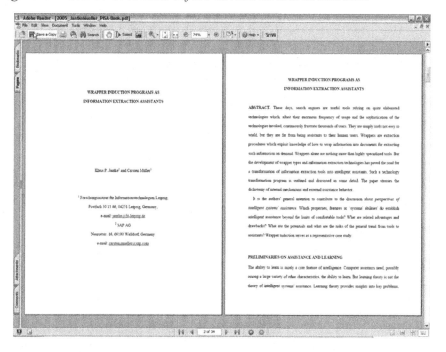

Apart from the existence of a taxonomy tree each document is also classified into other categories, the so-called "info-classes." These categories are built according to the content of the documents, for example, function documentation, procedure documentation and so on.

Wrappers can extract certain HTML-tags from the document according to which the category can be determined. In order to facilitate the navigation through the documentation, a guided   search for the "info-classes" was implemented as well (see Figure 8).

For the reader's convenience, an illustration will be supplied that demonstrates the interaction between LExIKON and TREK. This illustration shows how document objects can be enriched by additional attributes that are extracted by LExIKON wrappers.

We are selecting an arbitrary document which may be found anywhere in the Internet or in any business IT environment. For the present case study,

Figure 10. A document version in HTML/UTF-8 before transfer to the TREX index server

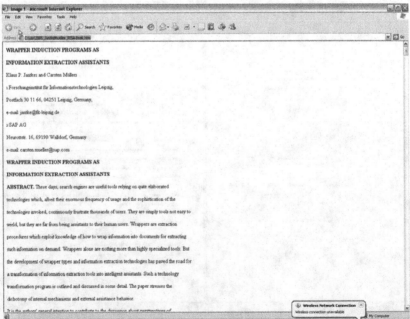

the authors have chosen this publication document itself in PDF format. The source document is displayed in Figure 9.

This document is received via HTTP-GET. The next preprocessing step transforms the source document into the HTML/UTF-8 format. The result is shown in Figure 10.

The document in the HTML/ITF-8 format (see Figure 10) contains the same information as its unprocessed version (see Figure 9). Such a transformation is needed as search engines can typically only further process plain text of HTML documents.To allow for better search results in the future, the document as shown in Figure 10 has to be further processed further it is handed over to the TREX index server.

This processing steps consists of a linguistic analysis by which the document is converted into a form which is suitable to be stored as the content component of an indexing object that can be inserted into the indexing object of TREX. In the conventional approach, this indexing object is an object file as shown in the leftmost screenshot in the back of Figure 11.

Figure 11. Variants of a indexing object without and with exploitation of LExIKON technology

When the authors' wrapper generation and metadata extraction technology is invoked, the idexing object object is enriched by annotations as shown in Figure 11. The rightmost screenshot in front of the display shows metadata in its lower frame. The attributes "abstract," "authors," and "title," are listed along with their corresponding values..

Figure 11 is displaying the two object versions of the same document when inspected under the TREX administration interface.

The feedback from SAP customers shows that it was possible to improve the search function of SAP Help Portal to a great extent by means of applying wrappers.

What has been outlined in the present section is the combination of two different technologies with the intention to gain some added value. In fact, a large part of the LExIKON computations is so sophisticated that it makes sense to hide it to the human user – it remains the assistantant's secret.

Steps toward a Science of Intelligent Assistance

Machina arithmetica in qua non additio tantum et subtractio sed et multiplicatio nullo, division vero paene nullo animi labore peragantur[2].

Gottfried Wilhelm Leibniz, 1685

From the general viewpoint of an investigation into the *Perspectives of Intelligent Systems' Assistance,* the present contribution may be seen as a case study, only. It exemplifies system's assistance within some particular application domain: information extraction from semistructured sources.

What are the characteristics of intelligent systems' assistance in this particular domain? What does establish systems' assistance under these circumstances? Which feature may be possibly generalized? What does the present case study tell us about intelligent systems' assistance, in general?

Information extraction is a problem of interest to a large number of users in literally every profession and in private areas, as well. Speaking about computer assistance for information extraction, the ultimate goals are assistants to users with varying profiles and with a largely varying computer literacy. A deeper understanding of communication and information technologies can not be assumed. Thus, the case under consideration is substantially different from application domains where specialists are to be supported by highly specialized computer assistants on scientific missions, for example.

Consequently, for the present application domain of information extraction, one easily identifies an easy to use intuitive human-computer interface as a first key characteristics of intelligent systems' assistance. The way in which computer assistants communicate with their human partners is a crucial issue. Novel research and development problems arise when the computer assistant has certain learning needs and, hence, has a desire to ask questions of its human cooperation partner (Jantke, Grieser, & Lange, 2004; Grieser G., Lange S., 2005).

In information extraction by wrapper induction, human users are usually not interested in the computer assistant's reasoning processes. To the human user, it does not matter how the currently employed wrapper looks like, and it is not relevant how the assistant did arrive at its current internal hypothesis. To say it explicitly:

- the computer assistant's reasoning processes are widely hidden to the human partner and go frequently far beyond human comprehension, and

- the results of computerized reasoning are not of interest in itself. They are frequently difficult to analyze and to interpret by humans.

Intelligent assistants perform a job humans could usually not do appropriately well by themselves. In areas where this does apply, human-computer cooperation may go far beyond the limits of conventional application of computerized tools.

The two points above may be paraphrased in different ways. One may stress, for instance, the assistant's need to have its own model of the world or, more precisely, of the part of the world it is dealing with. In the present case study, such an internal model is some concrete AEFS. Though AEFS are well-defined concepts with a clear semantics, they remain incomprehensible to the majority of computer users. That means that most users have only little chances to understand the "computer assistant's thinking."

This situation is substantially complicated by the fact that the information assistant's thinking is hypothetical in nature.

Every AEFS generated in response to the human user's inputs reflects the assistant's belief about the human's desires and implements an attempt to perform information extraction meeting the human user's needs.

This uncertainty of the assistant's reasoning is natural and by no means a mistake, because it is the way in which the assistant can learn what the user needs or wants. And the assistant's ability to learn is essential to the power of the assistance to the human it may offer.

When you cooperate with a partner who is learning, you must be aware of the possibility of mistakes made by your partner in accordance to the incompleteness of his learning process.

- When working together with intelligent assistants, assistants are rarely perfect. They may make mistakes that are corrected later.

As seen in the information extraction case study, intermediate mistakes made by the computerized assistant are a natural phenomenon in human-computer communication. The communication is especially organized in a way to resolve those problems (Jantke et al., 2004).

But this is not the place to blame a computerized assistant for possibly making mistakes. Especially in information gathering activities one frequently observes a human's behavior that may be circumscribed as mind shift. When getting involved in information extraction, humans may easily recognize that their interest is a little different than initially thought. So, their interest drifts from the original desires to what is finally considered satisfying. What we are sketching here in terms of the information extraction case study is just an instance of a more general phenomenon: wicked problems.

- Intelligent systems' assistance seems particularly relevant to wicked problems, that is, problems that are dynamic—due to the user's changing goals or due to dynamics of the environment like absence of persistence—such that solutions acceptable at one point in time may be no longer accepted at some later time point.

If human users have only tools available, they are facing all the difficulties of wicked problems and have themselves to find out how to change the tool application accordingly. In contrast, intelligent assistants should contribute to the user's efforts and alleviate treatment of wicked problems.

- With the introduction of intelligent systems' assistance, the problem arises of revising our perspective at IT systems' correctness. This may bring with it the need for a new approach to testing and evaluation. Intelligent assistants may be called "correct," if they do there job well over time.

Correctness cannot be established as a phenomenon which may be decided when checking the local input-output behavior of the system. First, there is a need for suitable concepts of correctness followed, second, by the necessity to develop related evaluation scenarios.

The authors do not consider it as a disadvantage, but as a promising perspective that, obviously, intelligent systems' assistance leads to new problems of science and technology.

Summary and Conclusion

The LExIKON system as described in the literature (Grieser et al., 2000, 2002; Grieser & Lange, 2001; Jantke, 2003a, 2003b; Lange et al., 2000) may already be seen as an intelligent assistant. It takes the user's requests formulated in a quite intuitive way and does a lot of information processing including inductive learning. As a result, it internally generates hypotheses taken as a basis of the information extraction service offered to the human user. These hypotheses are much too cumbersome to be communicated to the human user. Instead, the LExIKON system is negotiating the user's degree of satisfaction with certain extraction results. The human's complaints are processed toward the system's mind changes for serving the human better in the future.

From the outlined perspective, the LExIKON system may be truly seen as an intelligent assistant. The system's intelligence is mainly residing in its hidden learning functionality and in its communication skills. Instead of presenting largely unreadable code of wrappers written in AEFS, it is communicating about the extent to which the human desires are satisfied.

However nice such a service may appear, it is still somehow academic. The LExIKON technology has potentials to be exploited in numerous problem areas. The present chapter is intended to demonstrate the usage of the "pure"

LExIKON assistance in more application- oriented settings. Residing in an environment like TREX, it may contribute to transforming TREX into a more flexible, intelligent and, thus, helpful assistant to its human users. This is the direction in which the authors would like to continue their work.

Acknowledgment

The authors gracefully acknowledge a very fruitful cooperation with the former LExIKON research and development team with partners from the enterprises Bayerische Hypo-und Vereinsbank AG in Munich, r.z.w., cimdata AG in Weimar, Dr. Stephan & Partner in Ilmenau, and with partners from research groups at Darmstadt University of Technology, at the University of Koblenz-Landau, at the University of Leipzig, and at DFKI in Saarbrücken.

Bernd Thomas did a pioneering work on Island Wrappers. Gunter Grieser, Steffen Lange, and the first author of the present chapter invented the concept of AEFS which turned out to be essential. Kathrin Speich, Gunter Grieser and Jörg Herrmann contributed their own ideas to formal language learning for the sake of information extraction. Working in the enterprises mentioned above, Wilhelm Niehoff, Hans-Rainer Beick, and Andreas Stephan took care of an application orientation throughout all the time of LExIKON research.

For the present work with SAP, we have to thank Klaus Kreplin, Wolfgang Degenhardt, and the whole TREX team who allowed us to experiment with SAP TREX. Furthermore, we were able to benefit from their knowledge on search engines and information retrieval. With their help we turned LExIKON into an efficient assistant for SAP TREX and for many other SAP Solutions.

References

Angluin, D., & Smith, C.H. (1983). A survey of inductive inferences: Theory and methods. *Computing Surveys, 15*, 237–269.

Angluin, D., & Smith, C.H. (1992). Inductive inference. In S.C. Shapiro (Ed.), *Encyclopedia of artificial intelligence* (2nd ed., Vol. 1, pp. 672–682). John Wiley & Sons.

Baeza-Yates, R., & Ribeiro-Neto, B. (1999). *Modern information retrieval*. Addison-Wesley.

Chidlovskii, B. (2003, August 9-10). Information extraction from tree documents by learning subtree delimiters. In S. Kambhampati & C.A. Knoblock (Eds.), In *Proceedings of IJCAI-03 Workshop on Information Integration on the Web (IIWeb -03)* (pp. 3–8). Acapulco, Mexico.

Gold, E.M. (1965). Limiting recursion. *Journal of Symbolic Logic, 30*, 28–48.

Gold, E.M. (1967). Language identification in the limit. *Information and Control, 10*, 447–474.

Grieser, G., Jantke, K.P., & Lange, S. (2002). *Consistency queries in information extraction: Vol. 2533 of LNAI* (pp. 173–187). Springer-Verlag.

Grieser, G., Jantke, K.P., Lange, S., & Niehoff, W. (2000). LExIKON-Systemarchitekturen zur Extraktion von Information aus dem Internet. (LExIKON system architectures for the extraction of information from the interent.)In *Proceedings of the 42nd IWK* (pp. 913–918). Technische Universität Ilmenau.

Grieser, G., Jantke, K.P., Lange, S., & Thomas, B. (2000). A unifying approach to HTML wrapper representation and learning. In *Proceedings of the 3rd International Conference on Discovery Science* (LNAI 1967, pp. 50–64).

Grieser, G., & Lange, S. (2001). Learning approaches to wrapper induction. In *Proceedings of the 14th International Florida AI Research Society Conference* (pp. 249–253).

Grieser, G., & Lange, S., (2007). Interaction scenarios for information extraction. In R. Kaschek (Ed.), *Intelligent assistant systems: Concepts, techniques and technologies*. Hershey, PA: Idea Group Inc.

Hirschberg, D. (1975). A linear space algorithm for computing maximal common subsequences. *Communications of the ACM, 18*, 341–343.

Jain, S., Osherson, D., Royer, J.S., & Sharma, A. (1999). *Systems that learn.* The MIT Press.

Jantke, K.P. (2003a, March 5-7). Formalisms underlying intuitiveness in human-computer interaction. In Y. Tanaka (Ed.), In *Proceedings of the 3rd International Workshop on Access Architectures for Organizing and Accessing Intellectual Assets*, Sapporo, Japan.

Jantke, K.P. (2003b). Informationsbeschaffung im Internet. Lerntechnologien für die Extraktion von Information aus semistrukturierten Dokumenten. (Collecting information from the Internet. Learning technologies for the extraction of information from semi-structured documents). *Electrosuisse Bulletin SEV/VSE, 94*(1), 15–22.

Jantke, K.P. (2003c). Wissensmangement im Internet. Auf dem Weg zum Digitalen Assistenten für das e-Learning. (Knowledge Management in the Internet. On the road to Digital Assistance for E-Learning). *Global Journal of Engineering Education, 7*(3), 259–266.

Jantke, K.P., Grieser, G., & Lange, S. (2004, Sept. 29-Oct. 1). Adaptation to the learners' needs and desires by induction and negotiation of hypotheses. In M.E. Auer & U. Auer (Eds.), *International Conference on Interactive Computer Aided Learning* (CD-ROM), Villach, Austria.

Klette, R., & Wiehagen, R. (1980). Research in the theory of inductive inference by GDR mathematicians: A survey. *Information Sciences, 22*, 149–169.

Kushmerick, N. (2000). Wrapper induction: Efficiency and expressiveness. *Artificial Intelligence, 118*(1-2), 15–68.

Lange, S., Grieser, G., & Jantke, K.P. (2003). Advanced elementary formal systems. *TCS, 298*, 51–70.

Lange, S., Jantke, K.P., Grieser, G., & Niehoff, W. (2000). LExIKON: Lernszenarios für die Extraktion von Information aus dem Internet. In *Proceedings of the 42nd IWK* (pp. 901–906), Technische Universität Ilmenau.

Maedche, A., & Staab, S. (2001). Ontology learning for the Semantic Web. *IEEE Intelligent Systems, 16*, 72–79.

Muslea, I., Minton, S.N., & Knoblock, C.A. (2001). Hierarchical wrapper induction for semistructured information sources. *Autonomous Agents and Multi-Agent Systems, 4*, 93–114.

Soderland, S. (1999). Learning information extraction rules for semi-structured and free text. *Machine Learning, 34*(1-3), 233–272.

Stephan, A., & Jantke, K.P. (2002). *Wissensextraktion aus dem Internet mit Hilfe gelernter Extraktionsmechanismen.* (Knowledge Extraction from the Internet with the help of learned extraction mechanisms). In online 2002, Düsseldorf, Proc., Vol. VI, pages C612.01-C612.12. ONLINE GmbH.

Thomas, B. (2000a). T-wrapper. In *Proceedings of the 3ʳᵈ International Conference on Discovery Science* (pp. 50–64). LNAI 1967.

Thomas, B. (2000b). Token-templates and logic programs for intelligent Web search. *Journal of Intelligent Information Systems, 14*, 241–261.

Endnotes

[1]   On December 22, 2004, Google did return about 26,300 hits.

[2]   Leibniz, who may be seen as the true father in spirit of Artificial Intelligence, was dreaming of machines to free the human from routine work in thinking. The citation above might be read as follows: *For it is unworthy of excellent men to lose hours like slaves in the labor of calculation which could safely be relegated to anyone else if machines were used.* (See Computing Reviews, Vol. 45, No. 12, December 2004.) The science of intelligent assistance extends Leibniz's dream from machines used by anyone else to machines doing it by themselves.

Chapter IV

Modeling Confidence for Assistant Systems*

Roland H. Kaschek, Massey University, New Zealand

Abstract

An intelligent assistant system is supposed to relatively autonomously aid a master in problem solving. The way of doing so that is favored in this chapter involves master-assistant communication that leads to the assistant being exposed to a goal the master wants to achieve. The assistant—if that is possible—then creates problem solution procedures, the implementation of which is supposed to result in the goal being achieved. The assistant then chooses an implementation that can be expected to fit well its master dispositions. An assistant thus needs to know parts of its master's cognitive structure and to be capable of reasoning about it. The chapter proposes to use models as composite verdictive entities by means of which a master may refer to a domain of individuals. The concept of judgment is assumed to be the simple verdictive entity out of which models are composed. Models are used for representing cognitive states of masters. In particular, model extensions are considered, that is, models that are closed with respect to predicate negation of judgments, conjunction of judgments, and conditional judgments. The concept of confidence is formalized and applied to model extensions for deriving quantitative assertions about judgments. It is briefly discussed how the proposed theory of confidence in judgments can be used in intelligent assistant systems.

Introduction

Popper (1994) has in "The Logic of Scientific Discovery" aimed at explaining an approach to knowledge creation that is often used in the natural sciences. This approach uses the confirmation of implications from general theories as evidence for these theories being true. For example, effects that were forecasted on the basis of Einstein's Relativity Theory were considered as evidence for this theory being true after they could be confirmed.[1] Popper tried using **probability** theory for this work. Polya (1990), with the same intention, did that as well. However, it appears to be very unlikely that the required probability spaces could be defined in practical applications. It turns out that the key idea involved in that reasoning schema can be formulated without any reference to probability theory. A few axioms are proposed for formalizing consistency of confidences in a set of judgments. These axioms are inspired by probability theory and ideas regarding discourse regulation. With this approach one can give a precise meaning to Popper's idea restricted to individual judgments rather than to whole theories: assume a confidence in a set of judgments is consistent. Assume further that it is known that truth of a judgment U entails the truth of a judgment V and that V can be confirmed to be true. Then it is justified to be more confident about the conditional judgment U | V (i.e., U under the condition that V is true) than about U alone. In this meaning Popper's idea is proven to be correct in assertion 1 of Lemma 1. It is then, furthermore, a formula given for the confidence in U | V. This formula, that is, assertion 4 of Lemma 3, shows that the increase of the confidence is indirectly proportional to the confidence in V.

"Truth" in this chapter is considered as a culture depending concept for regulation of discourses. It thus is a purely methodological concept that in general may be beyond of what can be formally characterized. Truth is independent of confidence, as it is obviously possible to have no confidence at all in some of the judgments that during one's lifetime commonly are considered as true. Giordano Bruno was burned by the Catholic Church on the stakes for his beliefs in 1600. His faith shows that challenging the truths of one's time can be quite dangerous and that promoting alternative truths sometimes requires very profound confidence in these. However, the discourses considered in this chapter are assumed to not challenge the basic assertions to which commonly the predicate "true" is ascribed.[2] It is therefore here assumed that truth correlates with a confidence. The concept of "**truth**" used here is essentially the one of Janich (1996), that is, it is defined as the quality aspect of asserting speech that causes reasonable persons assent to the assertion made. A particular relationship between truth and confidence is going to be implicitly introduced in Definition 2. That, in fact, it is reasonable to conceive "truth" as culture dependent and thus depending on a particular choice of a social group that uses the true assertions for regulation of their discourses is very nicely illustrated by the article on independent thinkers in Gregory (1998, pp. 772). The source reports about independent thinkers in the 20th century such as Wilbur Glenn Voliva (the earth is a flat disc with the North Pole as its center and a wall of ice around it), Hans Hörbiger (ice is the most important material in the universe with the stars being gigantic blocks of ice), and Immanuel Velikovsky (planets can turn into comets and vice versa). Each had a significant number of followers. According to Gregory (1998) human history is full of independent thinkers. As is well-known they occasional make the majority of people follow (simplified versions of) their ideas, as was the case with Darwin and Einstein. The theories of independent thinkers can be quite hard to discuss as the problem with them may be that "one cannot argue because there is no common scientific ground at all" (Gregory, 1998, p. 773). A social group benefits from using "truth" for regulation of discourses in at least two ways. Firstly, a division of labor becomes possible such that mainly deliberately chosen individuals maintain what is considered as "true" in their domain of expertise while other individuals just use the respective maintained knowledge. Secondly, in discourses the true assertions can be used without being challenged and a consensus can be more easily achieved. Using "truth" for discourse regulation in practice can be considered as stimulating certain argumentative scenarios in a discourse. In practice this way of discourse regulation may be considered as not sufficiently efficient. Therefore "falsehood" or taboo can be considered as deterring from certain argumentative scenarios. The confidence axioms given implicitly support both approaches for discourse regulation.

Discourses can be conducted just for fun or for killing time, as is the case with small talk or flirts. However, discourse may have a particular subject. It is, for example, possible to focus in a discourse on what a given human wants or needs. In everyday life this is quite common, as humans are commonly perceived as being intentional. An assistant, in particular, needs to conduct such discourse, as an assistant needs to know what the master wants and be capable of aiding the master in the master's ambitions. As there is (at least currently) no way in which an assistant could find out what another human really wants, an assistant needs to rely on best guesses and assessing these in a justifiable and consistent way. The confidence calculus provided is supposed to serve the latter purpose. An assistant may, by using arbitrary means, generate best guesses (about what the master wants or what should be done) and then choose, by means of the results that are proven, the subset of the best guesses that will then be proposed to the master.

Chapter Outline

Assistant systems are briefly discussed in the section "Assistant Systems." Modeling cognitive structures of humans interacting with an intelligent assistant system in the role of a master is discussed in the section "Modeling the Master." The confidence calculus is introduced in the section "Reasoning about Models." In "Conclusions" the applicability of the mathematical apparatus introduced in this chapter to the design of Intelligent Assistant Systems is discussed. Finally in the section "Applicability of the Confidence Calculus in Assistant Systems" it is briefly discussed how the calculus could be applied. A few challenges for future research are provided in that section as well.

Assistant Systems

Intelligent assistant systems (IAS), following the discussion in the preface of this volume, in this chapter are user adaptive problem solving aids that understand what they do. The adaptation referred to in this definition concerns the capabilities of an IAS to learn and offer to its master a problem solving aid that is likely to be accepted. The term intelligence in this definition is used to refer the assistant's effectiveness and efficiency in proposing to the master an acceptable problem solving aid. It is supposed in this chapter that this intelligence can be implemented by means of plausible automated "reasoning" about models, which are abstract representations of the master. An IAS thus needs to incorporate a model of the master it is supposed to aid. The requirement that the IAS understands what it does is interpreted such that the IAS additionally includes a domain model that has been appropriately chosen.

Adaptiveness of an IAS to a master can be understood in terms of a set of master interface meta models being accessible to the assistant and up to its choice. An analysis of the ongoing interaction with the master can, as a first step, be used for choosing the most appropriate master interface meta model. In the second step, a particular instance of this meta model may be chosen and its parameters defined such that a particular master-interface becomes operative. Obviously this adaptation to the master can already be regarded as learning. The intelligence of the IAS with respect to adaptiveness would be measured in terms of how effectively the IAS adapts itself to the master and how efficiently it does so. The adaptiveness of an assistant to its master may concern the functionality provided as well as the quality of the provided functionality.

The assistant's adaptiveness towards the master is a kind of learning aptitude, that is, the learning aptitude to become more suitable to the master. This adaptiveness thus requires the master's feedback to be given and analyzed by the assistant. The learning capability from this feedback, that is, the interaction with the master requires the assistant to maintain a persistent session context. This session context functions as a framework for storing a subset of the mutable user, domain, and problem solving parameters. According to a respective heuristic the master's interaction with the assistant can then be analyzed and the mentioned parameters altered. Learning scenarios can be impacted by enabling the assistant to interact with several masters. This not only allows for more empirical observations being made and used for master adaptation but also enables grouping the masters into types and thus applying more sensitive analysis patterns to the master-assistant interaction. See, for example, Kaschek, Schewe, Thalheim, Kuss, and Tschiedel (2004) for a brief introduction to user-typing.

A problem within a particular domain of affairs can be understood as a negatively assessed difference between the current state of the domain and another state. For being capable of processing problems an assistant thus needs to have a meta model incorporated of the concept of "state of affairs" of that domain. Provided the assistant has a heuristic for generating problem solution procedures the assistant can create best guesses and use its reasoning capability to choose among them the procedure likely to be considered best by the master. An alternative to this is providing all best guesses to the user after labeling them with the confidence the assistant has in them. Obviously, as was suggested in Maes (1994), master adjustable threshold values for classifying confidence values as indicating false, true, and perhaps true judgments may be used as well for making the master-assistant cooperation more smooth.

Modeling the Master

In this chapter the master is considered from an abstract point of view, that is, only the master's cognitive models are considered as important. The cognitive models are entities that are used for referring to another entity, that is the original (Stachowiak, 1991). Stachowiak puts forward three main properties of models. These are firstly, the mapping property (each model is the model of something, its original); Secondly, the truncation property (models do in general lack some of the characteristics of the original); And thirdly, the pragmatic property (models are subdued to a purpose and their use for this purpose is only justified with respect to particular users, their objectives, applied techniques and tools, and period of time, etc.). With models one does not simply refer to originals. Rather, one manages to say something about the original. From practical modeling one knows that models are composite. Searching for a list of candidates for the indecomposable model ingredients one can hardly avoid taking note of Austin's Speech Act Theory. A preliminary list of speech act types was provided by him in Austin (1985). He distinguished utterances according to their illocutionary roles. He ended up with five kinds of speech acts, that is, verdictives (judging about something), exercitives (exercising power), commissives (taking responsibilities), behabitives (conduct in society such as apologizing, recommending, etc.), and expositives (explaining the function of utterances in a conversation or discussion).

Flechtner (1984) argues that sets of related judgments (see this concept's discussion later) can be considered sufficient for modeling human reasoning processes if they are extended by a modus that would allow to cover all modes of thought such as asking and so forth. It is presupposed in this chapter that it is sufficient to model verdicitive utterances for exhausting the concept of cognitive models. Later, cognitive models are considered to be sets of judgments. Johnson-Laird (1988, p. 455) gives a preliminary taxonomy of thought processes as associative (not goal-directed), calculative (goal-directed and deterministic), creative (goal-directed, nondeterministic, and lacking a precise starting point), deductive (goal-directed, nondeterministic, having a precise starting point, and nonincreasing the semantic information), and inductive (goal-directed, nondeterministic, having a precise starting point, and increasing semantic information). This, or similar coarse-granular models of thought for more sophisticated masters' models will be needed. In this chapter, however, the focus is on judgments, that is, the most fine-granular master models' aspects.

Though they are considered as the most elementary parts of models, judgments in themselves are not simple, that is, without a structure. Rather, they are composites. The theory of judgment that is followed in this chapter builds on the concept of "**notion**."[3] Notions are considered as cognitive entities that function as a representation of groups of words that, with respect to a given context, are used in the same way. This is a slightly generalized version of the view in Kamlah and Lorenzen (1996). Notions in this sense are abstract. So-called subject notions can serve as a template for referring to individuals in a domain. For each domain of individuals an extent is ascribed to a subject notion, that is, a set of individuals in that domain which are considered as instances of the notion. For example, for me, the notion "my car" had an empty extent until I bought a car 10 years ago while I was living in Austria. The extent was then a singleton set. Its element was a particular Ford car model, Fiesta. After having moved to Palmerston North, New Zealand, the extent of the concept "my car" has changed to a singleton set consisting of a Ford car model, Falcon.

According to Smith (1988 p.28) the extent of a notion is built around a prototype of the notion (such as an apple is considered as a prototype of fruit). Those individuals in the domain are then counted as belonging to the extent of a notion that are rather similar to the notion's prototype. Smith mentions three main functions of notions. They first promote "cognitive economy" by enabling us to refer to sets of entities with just one notion. Second, notions enable us to "go beyond the information given" by enabling us to relate an entity to notions that in our cognitive structure are related to the notion to the extent of which that entity is counted as belonging to. Third, notions can be combined into complex notions and thoughts. In Smith (1988 19,20), three ways of combining notions are discussed. These are first – modification, that is adjective-noun connection (for example "the black bird"); second – intensification, that is adverb-adjective combination (for example "the very large bird,"); and third – instantiation, that is, verb-noun connections (for example, "birds eat insects"). The first two ways of combining notions just refine the basic notion (in the examples this is the notion "bird") by combining it with a notion of a different status and result in a reduced extent. The third way of combining notions relates the basic notion to another one of equal status (i.e., "insect"). That way, something new is achieved, an assertion is made, and one can reason about whether one believes it to be true, sensible, or similar.

Judgments

With respect to the theory of judgments this chapter draws from Pfänder (1921). According to this theory, a judgment is an elementary act of ascription. In a **judgment**,[4] an agent A relates a predicate P in a way specified by a copula C to a subject s, that is referred to by a subject notion S. The predicate $U = U(S, P, C, A)$ is used to refer to this judgment. If the judging agent A is not relevant or obvious from the context, the judgment U may be represented by the predicate U(S, P, C). Judgments can be classified in the following, obviously independent, ways, that is, according to:

1. **Quality**, that is, the copula C may, for example, be used for ascribing a predicate to the subject or for denying it the predicate. The copulas used for that are "+" and "- " respectively.

2. **Modality**, that is, the degree $\mu \in [0,1]$ to which A ascribes the predicate to the subject s.

3. **Confidence**, that is, the degree $\gamma (U) \in [0,1]$ to which A is certain of U.

4. **Truth**, that is, the assertion created via the judgment is a true one. It is assumed within this chapter that an assertion is either true or false. The truth-values allocated to assertions are TRUE and FALSE respectively. The predicate τ is used for expressing the truth of a judgment U, that is, $\tau (U) =$ TRUE iff the judgment U is true.

For example, John might accredit the predicate "fair hair" to Linda. He might furthermore deny her the property "blue eyes." In these cases, the quality of judgment would be positive and negative, respectively. John may furthermore accredit the property "smart" to a high degree to Linda with a modality $\mu = 0.9$ and so expresses that he thinks she is very smart. Finally, John feels that he should deny Linda the property "well educated" but is not sure about that because, according to his prejudice, smart humans are well educated. John's confidence in the judgment (Linda, well educated, -, John) therefore might be as low as $\gamma = 0.1$.

For now, judgments are considered, on an individual basis, that is, one judgment is made at a time and this judgment is more or less independent of other judgments. Obviously this is a coarse grained model of how humans think. Some of the context dependency of human thought is incorporated into the model later on. For that end, the most important relationships between judgments will be analyzed. No revision of individual judgments is intended here.

For modeling more realistically how humans judge, the concept of judgment is extended. For example, it may be of importance that a judgment was made under particular conditions, while, for example, certain information was not available or that time was short for obtaining a result. To model things more realistically the concept of **conditional judgment** is introduced. A pair (U, κ) is called conditional judgment if U is a judgment that was made under the condition κ. Such a condition can be specified by a predicate involving the agent A, specified in the judgment. The initial case of judgment as discussed can be considered as a specific case of conditional judgment where the condition κ is a tautology. Two concepts are used in this chapter for modeling the contextuality of human thought. The first is "conditional judgment" and the second is "consistency of models." The conditional judgment $(U, \tau (V))$ is denoted as U | V. For judgments $U = (S,P,C,A)$ and $V = (T,Q,D,A)$ the conjunction UV is the judgment $((S,T),(P,Q),(C,D),A)$ that has the obvious meaning, that is, that P and Q are related to the extent of S and T in the ways specified by C and D, respectively.

Models

In this chapter a **model** M is a finite set of judgments. A more advanced discussion of the model concept is, for example, available in Kaschek (2005 p. 610-615). A basic predicate $\exists$ is used in some judgments. This existence predicate in this chapter is used with respect to a particular modeling task for ascribing to a judgment subject the property that it can be referred to independently of other subjects. In entity-relationship modeling (see Chen, 1976) the subjects to which one can refer to independently of other subjects are the entity types. In entity-relationship modeling one can only refer to relationship types or value types by presupposing a number of entity types that play a role in the relationship type or by presupposing an entity type that has values of the value type as a characteristic. Consider, for example, the following models:

- { (Joanna, $\exists$, +, Richard), (Joanna, sexy, +, Richard), (Joanna, blonde, -, Richard), (Joanna, smart, +, Richard) }.

- { (Employee, name, +, HR), (Employee, DOB, +, HR), (Employee, salary, +, HR), (Employee, $\exists$, +, HR), (Employee, creed, +, HR), (Thing20, IsA_Employee, +, HR), (Richard, IsA_name, +, HR), (Buddhism, IsA_creed, +, HR), (Thing20, Richard, +, HR), (Thing20, Buddhism, +, HR), ... }.

The first model says that Richard accredits "sexy" and "smart" to Joanna and denies "blonde" to her. In the second model HR stands for the Human Resources Division of some organization. The model expresses HR's view according to which there exists the concept "Employee." To this concept the predicates "name," "DOB," "salary," and "creed" are accredited. Furthermore, "Thing20" is an "Employee." The model additionally says that "Richard" is a "name," that "Buddhism" is a "creed" and that "Thing20" respectively has "Richard" and "Buddhism" as values for the predicates "name" and "creed."

Reasoning about Models

In this chapter, a simple approach is taken for modeling human cognitive states. Models are the basic concept employed. Contextuality of human thought to a limited extent is taken care of.

For this, two different concepts are used. Firstly, confidences are defined on models. That, to some extent, relates to each other the confidences put into individual judgments, as these judgments may be related. Secondly, conditional judgments and conjunctions of judgments are used to make a limited form of context dependency of individual judgments explicit. The interplay between these two concepts (i.e., confidences and combination of judgments) is then regulated by a number of axioms that specify what within this chapter is considered as a desirable cognitive state. The limited way of explicitly considering contextuality of human thought is, in particular, reflected in the definition of extension of a finite model as a model that is finite.

DEFINITION 1: Let M be a model. A **confidence** on M is a mapping $\gamma: M \to$ [0,1].

For each $U \in M$ the number $\gamma(U)$ is called the confidence in U. It is intended to use the natural order on [0, 1] for ordering the judgments in M. One would say that one is less confident about U than about V if $\gamma(U) < \gamma(V)$. The chapter focuses on extending confidence to composites of two judgments.

Judgments may be related to each other in the view of a judging individual. For example, under the influence of his judgment that the earth is spinning around the sun, Galilei might have made the judgment that the Lord does not exist, as at his time, many believed that due to Lordly creation, the earth was the center of the universe. Obviously, a relation being established between two judgments might depend on the truth of one or both of them.

Let M be a model, U, V$\in M$ be judgments with UV, U | V $\in$ M, and $\gamma: M \to$ [0,1] a confidence. For denoting that the truth of U entails the truth of V, the formula $U \Rightarrow V$ is used. The formula $U \equiv V$ denotes that $U \Rightarrow V$ and $V \Rightarrow U$. Obviously, $U \equiv UU$, for all judgments U. The formula $U \lozenge V$ denotes that U is true if V is false. Let $U = ((S, P, C, A), \kappa)$ be a conditional judgment[5], P* the negation of P, and *C the negation of C. Then obviously, $U^* \neq {}^*U$, but $*(U^*) = (*U)^*$, if one denotes the judgments (S, P*, C, A, κ), and (S, P, *C, A, κ) with U* and *U respectively. The judgment *(U*) is denoted as -U.

Obviously, pairs (M, γ) may be flawed. Some of these flaws can be expressed by elementary formulae like $(\gamma(V) \neq 0) \wedge (\gamma(V) < \gamma(U)) \wedge (U \Rightarrow V)$, or $(U \equiv V) \wedge (\gamma(U) \neq \gamma(V))$. It is intended to avoid such flaws by restricting to consistent models.

DEFINITION 2: Let M be a model and $\gamma: M \to$ [0,1] a confidence. Then γ is called **consistent** if the following assertions hold:

1. $\gamma (V \mid U) = 1$, for all $U, V \in M$ with $U \Rightarrow V$ and $V \mid U \in M$.

2. $\gamma (UV) = 0$, for all $U, V \in M$ with $U \lozenge V$ and $UV \in M$.

3. $\gamma (U^*) = 1 - \gamma (U)$, for all $U \in M$ with $U^* \in M$.

4. $\gamma (U) = \gamma (UV) + \gamma (UV^*)$, for all $U, V \in M$ with $UV, UV^* \in M$.

5. $\gamma (UV) = \gamma (V) \gamma (U \mid V)$, for all $V, V \in M$ with $U \mid V, UV \in M$.

6. $\gamma (UV) = \gamma (VU)$, for all $U, V \in M$ with $UV, VU \in M$.

In this chapter, the assertions 1. to 6. are referred to as axioms or as an axiom system. They are inspired by the formulae Polya (1990) draws from probability theory and used for reasoning about the likelihood of truth assertions. Clearly, if the truth of U entails the truth of V and one presupposes $\tau(U) = \text{TRUE}$ then confidence in V should be 1, therefore $\gamma (V, \tau (U)) = 1$, that is, axiom 1. Obviously, this axiom implies that $\gamma(U) = 1$ if $\tau (U) = \text{TRUE}$. This seems to be a reasonable assertion for discourses not challenging the actual system of true judgments. The assertion together with axiom 3 implies that $\gamma(U) = 0$ if $\tau (U) = \text{FALSE}$, for all judgments U. This shows that the axioms not only enable discourse regulation by means of stimulation. Rather, a taboo is also built in. Axiom 2 says that if U and V cannot both be true at the same time, then the confidence in UV should be zero. Obviously, this can be considered as requesting for a special kind of false judgment (i.e., one that is not true) the confidence in it to be zero. Axiom 3 says for each judgment that summing up the confidence in it and the confidence in its predicate negation yields 1. It is drawn from the probability theory assertion that the probabilities of an event and its complement sum to 1. Again, axiom 4 is motivated by probability theory. It uses the idea that any event with respect to any other event can be partitioned into two parts in which the second event happens or does not happen, respectively. The axiom trivially implies a limited version of axiom 2, that is, $\gamma(UU^*) = 0$, for all judgments U. Axiom 5 is motivated by the conditional probability formula and uses the conditional judgment (U, $\tau(V)$) instead of the symbol for the conditional probability. Axiom 6 simply reflects the assumption that the order in which judgments U and V are made does not impact the confidence in the combined judgment.

DEFINITION 3: Let M be a model. M is called **simple** if all judgments in M are unconditional and none of the judgments in M is a conjunction of other judgments in M. Denote $M \cup \{U^* \mid U \in M \}$ by M^*. Let M be a simple model. The **extension** $\varepsilon(M)$ of M is the smallest model O, such that the following assertions hold:

1. $M^* \subseteq O$.
2. UV,VU $\in$ O, for all U,V $\in M^*$, with U $\neq$ V.
3. U | V $\in$ O, for all U, V $\in M^*$, and V $\neq$ U.

DEFINITION 4: A pair (M,γ) of a simple model M and a confidence $\gamma : M \rightarrow [0,1]$ is called **consistent** if there is a consistent confidence $\gamma':\varepsilon(M) \rightarrow [0,1]$ that extends γ.

REMARK 1

The idea in defining consistent pairs (M,γ) is to provide a finite set of judgments, that is, $\varepsilon(M)$ that are related to each other in a sensible way and for which the axioms of DEFINITION 2 hold. It is assumed in this chapter that a human master who would care to undertake a meta discourse regarding the confidence calculus provided here would accept the axioms and thus, the lemmas that follow.

LEMMA 1

Let (L,γ_L) be consistent, $M = \varepsilon(L)$, and $\gamma : M \rightarrow [0,1]$ a consistent confidence extending γ_L, and U,V $\in$ M. Then the following assertions hold:

1. U $\equiv$ V implies $\gamma(U) = \gamma(V)$.
2. U $\Diamond$ V implies $\gamma(U) = 0$, or $\gamma(V) = 0$.
3. $\gamma(*U) = 1 - \gamma(-U)$.

Proof

Re 1: The axioms 5. and 6. imply that $\gamma(V)\,\gamma(V\,|\,U) = \gamma(U)\,\gamma(U\,|\,V)$ holds. Together with axiom 1. the hypothesis implies the assertion.

Re 2: Let U ◊ V. According to axiom 4. the equation $\gamma(U) = \gamma(UV) + \gamma(UV^*)$ holds. Due to axiom 2. and the hypothesis, this implies $\gamma(U) = \gamma(UV^*)$. Axiom 5. implies then that $\gamma(U) = \gamma(V^*)\,\gamma(UV^*)$. Axiom 3. implies then $\gamma(U) = (1 - \gamma(V))\,\gamma(U)$. Elementary arithmetic implies then $\gamma(U)\,\gamma(V) = 0$ and thus, the assertion.

Re 3: This is a trivial consequence of axiom 3.

Remark 2

This lemma is supposed to demonstrate relations between confidence and truth that are implicit in the axioms of Definition 2. The effort needed to actually confirm that $U \equiv V$ holds may be quite significant. The lemma is thus, not supposed to encourage doing the respective computations. Its assertions are rather interpreted such that (1), an intelligent human who holds that the truth of U entails the truth of V, and vice versa, should not distinguish by means of confidence the judgments U and V; (2) If U is true iff V is false, the confidence in one of these should be 0 because each of them is supposed to be either true or false.

Remark 3

Under certain assumptions one might consider assertion 3 of the lemma as more natural than axiom 3. Presuppose that for each judgment U holds $\gamma(U) = \gamma(-U)$, and that each predicate P there is a predicate Q with P = Q* and that for each copula C there is a copula D with C = *D and that both of these negations are idempotent, that is Q** = Q, **D = D. Then the axiom can be replaced by an axiom 3', that is, the assertion. The equation in axiom 3. can then be derived from axiom 3'. To see that, let U = (S,P,C,A), V = (S,Q,D,A). Assume that P=Q*, and C=*D. Then U* = (S, P*,C,A) = (S,Q,*D,A) = *V. Therefore, $\gamma(U^*) = \gamma(*V) = 1-\gamma(-V) = 1-\gamma((S, Q^*,*D,A)) = 1-\gamma(-U)$. Thus under the assumption made it does not matter whether the axiom or the assertion is presupposed. It is not obvious under what conditions copula negation can actually be considered as being idempotent.

Lemma 2

Let (L,γ_L) be consistent, $M = \varepsilon(L)$, and $\gamma : M \to [0,1]$ a consistent confidence extending γ_L, and U,V ∈ M. If U ⇒ V the following assertions hold:

1. $\gamma(U) \leq \gamma(U \mid V)$, and

2.   If $\gamma(V) \neq 1$, then $0 = \gamma(U \mid V^*)$.

Proof

Re 1: Let $U \Rightarrow V$. The axioms 5. and 1. together imply $\gamma(VU) = \gamma(U)$. Again axiom 5. implies that $\gamma(U \mid V)\, \gamma(V) = \gamma(UV)$. Axiom 6. and elementary arithmetic imply the assertion.

Re 2: Using the axioms 6., 5., and 1. one sees that $\gamma(UV) = \gamma(U)$ holds. Let $\gamma(V) \neq 1$ then $\gamma(V^*) \neq 0$ due to axiom 3. Axiom 5. implies that $\gamma(U \mid V^*)\, \gamma(V^*) = \gamma(UV^*)$. Axiom 4. implies that $\gamma(UV^*)) = \gamma(U) - \gamma(UV)$. Therefore $\gamma(UV^*) = 0$ and thus, the assertion holds. •

REMARK 4

There are several ways for deriving true judgments from a given one. First of all, the subject notion can be restricted. That obviously can be achieved for example by modification and intensification. It can also be achieved by instantiation if one uses the relationship between the notions established as a predicate being ascribed to certain entities in the extent of the basic notion. Everything that is counted as conforming to the restricted subject notion is also counted as conforming to the unrestricted one. Secondly, the predicate can be generalized. That leads to a more general predicate accredited to everything that is counted as conforming to the subject notion. Consequently, the derived judgments are true whenever the initial one is true. One can extend these ideas. A subject notion may be considered as an individual notion, such as "Napoleon Buonaparte." Exactly one thing would be counted as conforming to this notion. Other notions have a number of things that are counted as conforming to them. The "New Zealand residents by 3 March 2005" an example for the latter. Call the set of things that are counted as conforming to a notion the extent of that notion. The concept of judgment can be extended. A quantifier (such as the particularizer $\exists$ or the generalizer $\forall$) can be used for implying the kind of subset of the extent of the subject to which the predicate of a judgment is associated in the way specified by the judgment's copula. One can use the symbols "$\exists+$," "$\exists-$,""$\forall+$," and "$\forall-$" to denote respective copulas in the obvious meaning. Then, provided the extent of the subject notion is non-empty and the quantifier of a true judgment is the generalizer from the judgment another true judgment can be derived by replacing the generalizer by the particularizer.

Sub classing in object oriented languages can be understood as restricting the subject notion (for classes that can have objects) or relaxing the predicate (for classes that cannot have objects). It appears possible to also investigate copulas that are implied by a given copula and in that way, to study a further way of generalizing judgments. However, this is not intended here.

The lemma with respect to a judgment U can be interpreted as follows: (1) if the truth of a judgment V can be confirmed that is true whenever U is true, then this entitles for putting more confidence in U | V than in U; and (2) if the truth of a judgment V can be refuted that, however, is true whenever U is true, then this entitles for the confidence in U | V* to be equal to 0. This appears to be a generalization of the well-known modus tollens. See, for this term, for example, Brandt (2001, p. 55).

LEMMA 3

Let (L, γ_L) be consistent, $M = \varepsilon(L)$, and $\gamma : M \to [0,1]$ a consistent confidence extending γ_L, and $U, V \in M$. If $U \Rightarrow V$ the following assertions hold:

1. $\gamma(V) = \gamma(U) + (1 - \gamma(U)) \gamma(V | U^*) \geq \gamma(U)$.
2. If $\gamma(U) = 1$, then $\gamma(U) = \gamma(V)$.
3. If $\gamma(U) \neq 1$, then $\gamma(V | U^*) = (\gamma(V) - \gamma(U)) / (1 - \gamma(U))$.
4. If $\gamma(V) \neq 0$ then $\gamma(U | V) = \gamma(U) / \gamma(V)$.

Proof

Re 1: Axioms 5. and 1. imply that $\gamma(VU) = \gamma(U) \gamma(V | U) = \gamma(U)$ holds. Axiom 4. implies that $\gamma(V) = \gamma(VU) + \gamma(VU^*)$ and therefore, that $\gamma(V) = \gamma(U) + \gamma(U^*)$ holds. Again applying axiom 5. results in $\gamma(V) = \gamma(U) + \gamma(U^*) \gamma(V | U^*)$. Using axiom 3. proves the assertion.

Re 2. & 3: Both assertions follow immediately from assertion 1.

Re 4: This follows from axioms 6., 5., and 1.

REMARK 5

Assertion 4 is the adapted version of the conditional probability formula.

REMARK 6

Another interpretation of the axiom system in Definition 2 may be the following. Let D be a domain of individuals and Ω its set of states. Let it be such that D is always in exactly one state. Let $\Sigma_U \subseteq \Omega$ and assume that an agent A wants to characterize exactly the states in Σ_U by a judgment U in the sense that D is in one of the states in Σ_U iff U is true. However, not only humans err. Agents might be wrong too. For simplifying the notation the set of states of D that corresponds to $\tau(U) =$ TRUE, is denoted by $\tau(U)$. Slightly adapting the standard definition recalled in Johnson-Laird (1988, p. 435), the **semantic information** $\iota(U)$ represented by U is understood as the capacity of the judgment U that includes the states in Σ_U in $\tau(U)$, and excludes the states in $\Omega \backslash \Sigma_U$ from $\tau(U)$. Assume that $\iota(U)$ is characterized by the axiom system in DEFINITION 2. The axioms in DEFINITION 2—maybe apart from axiom 5—seem then to be obvious choices. Also, assertions 1 and 2 of Lemma 1 appear to be sensible. To show that also assertion 1 of Lemma 2 is sensible few further preparations are needed.

Let U be the set of all judgments. For each $U \in U$ let Σ_U be the set of states of D that U is supposed to characterize. Let $\sim = \{(X, Y) \in U \times U \mid \tau(X) = \tau(Y)\}$. Then $\sim$ is trivially an equivalence relation on U and the factor set U $/ \sim$ is denoted as U^*. On this factor set, a relation "$\leq$" can be defined by $[X] \leq [Y]$ iff inclusions (1) $\Sigma_X \cap \tau(X) \subseteq \Sigma_Y \cap \tau(Y)$, and (2) $(\Omega \backslash \Sigma_Y) \cap \tau(Y) \subseteq (\Omega \backslash \Sigma_X) \cap \tau(X)$ hold. It is trivial to show that this relation is a partial order on U^*, that is, it is reflexive, antisymmetric, and transitive. If judgments X, Y $\in U$ exist with $\Sigma_X = \emptyset$ and $\tau(X) = \Omega$, and $\Sigma_Y = \Omega$ and $\tau(X) = \Omega$ then $[X]$, $[Y]$ is the minimum and maximum element of U^* respectively. Consider the confidence in a judgment U in the naive sense and denote this confidence by $\gamma^*(U)$. It appears then as reasonable to assume that $[X] \leq [Y]$ implies that $\gamma^*(X) \leq \gamma^*(Y)$. Also, if one assumes that U, V $\in U$, U $\Rightarrow$ V, and $\tau(V) =$ TRUE, then it is reasonable to assume $[U] \leq [U \mid V]$ and thus $\gamma^*(U) \leq \gamma^*(U \mid V)$, that is assertion 1 of Lemma 2.

*Table 1. Judgments J of ε(**M**) together with their confidences γ assuming α ≠ 1 and β ≠ 0 elements*

J	γ	J	γ
U	α	V	β
UV	α	VU	α
VU	α	VU*	β - α
U | V	α / β	U | V*	0
V | U	1	V | U*	(β - α) / (1 - α)

J	γ	J	γ
U*	1 - α	V*	1 - β
(U*)V	β - α	UV*	0
(U*)V*	1 - β	(V*)U*	1 - β
U* | V	(β - α) / β	U* | V*	1
V* | U	0	V* | U*	(1 - β) / (1 - α)

EXAMPLE

In the classical science fiction TV series "Starship Enterprise" humans are allied with a number of other forms of intelligent life in the so-called Federation. Among them are the Vulcanians. Vulcanians are known to be extremely rational and to have no emotions. The Vulcanian Spock serves as First Officer on the Enterprise under Captain Kirk, a human. Spock's father is known to be a "pure" Vulacnian while his mother is known to be human. Let U = (Spock, v, +,F) and V = (Spock,e,+,F), where the predicates v and e mean Vulcanian and emotionless respectively and the Federation is abbreviated with F. Assuming that γ (U) = 0.3 and γ (V) = 0.5 hold, implies, according to the lemma, that γ (U | V) = γ (U) / γ (V) = 0.6 holds. Thus, the confidence in the judgment that Spock is a Vulcanian has doubled due to knowing that Spock is emotionless. It can be shown that in this situation it is more reasonable (in the sense of consistent model-confidence pairs) to be convinced of U | V rather than U* | V. To show that, the extension ε(**M**) and a consistent confidence on it will be determined.

The confidences in the table were, of course, computed with the formulae given in the axioms or the lemmas. The easy proofs are omitted from this chapter. It seems that, l a number of consistent confidences on the extension of a simple model might continue a confidence defined on that simple model. The situation here is, however, more specific. As we have U $\Rightarrow$ V we have γ (V | U) = 1. It turns out that on the extension $\varepsilon(M)$ there is only one consistent confidence that fits U $\Rightarrow$ V. Regarding whether to consider Spock as a Vulcanian, the example allows now to conclude that γ (U* | V) = 0.4, which is significantly smaller than γ (U | V) = 0.6. Thus, given the data discussed here it is more reasonable to consider Spock as a Vulcanian, than it is to consider him as something different. An assistant could, therefore, based on the model and data used here, propose to a Starfleet Captain who expects Spock to board his ship to welcome Spock according to the Vulcanian habits.

Applicabilty of the Confidence Calculus in Assistant Systems

The IAS was assumed to be a user adaptive, intelligent, and domain specific problem solving aid that understands what it does. This seems to suggest that an IAS incorporates a domain model, a user model, a set of problem models and for each of the problem models, a heuristic for creating candidate problem solution procedures. The domain model and the user model will obviously contain sets of assertions that in a given state of affairs of a problem solving session are true or false, respectively. A reasoning component of an IAS may additionally, on request, identify sets of true and false assertions respectively in the mentioned models.

In order to store instantiations of these basic models an IAS must be expected to maintain a persistent session context. Data mining techniques can be used for identification of interaction patterns. Machine learning techniques can be used for providing the parameter values of basic models with mutable parameters. Both of these can be used as input in a heuristic for creating best guesses for master proposals. If an assistant has capabilities to interact with more than one master or communicate with other assistants, then best guesses can be generated that are drawn from the analysis of interactions that involve more than one master. In this case, user-typing may be helpful for keeping the best guesses sufficiently specific. An IAS may perform a heuristic or algorithmic analysis of the ongoing master interaction and henceforth update the basic models. The relative frequency, in which a user performs a particular activity, provided the session context falls into a given category, can be used to estimate the value of the master's confidence in that activity for that session context category. Obviously, this is a situation that can be modeled as a conditional judgment. Similarly, an assistant system can monitor the user's responses to its suggestions and in this way, obtain an estimation of the confidence in its suggestions. The formula given in Table 1 can be used for calculating the confidences in combined and in particular in conditional judgments. As was shown in the example the provided tables' formulae may allow discriminating between suggestions that could be made to the master.

Future work regarding the theory proposed in this chapter should include:

1. Prove that none of the axioms (and in particular axiom 4) can be implied from the others.

2. Design an algorithm for creation of the extension of a simple finite model.

3. Obtain an overview about the consistent confidences on the extension of a model that extend a given confidence defined on the model.

4. Create versions of the axiom system that do not support discourse regulation by stimulation or by deterrence respectively.

5. Relate the consistent confidences theory to the work done regarding "belief revision."

6. Create and evaluate an IAS prototype that employs the consistent confidences theory.

References

Austin, J.L. (1985). *How to do things with words* (2nd ed. In German). Stuttgart: Philip Reclam jun.

Banker, R., Datar, S., Kemerer, C., & Zweig, D. (1993). Software complexity and maintenance costs. *Communications of the ACM, 36*(11), 81–94.

Brandt, R. (2001). *Philosophie: eine Einführung* (Philosophy: An introduction). Stuttgart: Philipp Reclam jun. GmbH & Co.

Chen, P. (1976). The entity-relationship model: Toward a unified view of data. *ACM Transactions on Database Systems*, *1*(1), 9–37.

Flechtner, H.J. (1984). *Grundbegriffe der Kybernetik* (Foundations of Cybenetics). München: Deutscher Taschenbuch Verlag GmbH & Co. KG.

Gregory, R.J. (Ed.). (1998). *The Oxford companion to the mind*. Oxford: Oxford University Press.

Janich, P. (1996). *Was ist Wahrheit?* (What is truth?) München: Verlag C.H. Beck.

Johnson-Laird, P.N. (1988). A taxonomy of thinking. In R.J. Sternberg & E.F. Smith (Eds.), *The psychology of human thought*. Cambridge: Cambridge University Press.

Kamlah, W., & Lorenzen, P. (1996). *Logische Propädeutik: Vorschule des vernünftigen Redens* (Logical propaedeutics: A pre-school of sensible discourse). Stuttgart: Verlag J.B. Metzler.

Kaschek, R. (2005). *Modeling ontology use for information systems*. In K.D. Althoff, A. Dengel, R. Bergmann, M. Nick, & T. Roth-Berghofer (Eds.), *Professional knowledge management*. Berlin: Springer Verlag.

Kaschek, R., Schewe, K.D., Thalheim, B., Kuss, T., & Tschiedel, B. (2004). Learner typing for electronic learning systems. In Kinshuk, C.K. Looi, E. Sutinen, D. Sampson, I. Aedo, L. Uden, & E. Kähkönen (Eds.), *The 4th International Conference on Advanced Learning Technologies* (pp. 375–379). Los Alamitos, California.

Kuhlen, R. (1999). *Die Konsequenzen von Informationsassistenten: was bedeutet informationelle Autonomie oder wie kann Vertrauen in elektronische Dienste in offenen Informationsmaerkten gesichert werden?* (The consequences of information essistants: What does informational autonomy mean, or how can trust in electronic services in open information markets be secured?). Frankfurt am Main: Suhrkamp Taschenbuch Verlag; Suhrkamp Taschenbuch Wissenschaft.

Kuhn, T.S. (1996). *The structure of scientific revolutions* (3rd ed.). Chicago: The University of Chicago Press.

Maes, P. (1994). Agents that reduce work and information overload. *Communications of the ACM*, *37*(7), 31–40, 146.

Pfänder, A. (1921). *Logik*. (*Logic*). Halle a. d. Saale: Verlag von Max Niemeyer.

Popper, K.R. (1994). *Logik der Forschung* (10th ed.). (*The logic of scientific discovery*).Tübingen: J.C.B. Mohr (Paul Siebeck).

Polya, G. (1990). *Mathematics and plausible reasoning*. Princeton: Princeton University Press.

Smith, E.F. (1988). Concepts and thought. In R.J. Sternberg & E.F. Smith (Eds.), *The psychology of human thought*. Cambridge: Cambridge University Press.

Stachowiak, H. (1992). Modell. (*Model*)In H. Seiffert & G. Radnitzky (Eds.), *Handlexikon Zur Wissenschaftstheorie* (pp. 219–222). München: Deutscher Taschebuch Verlag GmbH & Co. KG.

Endnotes

[1]   That is for example the case with respect to curvature of space due to the impact of large masses such as the sun.

[2]   Restricted to scientific discourse this chapter thus in Kuhn's terminology would deal with "normal science". (See for example Kuhn, 1996.)

[3]   I use the word concept as a synonym of notion.

[4]   The concept is generalized into "conditional judgment" for describing certain relations between judgments.

[5]   It may as well be denoted as (S, P, C, A, κ).

[*]   I thank Nadav Katz and Alexei Tretiakov for proofreading this chapter.

Chapter V

Intelligent Support for Building Knowledge Bases for Natural Language Processing

Son Bao Pham, University of New South Wales, Australia

Achim Hoffmann, University of New South Wales, Australia

Abstract

In this chapter we discuss ways of assisting experts to develop complex knowledge bases for a variety of natural language processing tasks. The proposed techniques are embedded into an existing knowledge acquisition framework, KAFTIE, specifically designed for building knowledge bases for natural language processing. Our intelligent agent, the rule suggestion module within KAFTIE, assists the expert by suggesting new rules in order to address incorrect behavior of the current knowledge base. The suggested rules are based on previously entered rules which were "hand-crafted" by the expert. Initial experiments with the new rule suggestion module are very encouraging as they resulted in a more compact knowledge base of comparable quality to a fully hand-crafted knowledge base. At the same time the development time for the more compact knowledge base was considerably reduced.

Introduction

Domain experts face a number of challenges in building knowledge bases. These include the articulation of their knowledge in a given knowledge representation language, as well as to ensure the integrity of the rules they enter.

In articulating their knowledge it is important that they find the right level of generality to ensure that the resulting knowledge base is performing the intended function. Furthermore, finding the proper level of generality is critically important to keep the resulting knowledge base within a manageable size and hence allowing users to build a quality knowledge base within a feasible time frame. We developed a knowledge acquisition framework, KAFTIE (Pham & Hoffmann, 2004b), which allows experts to articulate knowledge for a variety of natural language processing tasks. The knowledge is articulated in form of rules at a wide range of levels of generality. At the same time our KAFTIE ensures the integrity of the rules being entered. This chapter introduces an intelligent agent that helps the expert to articulate new rules by generating plausible rule suggestions from which the expert can choose a rule and/or edit a suggested rule to suit their intentions. We present very encouraging initial experimental results using the intelligent agent and discuss the reasons for the positive results. To introduce our intelligent agent within KAFTIE, we first need to present the basic concepts of KAFTIE and the underlying knowledge acquisition methodology.

The remainder of the chapter is structured as follows: We will first give an example application we built using KAFTIE to motivate the subsequent description of our KAFTIE framework. We will then describe the underlying methodology of our framework and illustrate the process by giving examples on how the knowledge base evolves. Subsequent sections discuss the rule suggestion techniques we have developed so far and present our initial experimental results with the intelligent assistant for the knowledge acquisition process. The final section contains a discussion and the conclusions.

An Example Application for KAFTIE

To motivate the following description of KAFTIE, let us give an example of an NLP application, which has been developed with KAFTIE (see Pham & Hoffmann, 2004a). Knowing the advantages and disadvantages of a particular concept or algorithm is important for every researcher. It helps researchers in learning a new field or even experienced researchers in keeping up to date. Unfortunately, such information is usually scattered across many papers. Survey papers are generally written on an irregular basis, and hence up-to-date surveys may not be available. Furthermore, in new and emerging fields, often survey papers do not exist at all. Having a tool that could collect all the relevant information for a concept of interest would therefore be of tremendous value.

For example, suppose we want to check if a particular algorithm is suitable for our task at hand, such a tool could go through available papers and extract sentences together with the contexts that mention the advantages and disadvantages of the algorithm. This would make our task much simpler. We only have to look at those extracted sentences rather than going through a large number of entire papers. The example application we consider in this chapter is to extract advantages of concepts or actions, that is, positive attributions of the concepts/actions, in technical papers.

An advantage is detected when a positive sentiment is expressed towards the concept or action. For example, given the following sentences:

There is some evidence that randomizing is better than bagging in low noise settings.

It is more efficient to use knowledge acquisition to solve the task.

We would like to detect that the algorithm *randomizing* and the action *to use knowledge acquisition to solve the task* have been mentioned with a positive sentiment. Analysis of positive sentiments towards a concept is a challenging task that requires deep understanding of the textual context, drawing on common sense, domain knowledge and linguistic knowledge. A concept could be mentioned with a positive sentiment in a local context but not in a wider context. For example:

We do not think that X is very efficient.

If we just look at the phrase "*X is very efficient*," we could say that *X* is of positive sentiment, but considering its wider context it is not.

Methodology

In this section we present the basic idea behind ripple down rules upon which our approach is based. Our KAFTIE framework and its implementation will be explained subsequently.

Knowledge Acquisition with Ripple Down Rules

Ripple down rules (RDR) is an unorthodox approach to knowledge acquisition. RDR does not follow the traditional approach to knowledge based systems (KBS) where a knowledge engineer together with a domain expert perform a thorough domain analysis in order to come up with a knowledge base. Instead a KBS is built with RDR incrementally, while the system is already in use. No knowledge engineer is required as it is the domain expert who repairs the KBS as soon as an unsatisfactory system response is encountered. The expert is merely required to provide an explanation for why in the given case; the classification should be different from the system's classification. This approach resulted in the expert system PEIRS used for interpreting chemical pathology results (Edwards, Compton, Malor, Srinivasan, & Lazarus, 1993). PEIRS appears to have been the most comprehensive medical expert system yet in routine use, but all the rules were added by a pathology expert without programming or knowledge engineering support or skill whilst the system was in routine use. Ripple Down Rules and some further developments are now successfully exploited commercially by a number of companies.

Figure 1. An example SCRDR tree with simple rule language to classify a text into positive or negative class. Node 1 is the default node. A text that contains excellent is classified as positive by Node 2 as long as none of its exception rules fires, that is, the text does neither contain not, neither nor far from so Node 3,5,6 would not fire. A text that has not excellent is classified as negative by Node 3 while it is classified as positive by Node 4, if it contains excellent but not. If it contains far from excellent then it is classified as negative by Node 6.

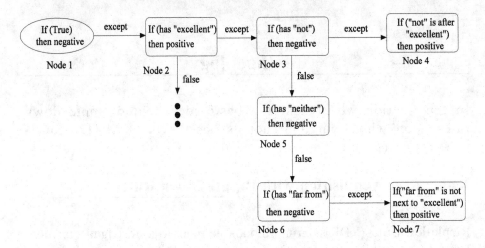

Single Classification Ripple Down Rules

A single classification ripple down rule (SCRDR) tree is a finite binary tree with two distinct types of edges. These edges are typically called *except* and *if not* edges (see Figure 1). Associated with each node in a tree is a *rule*. A rule has the form: *if A then B* where *A* and *B* are called the *condition* and the *conclusion*. Cases in SCRDR are evaluated by passing a case to the root of the tree. At any node in the tree, if the condition of a node *N*'s rule is satisfied by the case, the case is passed on to the exception child of *N*. Otherwise, the case is passed on the *N*'s if-not child. The conclusion given by this process is the conclusion from the last node in the RDR tree which fired. To ensure that a conclusion is always given, the root node typically contains a trivial condition which is always satisfied. This node is called the *default* node. A new node is added to an SCRDR tree when the evaluation process returns a wrong conclusion. The new node is attached to the last node evaluated in the tree. If the node has no exception link, the new node is attached using an exception link, otherwise an *if not* link is used. To determine the rule for the new node, the expert formulates a rule which is satisfied by the case at hand. Importantly, new node is added only when its rule is consistent with the knowledge base that is, all cases that have been correctly classified by existing rules will not be classified differently by the new rule.

Our KAFTIE Framework

We use SCRDR for building knowledge bases (KBs) in the KAFTIE framework. While the process of incrementally developing knowledge bases will eventually lead to a reasonably accurate knowledge base, provided the domain does not drift and the experts are making the correct judgments, the time it takes to develop a good knowledge base depends heavily on the appropriateness of the used language in which conditions can be expressed by the expert.

Some levels of abstraction in the rule's condition are desirable to make the rule expressive enough in generalizing to unseen cases. To realize this, we use the idea of annotations where phrases that have similar roles (belong to the same concept) are deemed to belong to the same annotation type. Annotations contain the annotation type, the character locations of the beginning and ending positions of the annotated text in the document, and a list of feature value pairs.

Finite State Grammars over Annotations

Finite state grammars have been used successfully in many applications. Their clear advantages are being declarative and efficient. Having a declarative language that enables experts to specify perspicuous rules is important in our approach. Conventionally, finite state operations are defined over a character input making it difficult to define grammars involving syntactic constituents.

Recently, there is a strong trend in using finite state grammars over annotations. Transductions are incorporated resulting in finite state transducers (FST) to enable the posting of new annotations relevant to the match of the finite state grammar. This is a feature that is utilized in our approach to record result of the match for every rule. FST have been used for various tasks: recognizing part-of-speech tags (Roche & Schabes, 1995), FS approximations to phrase structure grammars (Pereira & Wright, 1997), recognizing syntactic structures (Abney, 1996; Ait-Mokhtar & Chanod, 1997) and information extraction (Hobbs, Appelt, Bear, Israel, Kameyama, Stickel, & Tyson, 1997). Our approach differs by offering a systematic way of acquiring and structuring finite state grammars to effectively avoid potential conflicts among them.

Rule Description

A rule is composed of a condition part and a conclusion part. The following is an example of a rule in KAFTIE:

Condition:
> ({*Noun*}):Noun1 {*VG.voice* == active} {*Noun*}

Conclusion:
> **Class:** true
> **Concept annotation:** Noun1

A condition is a regular expression pattern over annotations. It can also post new annotations over matched phrases of the pattern's sub-components. Effectively, the rule condition contains a finite state transducer. The rule's condition contains the pattern:

{*Noun*} {*VG.voice* == active} {*Noun*}

This pattern would match phrases starting with a *Noun* annotation followed by a *VG* annotation, which must have feature *voice* equal to *active*, followed by another *Noun* annotation. The rule's condition also has a transduction which would post a *Noun1* annotation over the first *Noun* annotation when a piece of text is matched by the pattern.

As annotations have feature value pairs, we can impose constraints on annotations in the pattern by requiring that a feature of an annotation must have a particular value. For example:

VG.voice == active
Token.string == increase

A piece of text is said to satisfy the rule condition if it has a substring that satisfies the condition pattern.

The rule's conclusion contains the classification of the input text. In our task, it is *true* if the text mentions an advantage or a positive aspect of a concept/term and *false* otherwise. Besides classification, our framework also offers an easy way to do information extraction. Since a rule's pattern can post annotations over components of the matched phrase, extracting those components is just a matter of selecting appropriate annotations. In this work, we extract the concept/term of interest whenever the case is classified as containing a positive aspect by specifying the target annotation.

The rule's conclusion contains a classification and an annotation to be extracted. Notice that the pattern has two *Noun* components so the matched phrases would have two different *Noun* annotations. As there is a transduction to post a new annotation, called *Noun1*, over the first *Noun* annotation, we can uniquely extract the target phrase in the conclusion.

In regards to whether a new exception rule needs to be added to the KB, a conclusion is deemed to be incorrect if either part of the conclusion is incorrect.

Annotations and Features

- **Built-in annotations:** As our rules use patterns over annotations, the decision on what annotations and their corresponding features should be is important for the expressiveness of rules. Following annotations and features make patterns expressive enough to capture all rules we want to specify for various tasks.

We have *Token* annotations that cover every token with *string* feature holding the actual string, *category* feature holding its part of speech and *lemma* feature holding the token's lemma form.

As a result of the *Shallow Parser* module, which will be described in the next section, we have several forms of noun phrase annotations ranging from simple to complex noun phrases, for example, *NP* (simple noun phrase), *NPList* (list of *NP*s) and so forth. All forms of noun phrase annotations are covered by a general *Noun* annotation.

There are also *VG* (verb groups) annotations with *type, voice, headVerbPos, headVerbString,* and so forth, features and other annotations, for example, *PP* (prepositional phrase), *SUB* (subject), *OBJ* (object).

Take an example:

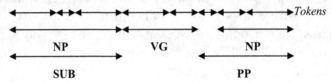

Decision tree learners perform well in noisy domains

The sentence is shown with all built in annotations (result of the Shallow Parser) covering their corresponding text spans. As an alternative way of representing a text with covering annotations, we use annotations names with brackets surrounding the corresponding text. The sentence with *NP* annotations will be represented as:

[NP *Decision tree learners* NP] *perform well in* [NP *noisy domains* NP]

An important annotation that makes rules more general is *Pair* which annotates phrases that are bound by commas or brackets. With this annotation, the following sentences:

[Noun *The EM algorithm* Noun] *is* [LexGoodAdj *effective* LexGoodAdj]...
...[Noun *the algorithm* Noun] [Pair *, in noisy domains,* Pair] *is* [LexGood-Adj *efficient* LexGoodAdj]...

could be covered by the following pattern where the *Pair* annotation is declared optional:

$$\{Noun\}(\{Pair\})?\{Token.lemma{=}{=}be\}\{LexGoodAdj\}$$

Every rule that has a non-empty pattern would post at least one annotation covering the entire matched phrase. Because rules in our knowledge base are stored in an exception structure, we want to be able to identify which annotations are posted by which rule. To facilitate that, we number every rule and enforce that all annotations posted by rule number x should have the prefix *RDRx*. Therefore, if a rule is an exception of rule number x, it could use all annotations with the prefix *RDRx* in its condition pattern.

- **Custom annotations:** Users could form new named lexicons during the knowledge acquisition process. The system would then post a corresponding annotation over every word in such a lexicon. Doing this makes the effort of generalizing the rule quite easy and keeps the rules compact.

Annotation Constraints

A set of annotations can be seen as a lattice in terms of their indices and relative priorities. To enrich the power of the condition language beyond just a matching of linear sequence of annotations and their corresponding features, ability to query the upper/lower context of an annotation in the lattice is needed.

Apart from the requirement that an annotation's feature must have a particular value, we define extra constraints on annotations namely *hasAnno*, *underAnno,* and *hasString*. We will now explain what these constraints are and their motivations.

hasAnno (*underAnno*) requires that the text covered by the annotation must contain (be contained by) another specified annotation. For instance:

$$\{NP.underanno == SUB\}$$

only matches *NP* annotations that are under a *SUB* annotation that is, covering a substring of a *SUB* annotation. This is used to differentiate a subject *NP* from other *NP*s.

hasString is used to constrain an annotation to contain a certain string:

{*NP.hasString* == excellent}

This pattern matches *NP* annotations containing the token string *excellent*. Alternatively, the token string and its synonyms can be used to form a custom semantic lexicon and the *hasAnno* constraint will be used instead:

{*NP.hasAnno* == LexGoodAdj}

assuming the token string *excellent* is in the *LexGoodAdj* lexicon.

For example, let's consider the following rule condition:

(
({*NP*}):Noun1 {*VG.voice*==active}({*NP.hasAnno*==LexGoodAdj}):Noun2
):MATCH

This pattern would match phrases starting with a *NP* annotation followed by a *VG* annotation (with feature *voice* having value *active*) followed by another *NP* annotation, which must also contain a *LexGoodAdj* annotation as its substring.

When a phrase satisfies the rule condition, a *MATCH* annotation would be posted over the whole phrase, and *Noun1*, *Noun2* annotations will be posted over the first and second *NP* in the pattern respectively. Note that *Noun1* is not used in the condition part, but it could be used later in the conclusion part or in the exception of the current rule.

The following sentence matches the rule condition because *useful* is annotated as a *LexGoodAdj* annotation, being a custom built lexicon containing terms indicating a positive sentiment:

[NP *Parallelism* NP][VG *is* VG][NP *a* [LexGoodAdj *useful* LexGoodAdj] *way* NP] *to speed up computation.*

This sentence triggers the posting of the following new annotations:

[MATCH *Parallelism is a useful way* MATCH]
[Noun1 *Parallelism* Noun1]
[Noun2 *a useful way* Noun2]

However, the following sentences do not match:

1. [NP *Parallelism* NP] [VG *is* VG] [NP *a method* NP] *used in our approach.*

2. [NP *Parallelism* NP] [VG *has been shown* VG] [VG *to be* VG] *very useful.*

Sentence (1) matches *{NP}{VG}{NP}* , but it does not satisfy the annotation constraint of the second *NP*. Sentence (2) does not match the pattern.

The Knowledge Acquisition Process in KAFTIE

The knowledge acquisition process goes through a number of iterations. The user gives a text segment (e.g., a sentence) as input to the KB. The conclusion (e.g., classification) is suggested by the KB together with the *fired* rule *R* that gives the conclusion. If it is not the default rule, annotations posted by the rule *R* are also shown (see the next Example section) to help the user decide whether the conclusion is satisfactory.

If the user does not agree with the KB's performance, there are two options of addressing it: adding an exception rule to rule *R* or modifying rule *R* if possible. In either case, the user's decision will be checked for consistency with the current KB before it gets committed to the KB. To create a new exception rule, the user only has to consider why the current case should be given a different conclusion from rule *R*. This effort does not depend on the knowledge base size.

Modification of existing rules in the KB is not normally done with RDR as it is viewed that every rule entered to the KB has its reason for being there. However, we find that in many natural language applications it is desirable to modify previously entered rules to cover new cases.

Implementation

We built our framework using GATE (Cunningham, Maynard, Bontcheva, & Tablan, 2002). A set of reusable modules known as ANNIE is provided with GATE. These are able to perform basic language processing tasks such as part-of-speech (POS) tagging and semantic tagging. We use *Tokenizer, Sentence Splitter, Part-of-Speech Tagger, and Semantic Tagger* processing resources from ANNIE. *Semantic Tagger* is a JAPE finite state transducer that annotates text based on JAPE grammars. Our rule's annotation pattern is implemented as a JAPE grammar with some additional features facilitating our annotation constraints.

We also developed additional processing resources for our task:

* **Lemmatizer:** A processing resource that automatically puts a *lemma* feature into every Token annotation containing the lemma form of the token's string (Porter, 1980). Lemmatizer uses information from Word-Net (Fellbaum, 1998) and the result from the POS Tagger module.

*Figure 2. Rule interface:a new rule where the rule is automatically checked for consistency with the existing KB before it gets committed. Annotations including those created by the Shallow Parser module are shown in the tree in the **structure** box.*

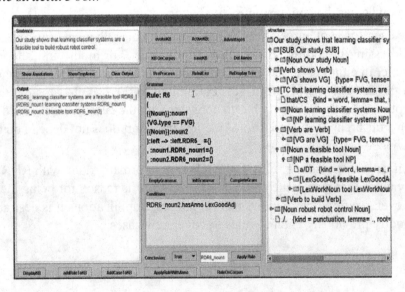

- **Shallow Parser:** A processing resource using JAPE finite state transducer. The shallow parser module consists of cascaded JAPE grammars recognizing noun groups, verb groups, propositional phrases, different types of clauses, subjects and objects. These constituents are displayed hierarchically in a tree structure to help experts formulate patterns (see Figure 2).

All these processing resources are run on the input text in a pipeline fashion. This is a pre-processing step which produces all necessary annotations before the knowledge base is applied on the text.

Examples of how to Build a Knowledge Base

The following examples are taken from the actual KB. Suppose we start with an empty knowledge base for recognizing advantages. That is, the KB would only contain a default rule which always produces a *false* conclusion. When the following sentence is encountered:

Our study shows that [Noun *learning classifier systems* Noun][VG *are* VG][Noun *a* [LexGoodAdj *feasible* LexGoodAdj] *tool* Noun] *to build robust robot control.*

Our empty KB would initially use the default rule to suggest it does not belong to the *Advantages* class. This can be corrected by adding the following rule to the KB:

Rule: R6
    (({*Noun*}):RDR6_noun1 {*VG.type*==FVG}
    ({*Noun.hasAnno* == LexGoodAdj}):RDR6_noun2):RDR6
Conclusion:
    Class: true
    Target Concept: RDR6_noun1

This rule would match phrases starting with a *Noun* annotation, followed by a *VG* annotation (with feature *type* equal to *FVG – finite verb group*) followed by a *Noun* annotation. Furthermore, the second *Noun* annotation must contain a *LexGoodAdj* annotation covering its substring. As there is a *LexGoodAdj* annotation covering the token *feasible*, the phrase *learning classifier systems are a feasible tool* is matched by *R6* and *learning classifier systems* is extracted as the concept of interest.

When we encounter this sentence:

*Given a data set, it is often not clear beforehand which **algorithm will yield the best performance.***

Rule *R6* suggests that the sentence mentions *algorithm* with a positive sentiment (the matched phrase is highlighted in boldface and will be annotated with *RDR6* by rule *R6*) which is not correct. The following exception rule is added to fix that:

Rule:R32

> ({*Token.lemma*==which} {*RDR6*}):RDR32

Conclusion:

> **Class:** false

This rule says that if the phrase matched by rule *R6* follows a *which* token, then the sentence containing it does not belong to *Advantages* class. However, when we encounter the following sentence:

*The latter approach searches for the subset of attributes over **which naïve Bayes has the best performance.***

Rule *R6* suggests that *naive Bayes* has been mentioned with a positive sentiment but its exception rule, *R32*, overrules the decision because the phrase that matches *R6* (annotated by *RDR6*) follows a token *which*. Obviously, *naive Bayes* should be the correct answer since the token *which* is used differently here than in the context in which *R32* was created. We can add an exception to *R32* catering for this case:

Rule:R56

> ({*Token.string*==over} {*RDR32* }):RDR56

Conclusion:

> **Class:** true
> **Target Concept:** RDR6_noun1

Automatic Rule Suggestions

Support for the process of creating rules is certainly desirable. A new rule is created only when the KB gives the new case an incorrect conclusion. In a fully manual mode, experts have to identify a phrase in the text at hand which justifies why the text should be classified differently. A rule then has to be crafted to match the identified phrase while being consistent with the existing KB.

In order to alleviate the cognitive load in the process of creating the right pattern to match the identified phrase, we propose algorithms that provide rule recommendations to the experts. Our Rule Suggestion Module (RSM) comes in three forms, that is, suggestion of new patterns, of similar existing patterns, and of lexicons.

New Patterns

We describe how experts are helped in creating new patterns, that is, rules' conditions. Given a selected phrase, patterns at annotation level, not including annotations' constraints, that match exactly the phrase are generated. The list of patterns is then sorted in the order of increasing number of annotations before presenting to the users. Among patterns having the same number of annotations, the ones with higher level annotations are ranked higher. For example, *NP* annotation is ranked higher than *Token* annotation. The motivation behind this heuristic is that patterns using higher level annotations are more likely to generalize to cover more cases. Furthermore, higher level annotations tend to cover longer text span, hence resulting in shorter and simpler patterns. From the list of proposed patterns, experts can choose one that they deem most appropriate. Note that these patterns do not have constraints on their annotation components, hence are very general. Experts have a choice of specializing the pattern by specifying constraints on annotations' attributes. For each annotation, a list of possible attribute constraints will be presented to the experts through a user friendly interface.

Similarity Measure for Rule Modification

We describe how changes to existing rules are recommended to experts in order to correctly classify a new case using rule similarity measure. Given the selected phrase in the new text, existing rules in the KB are checked to see if they *nearly* match the phrase (see Figure 3). The similarity measure between an existing rule and the text at hand is computed using an edit distance function (Cohen, Ravikumar, & Fienberg, 2003). It is the minimal cost required to change the rule's pattern so that it matches exactly the selected phrase. Possible operators over annotation components are deletion, insertion and replacement. We use nonuniform weights depending on what annotations are involved in the operation. For example, the cost of changing a *NP* to a *Noun* is less than changing a *VG* to a *Noun*. Existing rules are then sorted in the order of decreasing similarity or increasing order of edit distance value. Each of those rules is coupled with corresponding changes to its pattern to match the selected phrase. Experts can choose a suggestion they deem most appropriate.

Let's look at concrete examples to see how the rule suggestion feature works. Suppose we have a pattern:

$\{SUB\}$ $\{VG.type == \text{FVG}\}$ $\{LexGoodAdj\}$

Figure 3. Similar rules: in the increasing order of similarity to the relevant phrase in the current sentence together with corresponding modifications.

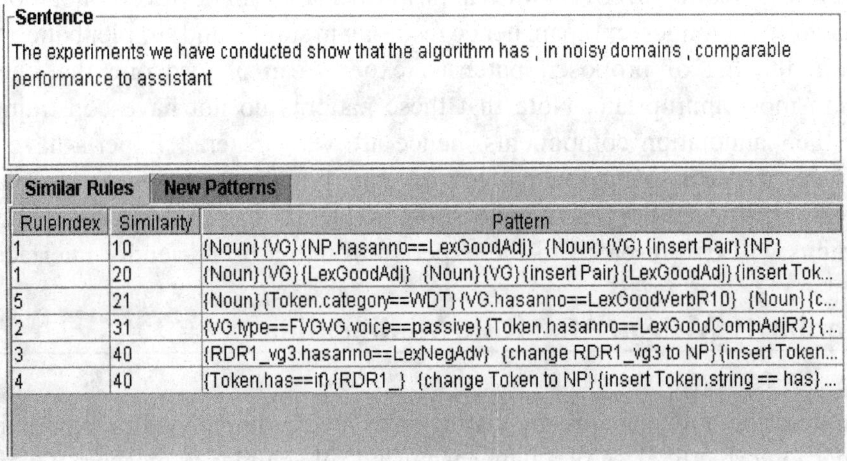

Sentence

The experiments we have conducted show that the algorithm has , in noisy domains , comparable performance to assistant

Similar Rules	New Patterns	
RuleIndex	Similarity	Pattern
1	10	{Noun}{VG}{NP.hasanno==LexGoodAdj} {Noun}{VG}{insert Pair}{NP}
1	20	{Noun}{VG}{LexGoodAdj} {Noun}{VG}{insert Pair}{LexGoodAdj}{insert Tok...
5	21	{Noun}{Token.category==WDT}{VG.hasanno==LexGoodVerbR10} {Noun}{c...
2	31	{VG.type==FVGVG.voice==passive}{Token.hasanno==LexGoodCompAdjR2}{...
3	40	{RDR1_vg3.hasanno==LexNegAdv} {change RDR1_vg3 to NP}{insert Token...
4	40	{Token.has==if}{RDR1_} {change Token to NP}{insert Token.string == has} ...

to match the sentence:

[SUB [Noun Parallelism Noun] SUB] [VG is VG] [LexGoodAdj useful LexGoodAdj] to speed up computation.

Notice that the first component of the pattern could also be *Noun* instead of *SUB*. Deciding between *Noun* and *SUB* without looking at more cases is impossible. Rule modification using similarity measure could be used to defer this decision until we have enough information. Now if we encounter:

The experiments we have conducted show that [Noun SVM Noun] [VG is VG] [LexGoodAdj excellent LexGoodAdj].

The pattern does not match the sentence. Suppose experts select the phrase *SVM is excellent*, the system would propose the pattern as very similar, suggesting a change of *SUB* to *Noun* so that the new sentence will be covered. So the newly modified pattern can be either:

{Noun} {VG.type == FVG} {LexGoodAdj}

or

({SUB}|{Noun}){VG.type == FVG} {LexGoodAdj}

The new sentence:

[Noun Adaboost Noun] [Pair , in noisy domain, Pair] [VG is VG] [LexGoodAdj superior LexGoodAdj] to other algorithms.

will not be matched by the pattern. An insertion of a *Pair* annotation to the pattern is suggested to match the sentence:

({SUB}|{Noun})({Pair})? {VG.type == FVG} {LexGoodAdj}.

Suggested rule modification has several advantages. First, it makes the task of creating a new rule easier as it is less important that experts worry if their choice of annotations or their constraints are too general or too specific. Second, by allowing an existing rule to be modified to cover the new case we make the KB more compact and generalize better. Suppose instead of modifying an existing rule, we create a new rule to cover the new case. Since the new rule is similar to an existing rule, its exception rules subtree is likely to be similar to the exception rules subtree of the similar existing rule. Furthermore, we need to see enough data for the exception rules subtree to be created while the exception rules of the existing similar rule could be reused for free without seeing any more data. Suryanto and Compton (2004) proposed a way to generalize existing rules in RDR knowledge bases by discovering new intermediate predicates. In this work, however, only a predefined list of features and features' values are considered with boolean operators to create a rule's condition. In contrast, our work tackles the domain of natural language which has an arbitrary large number of features. Using patterns as the language for the rule's condition is also more expressive than using just boolean operators over feature-value constraints.

Lexicon Suggestions

As described in custom annotations section, lexicons are used in generating annotations for specifying patterns. Reusing lexicon is an effective way of generalizing patterns over unseen cases. Given existing synonym resources, for example, Wordnet (Fellbaum, 1998) and algorithms that populate a lexicon using a few seed words (Phillips & Riloff, 2002; Stevenson & Greenwood, 2005), an important issue is to decide what and when new lexicons are needed for the task at hand. We describe heuristics that suggest when a new lexicon should be created or when an existing lexicon should be expanded while experts are building the KB incrementally. The heuristics are based on changes suggested by the Rule Recommendation module when an existing rule is modified. **Creating a new lexicon:** When a change involves features of *Token*, a new lexicon will be recommended. For example, suppose a pattern has a component:

{*Token.string* == useful}

and features of the *Token* are recommended to be changed to cover the token *appropriate* then a new lexicon containing *useful, appropriate* can be created.

- **Expanding an existing lexicon:** When a lexicon annotation is suggested to be changed to *Token* annotation, the lexicon can be expanded by including the token string. For example, for the pattern:

$\{Noun\}(\{Pair\})?\{VG.type == FVG\}\{LexGoodAdj\}.$

to match the phrase:

[Noun *this algorithm* Noun] [VG *is* VG] *elegant*

where the word *elegant* is not in the lexicon *LexGoodAdj*, *LexGoodAdj* is suggested to be changed to *Token*. In this situation, the token *elegant* could be added to the lexicon *LexGoodAdj*.

Experimental Results

We built two knowledge bases (KBs) with and without the Rule Suggestion Module for the task of extracting positive attributions from scientific texts described in the Example section. 16 technical papers in the area of machine learning from different authors were randomly selected for building the knowledge bases.

Following is the procedure to build a KB:

Create an empty SCRDR knowledge base.

1. Take one case from the training corpus as an input to the KB: a sentence in this task
2. The KB gives a conclusion for this sentence that is, the classification (true or false depending on whether the sentence contains a positive attribution) and the extracted phrase if it belongs to the true class. The conclusion of the sentence is shown to the expert for validation. If the expert agrees with the KB's conclusion, then go back to step 2. If the expert disagrees then go to next step.

3.   The expert can either create a new exception rule or modify an existing rule to correct the misclassification.

4.   Repeat step 2.

The first KB, called *basic KB*, is built without using the Rule Suggestion Module (RSM) while the second KB, called *assisted KB*, is built using the RSM in step 3. Notice that every time a KB performs unsatisfactorily on a new case, a knowledge acquisition session is carried out by the expert in step 4. A knowledge acquisition session does not necessarily result in a new rule added to the KB as an existing rule could be modified instead. Therefore, when comparing the two KBs, it is important that we consider the actual number of knowledge acquisition sessions incurred rather than just the number of rules in the KBs.

The *basic KB* comprises 74 rules with 59 rule modifications. In other words, 133 knowledge acquisition sessions occurred during the process of building

*Figure 4. Precision, Recall and F-measure on the test data of the **basic KB** as more rules are incrementally added to the KB. A rule can comprise several Knowledge Acquisition sessions.*

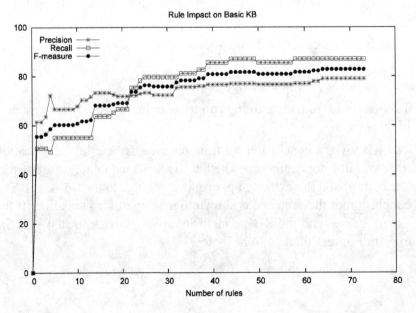

*Figure 5. Precision, Recall and F-measure on the test data of the **assisted
KB** as more rules are incrementally added to the KB. A rule can comprise
several Knowledge Acquisition sessions.*

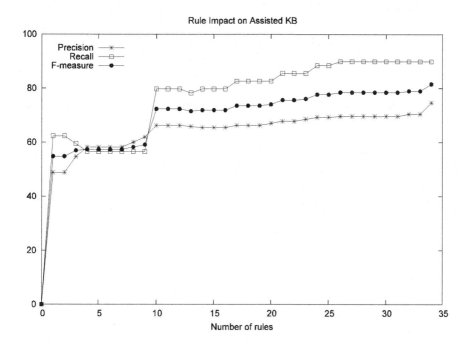

the *basic KB*. This KB has been evaluated with an F-measure of around 80%
on an unseen test corpus. It has been shown that this KB outperforms other
machine learning algorithms trained on the same data used for building the
KB (Pham Hoffmann, 2004a).

With the RSM, the *assisted KB* consists of 34 rules and 43 modifications.
Effectively, it is built using 77 experts knowledge acquisition sessions. On
the same test corpus, the *assisted KB* has a similar performance as the basic KB. It can be seen that the *assisted KB* is 54% more compact than the
basic KB. Furthermore, *assisted KB* observes a 42% reduction in the number of knowledge acquisition sessions required compared to the *basic KB*.
As shown in the Figure 4 and Figure 5, the *assisted KB* takes fewer number
of rules to achieve a similar level of performance as the *basic KB*. Notice
that a rule is a result of one or more knowledge acquisition sessions. Even
though the *assisted KB* achieves an F-measure of around 75% with only 10

rules, this is in fact a result of approximately 35 KA sessions as shown in the Assisted KB KA Impact figure.

Compared with lexicons used by the *basic KB*, the *assisted KB* has seven more lexicons which were recommended by the RSM. Among them, three lexicons are reused in more than one rule.

It suggests that with the RSM, it is quicker and requires less effort to build a knowledge base with reasonable performance.

Experience with RSM in the Knowledge Acquisition Process

The experts' task could be characterized by the two somewhat overlapping phases namely *text understanding* and *rule formulation*. In the *text understanding* phase, experts try to study the text to make a decision whether the text should be given a particular conclusion. In the task of extracting positive

*Figure 6. Precision, Recall and F-measure on the test data of the **assisted KB** as Knowledge Acquisition sessions are carried out.*

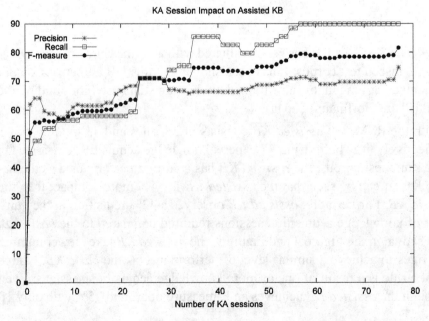

attribution, the conclusion is the type of the sentence and its relevant phrase. *Rule formulation* phase is to create a rule in KAFTIE language to justify for the chosen conclusion. It is difficult to completely separate these two phases as in order to make a decision in the *text understanding* part, experts probably already think about a rule covering this case, at least subconsciously.

As shown in the previous section, the RSM helps in building a more compact KB. A more compact KB also means a better generalization capability. An important benefit that the RSM brings in is the reduction in cognitive effort required to build the KB in both two phases.

In the *rule formulation* phase, the expert usually tries to remember if a similar rule has been entered before or searchs for similar rules in the KB. If a similar rule cannot be found, a new rule has to be created. Looking for a similar existing rule requires a lot of effort. Experts would have to recall what rules have been created. It gets even harder when there are more than one expert involved in building the KB or when the KB is large. With the RSM in place, experts merely have to inspect a proposed list of similar rules together with actions on how to modify them to cover the new case. If a suggested rule is deemed appropriate by the expert, the expert can modify the existing rule accordingly. Even when experts are not satisfied with the RSM's suggestions, at least the expert would have some ideas on what the new rule for this case might look like. When a new exception rule has to be created, most of the time the pattern experts select are in the top 5 of the list recommended by the RSM. Though the patterns recommended by the RSM are at annotations level only, specifying features constraints on those annotations is easy as the system automatically checks whether the pattern cover the current new case. Notice that with only one example at hand to create a rule, it is challenging to decide what level of generality the rule should be. This problem is alleviated by the RSM as when the KB performs incorrectly on a new case because a previously entered rule was too general or too specific, the RSM would be able to find this rule and suggest appropriate modifications. Moreover, after a new rule is committed to the KB, experts can simply "forget" that rule as the RSM will bring it back if the need arises. While it is possible that modifying an existing rule might over-generalize, with our approach it can always be fixed by experts adding more exception rules later. As can be seen in Figure 6, the precision or recall measures sometimes go down as a result of a knowledge acquisition session, being either a rule addition or a rule modification. Overall, however, an upwards trend is maintained as errors made by previous KA sessions are patched up by later KA sessions. Also, unseen cases covered by a generalization would not have been interpreted if there was no generalization and would require a new rule anyway. When a KB performs incorrectly on a new case by a non default rule, the matched phrases and annotations posted by the rule on the case can be seen as explanation for the KB's conclusion. In contrast, the default rule can only provide the default conclusion. Intuitively, it makes the *text understanding* phase easier when the KB already makes a conclusion with some explanation in the form of matched phrases. Therefore, it can even be advantageous to over-generalize a rule to cover a new case, even where it is known that the rule represents an incorrect conclusion. However, there may be domains/tasks where it is preferable to give no conclusion or when the default conclusion is already correct.

Discussion and Future Work

We proposed an intelligent agent that supports the construction of a complex knowledge base suitable for a variety of NLP tasks. Experimental results have shown that with the help of our Rule Suggestion Module (RSM), a more compact KB can be built with considerably fewer rules and, hence, with fewer rule acquisition interactions between the system and the expert. Consequently, the overall time spent by the expert was reduced. More importantly, however, the cognitive load on the expert is considerably reduced when a new rule needs to be entered. This allows the expert to continue with the task of improving the knowledge base for a longer period of time without the need for longer breaks.

Furthermore, using the Rule Suggestion Module a more compact knowledge base was built while maintaining the same performance (accuracy) as the knowledge base originally built without the assistance of the RSM.

It appears that one reason for the fewer rules needed in the RSM assisted construction of a KB is the better generalization of the rules entered and modified by the RSM compared to the rules entered "from scratch" by the expert directly. This is somewhat surprising, as the suggested rules are all based on previously entered rules which had to be developed by the human expert. We believe that in practice it is too difficult for the expert to remember the previously entered rules that would allow the expert to "manually" enter the *similar* rules which otherwise were developed with the help of the RSM.

Another question is why the previously entered rules on which the automatic rule suggestions are based lead to a more compact KB. We believe the reason lies in the fact that the previously entered rules reflect previously seen problem instances (text segments). By using an edit distance metric in the Rule Suggestion Module, a more general rule is suggested that covers both, the previously seen problem instance as well as the current case for which a new rule is required. This is in contrast to rules which are entered without the automatic assistance which are more likely not to cover the previously seen case as the expert focuses on the current case when coming up with a new rule.

If this is the case, our Rule Suggestion Module will not only provide useful support for building knowledge bases for natural language processing tasks as in KAFTIE. The RSM may be a useful addition to most knowledge acquisition systems based on an incremental knowledge acquisition framework, such as ripple down rules. Whether it would be possible to use a general purpose edit-distance remains to be seen. This explanation suggests that the positive effect of the RSM in resulting in a more compact KB is likely to be even more pronounced the larger the knowledge base grows because rules entered later are taking an increasing number of cases into account, thus becoming increasingly general. Of course, depending on the requirements of the domain, this effect of leading to increasingly general rules may also lead to overly general rules for which in turn exception rules would need to be developed once exception cases are presented to the expert. We suspect that indeed the RSM will allow one to build large knowledge bases even more effectively than the help RSM provided in the presented case study. However, further research is needed to gain more detailed insight into how far the RSM will be able to assist in building increasingly more compact KBs compared to the "manual" knowledge acquisition approach.

References

Abney, S. (1996). Partial parsing via finite-state cascades. *Natural Language Engineering*, *4*(2), 337–344.

Ait-Mokhtar, S., & Chanod, J.P. (1997). Incremental finite-state parsing. In *Proceedings of the 5th Conference on Applied Natural Language Processing* (pp 72–79). Washington, DC.

Cohen, W.W., Ravikumar, P., & Fienberg, S. (2003). A comparison of string distance metrics for name-matching tasks. In *Proceedings of IJCAI-03 Workshop on Information Integration on the Web (IIWeb-03)* (pp.73–78). Acapulco, Mexico.

Cunningham, H., Maynard, D., Bontcheva, K., & Tablan, V. (2002). Gate: An architecture for development of robust HLT applications. In *Proceedings of the 40ᵗʰ Annual Meeting of the Association for Computational Linguistics (ACL)* (pp. 168–175). Philadelphia.

Edwards, G., Compton, P., Malor, R., Srinivasan, A., & Lazarus, L. (1993). PEIRS: A pathologist maintained expert system for the interpretation of chemical pathology reports. *Pathology, 25*, 27–34.

Fellbaum, C. (Ed.). (1998). *WordNet: An electronic lexical database*. Cambridge, MA: MIT Press.

Hobbs, J., Appelt, D., Bear, J., Israel, D., Kameyama, M., Stickel, M., & Tyson, M. (1997). FASTUS: A cascaded finite-state transducer for extracting information from natural-language text. In E. Roche & Y. Schabes (Eds.), *Finite-state language processing* (pp. 383–406). Cambridge, MA: MIT Press.

Pereira, F., & Wright, R. (1997). Finite-state approximation of phrase structure grammars. In E. Roche & Y. Schabes (Eds.), *Finite-state language processing* (pp. 149–174). Cambridge, MA: MIT Press.

Pham, S.B., & Hoffmann, A. (2004a). Extracting positive attributions from scientific papers. In *Proceedings of the 7ᵗʰ International Conference on Discovery Science* (pp. 169–182). Italy.

Pham, S.B., & Hoffmann, A. (2004b). Incremental knowledge acquisition for building sophisticated information extraction systems with KAFTIE. In *Proceedings of the 5ᵗʰ International Conference on Practical Aspects of Knowledge Management* (pp. 292–306), Vienna, Austria.

Phillips, W., & Riloff, E. (2002). Exploiting strong syntactic heuristics and co-training to learn semantic lexicons. In *Proceedings of the 2002 Conference on Empirical Methods in Natural Language Processing (EMNLP)* (pp. 125–132). Pennsylvania.

Porter, M. (1980). An algorithm for suffix stripping. *Program, 14*(3), 130–137.

Roche, E., & Schabes, Y. (1995). Deterministic part-of-speech tagging with finite-state transducers. *Computational Linguistics, 2*(21), 227–253.

Stevenson, M., & Greenwood, M. (2005). A semantic approach to IE pattern induction. In *Proceedings of the 43rd Annual Meeting of The Association for Computational Linguistics (ACL)* (pp. 379–386). Ann Arbor, Michigan.

Suryanto, H., & Compton, P. (2004). Invented predicates to reduce knowledge acquisition. In *EKAW2004 – Proceedings of the 14th International Conference on Knowledge Engineering and Knowledge Management* (pp. 293–306). UK.

Chapter VI

Formalization of User Preferences, Obligations and Rights

Klaus-Dieter Schewe, Massey University, New Zealand

Bernhard Thalheim, Christian Albrechts University Kiel, Germany

Alexei Tretiakov, Massey University, New Zealand

Abstract

The aim of this chapter is to formalize user preferences, obligations, and rights in the context of Web information systems (WISs), and to indicate how this formalization can be used to reason about WIS specifications. This problem is approached on two levels of abstraction. On a high level a WIS is represented by a storyboard, which itself can be represented by an algebraic expression in a Kleene algebra with tests (KAT). Preferences can be formalized using the equational theory of KATs, which enable sophisticated propositional reasoning that can be applied to WIS personalization. Obliga-

tions and rights give rise to a propositional deontic logic. On a lower level of abstraction detailed state specifications are added using extended views. This amounts to replacing KATs by higher-order dynamic logic, using a higher-order deontic logic, and the formalization of proof obligations.

Introduction

Web information systems (WISs) are an important class of data-intensive systems with a lot of applications in e-business (Schewe, Kaschek, Wallace, & Matthews, 2005), e-learning (Schewe, Thalheim, Binemann-Zdanowicz, Kaschek, Kuss, & Tschiedel, 2005), information services (Feyer, Schewe, & Thalheim, 1998), and many more. Each WIS provides a dialogue between the system and the users, the latter ones being very often unknown to the designers. Each user uses the system to perform a certain task, some of which may only be realized by a joint effort of several users.

One problem we are confronted with in WISs is to be aware of user preferences and goals such that the system can be set up in way that permits an automatic customization to these preferences and goals. In order to do so we have to formalize the user preferences, which of course depend on a classification of users into *user profiles* or user types.

Furthermore, not all users are eligible to perform or contribute to the same tasks. This requires another classification of users according to their *roles*, and each role determines the rights and obligations of users in this role.

The aim of this chapter is to formalize user preferences, obligations, and rights and to indicate how this formalization can be used to reason about the WIS specification. For this purpose we adopt the co-design approach from Schewe and Thalheim (2005) to WIS design. On a high-level of abstraction the major modeling activity is *storyboarding* (Kaschek, Schewe, Wallace, & Matthews, 2004; Schewe & Thalheim, 2005; Thalheim & Düsterhöft, 2001), which consists of defining the *story space*, the *actors*, and the *tasks*. The system is considered as a set of abstract locations called *scenes*, between which users navigate. On their paths (called *stories*) through these scenes the users execute *actions*. This leads first to modeling story spaces by directed labeled graphs that are further refined by story algebras (Schewe & Thalheim, 2004; Thalheim & Düsterhöft, 2001). Actor modeling comprises user profiling, role modeling, plus modeling information portfolios. However, information portfolios are treated as part of supporting information for scenes (Schewe & Thalheim, 2005). We will present the gist of storyboarding in the next section.

In particular, we will formalize obligations and rights as part of user roles (Schewe & Thalheim, 2005) using a propositional variant of deontic logic (Eiter & Subrahmanian, 1999). This permits expressing deontic constraints already on a high level of abstraction. Furthermore, preferences will be associated with user profiles or user types (Schewe & Thalheim, 2005).

In Schewe and Thalheim (2004) it was actually shown that story algebras carry the structure of Kleene algebras with tests (Kozen, 1997), thus term rewriting can be applied to reason about story spaces, in particular, as KATs subsumes propositional Hoare logic (Kozen, 1999). In Schewe and Thalheim (2004) this was applied to personalization with respect to user preferences, which can be formalized by equations, and user goals, which can be formalized by postconditions. However, it was left open where the preferences were to be taken from. According to this model several dimensions are used to characterize user properties and for each dimension a usually ordered set of values is provided. A user profile is determined by values for each of the dimensions, whereas a user type combines several value combinations. While this is an accurate approach in accordance with more application oriented approaches, for example, learner modeling for e-learning systems, it bears the risk of having to define too many user types. Preferably, it would be better, if equations that express preferences would be made explicitly depending on values of some dimensions. This avoids identifying the user types and may be used to determine evolving user-specific story spaces. However, it is very unlikely that user types are compositional, so that we must expect non-monotonicity in personalization using such an approach. We will demonstrate this approach to personalization in another section.

Obligations and rights that are associated with roles have been formalized in Schewe and Thalheim (2005) using a propositional variant of deontic logic (Eiter & Subrahmanian, 1999). This permits expressing deontic constraints already on a high level of abstraction. However, all these high-level propositional approaches to formalizing preferences, goals, obligations, and rights with their reasoning facilities provide only a first and rather coarse handling of the problem. In order to fully capture the problem we have to look at a finer level of detail taking the data content and the functionality that is available at each scene into account. For this, the method in Schewe and Thalheim

(2005) provides *media types* that are extended views on some underlying database schema. The data model for this schema is of minor importance as long as the query language used for the views is expressive enough. For instance, it is well possible to assume that the database schema is modeled using HERM (Thalheim, 2000), while the query language constructs rational trees (Schewe & Thalheim, 2005).

One of the extensions to the views captures explicitly adaptivity to users, channels, and end-devices by using cohesion pre-orders or proximity values, which both enable a controlled split of information. For our purposes here, however, the extension by operations is a greater importance. As briefly indicated in Schewe (2004) the media types permit the refinement of propositional conditions in the story algebra by formulae in higher-order logic, while the operations refine the actions in the story space. These operations can be modeled as abstract programs, so that the whole story space will be refined by expressions of higher-order dynamic logic (Harel, Kozen, & Tiuryn, 2000). This can be used to set up proof obligations for personalization, static and dynamic consistency, and story space correctness (Schewe, 2004).

With respect to obligations and rights, the deontic constraints associated with the storyboard can be refined as well using the full power of deontic logic for agents (Eiter & Subrahmanian, 1999; Elgesem, 1997; Nute, 1997). Similar use of deontic logic has been made in Broersen, Wieringa, and Meyer, 2002; Dignum, Meyer, Wieringa, and Kuiper, 1996; and Wieringa and Meyer, 1991, 1993. In particular, we obtain a level of granularity that will allow us to model the cooperation of actors including messaging and task delegation. The non-monotonicity requests to take defeasibilty into account as well (Antoniou, Billington, Governatori, & Maher, 2001). In the last section before the conclusion we will present this refined approach to the problem of formalizing preferences, obligations, and rights.

Storyboarding

A *storyboard* describes the ways users may choose to interact with the system. It consists of three parts: a model of the story space, a model of actors, and a model of tasks. The *story space* describes the paths users follow while navigating through the WIS. These paths are the *stories*. Actors are groups of users with the same behavior, which leads to modeling *user profiles* and *roles*. *Tasks* link the actions of the story space with the actors, but we will not discuss tasks in this chapter.

Story Spaces

On a high level of abstraction we may think of a WIS as a set of abstract locations, which abstract from actual pages. A user navigates between these locations, and on this navigation path s/he executes a number of actions. We regard a location together with local actions, that is, actions that do not change the location, as a unit called *scene*.

Then a WIS can be described by an edge-labeled directed graph, in which the vertices represent the scenes, and the edges represent transitions between scenes. Each such transition may be labeled by an action executed by the user. If such a label is missing, the transition is due to a simple navigation link. The whole graph is then called *story space*. Scenes may be atomic or complex. In the latter case the scene itself represents another set of abstract locations, between which users can navigate. This gives rise to a multilayer model.

Example 1.

Figure 1 shows the graph of a story space for online loan applications. We numbered the scenes and the actions, so referring to this example we only talk of scene s_i and action α_j. In addition, scenes and actions are named, and the names have been chosen in a way to be understandable without deeper explanation.

The scene $s_0 = start$ is the start scene, that is, a user using the WIS will start here. Only one action $\alpha_1 = enter\_load\_system$ can be chosen in this scene. This action leads to a transition to scene $s_1 = type\_of\_loan$, in which general information about loans will be provided. A user has several actions to choose from in this scene. The actions $\alpha_7 = select\_personal\_loan$ and $\alpha_{13} = select\_mortgage$ lead to the scene $s_2 = applicant\_details$, the starting scene for the core of a loan application. Alternatively, a user may choose the action $\alpha_2 = look\_at\_loans\_at\_a\_glance$ requesting an overview on all available loans with a short description for each, which will be done in scene $s_{10} = loan\_overview$. From here a simple transition without action, indicated by the label skip leads back to the scene s_1.

Figure 1. A story space for online loan application

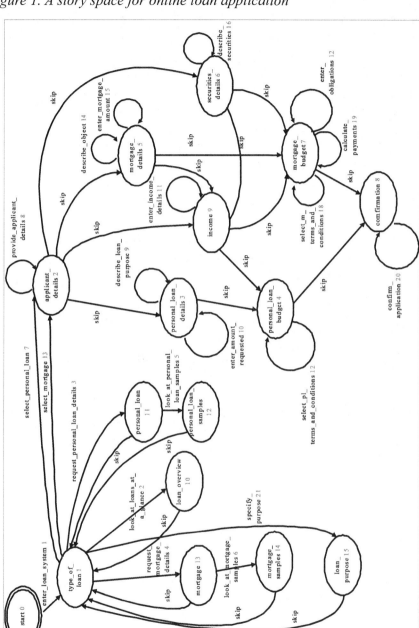

Similarly, actions $\alpha_3 = request\_personal\_loan\_details$ and $\alpha_3 = request\_mortgage\_details$ to scenes $s_{11} = personal\_loan$ and $s_{13} = mortgage$, respectively, in which details about a particular personal loan or mortgage will become available. In both cases a user can navigate back to scene s_1, or request samples for the personal loan or mortgage by choosing the action $\alpha_6 = look\_at\_personal\_loan\_samples$ in scene s_{11} or $\alpha_6 = look\_at\_mortgage\_samples$ in scene s_{13}, respectively, which will lead to scene $s_{12} = personal\_loan\_samples$ or $s_{14} = mortgage\_samples$, respectively. The last action $\alpha_{21} = specify\_purpose$ in scene s_1 takes a user to scene $s_{15} = loan\_purpose$, in which advice on suitable loans for a specified purpose can be sought.

The part of the story space starting from scene s_2 deals with gathering applicants' details, details of the selected mortgage or personal loan such as the amount requested, terms and conditions and securities, details concerning the income of the applicants, and finally a confirmation of the application. It can be understood in the same way, as the names of scenes and actions are self-explanatory—using "pl" and "m" as shortcuts for personal loan and mortgage, respectively.

At a finer level of detail we would like to extend the story space and indicate, under which conditions an action or scene transition can or must be executed and what will be the effect of an action. In doing so we associate a *precondition* with each action to specify exactly, under which conditions an action can be executed. Such preconditions can be easily expressed on the basis of propositional logic. That is, we take a set $\{\varphi_1, \ldots \varphi_n\}$ of atomic propositions and complete this to a propositional logic defining the set Φ of *propositional formulae* in the usual way, that is:

- Each atomic proposition φ_i is a proposition in Φ.
- If $\varphi, \psi \in \Phi$, then also $\neg\varphi$, $\varphi \wedge \psi$, $\varphi \wedge \psi$, and $\varphi \rightarrow \psi$ are propositions in Φ.

Thus, the *precondition* of an action α is a proposition $Pre(\alpha) \in \Phi$. A user can only choose the action α and execute it, if the precondition $Pre(\alpha)$ is satisfied in the current state of the WIS.

In a similar way we associate a *postcondition* $Post(\alpha) \in \Phi$ with each action α to specify exactly, which effects the action will have. That is, if the actionn α is selected and executed, the resulting state of the WIS will satisfy the proposition $Post(\alpha)$.

Example 2.

Take another look at the story space represented by Figure 1, in particular at the action α_{13} = *select_mortgage*. In this case we may want that a user can only execute this action, if s/he has received the necessary information about available mortgages, that is, mortgages must be known. This can be simply formalized by requesting *Pre(select_mortgage)=mortgages_known* using an atomic proposition. The interpretation of this atom should be that a user knows about mortgages.

Analogously, we may set *Post(select_mortagage)=mortgage_selected*, which states that after executing α_{13} a mortgage has been selected.

Plots

The introduction of pre and postconditions of actions opens a new perspective to the story space. We may look at the *plot*, which gives a detailed, yet still high-level specification of functionality. In addition to pre and postconditions, actions can be executed sequentially or in parallel, they can be iterated, and if several actions are available, users can choose between them. These extensions should also become part of the plot. These possibilities to combine actions lead to operators of an algebra, which we will call a *story algebra*. Thus, we can describe a story space by an element of a suitable story algebra.

Let us take now a closer look at the storyboarding language SiteLang (Thalheim & Düsterhöft, 2001), which defines a story algebra that captures the details of plots. For this we take the set A of actions and the set S of scenes as the basis for defining the set of *processes* $P = P(A,S)$ determined by A and S.

The set of *processes* $P = P(A,S)$ determined by the set of actions A and the set of scenes S and the extension of the scene assignment σ to a partial mapping $\sigma: P \rightarrow S$ are inductively defined as follows:

- Each action $\alpha \in A$ is also a process
- *skip* (or 1) is a process with no effect
- *fail* (or 0) is a process that is not executable
- If p_1 and p_2 are processes, then also the *sequence* $p_1 p_2$ is a process
- If p_1 and p_2 are processes, then also the *choice* $p_1 + p_2$ is a process
- If p is a process, then also the *iteration* p^* is a process

- If p is a process and φ is a Boolean condition, then the *guarded process* φp and the *post-guarded process* $p\varphi$ are processes.

We would like to define also the *parallel process* $p_1 \| p_2$. However, as we are mainly interested in the stories, we can consider $p_1 \| p_2$ as a shortcut for $p_1 p_2 + p_2 p_1$, that is, we just state that the order of the component processes does not matter.

A plot may contain Boolean conditions. The rationale behind this is that such a condition can be identified with a test that checks the condition. In particular, we write $\varphi + \psi$ for the disjunction of conditions φ and ψ, $\varphi \cdot \psi$ for their conjunction, and $\bar{\varphi}$ for a negated condition. This unusual notation is in accordance with the notation for Kleene algebras with tests, which we will exploit in the next section. In particular, the overloaded use of + for disjunction and choice, · for conjunction and sequence, 1 for true and *skip* skip, and 0 for false and *fail* does not lead to conflicts.

Example 3.

A plot expression for the detailed loan application in Figure 1 can be described as follows:

$$\alpha_1((\varphi_0(\alpha_{21}\,\varphi_{13}+1)\alpha_2 + \varphi_1\,\varphi_3(\alpha_5+1)\,\varphi_3 + \varphi_2\alpha_4(\alpha_6+1)\alpha_4)^*\,\varphi_5)(\alpha_1\,\varphi_6+\alpha_{13}\,\varphi_7)$$
$$\varphi_6\alpha_8(\alpha_8+1)\alpha_9\alpha_{10}\alpha_{11}\alpha_{12}\alpha_8+\varphi_7\alpha_8\alpha_8{}^*\alpha_{14}\alpha_{15}\alpha_{16}{}^*\alpha_{11}\alpha_{17}(\bar{\alpha}_{12}\alpha_{18}\varphi_{19})^*\varphi_{12}\alpha_{18}\varphi_9)$$

Box A.

φ_0 = *information_loan_types_needed*	φ_1 = *information_personal_loans_needed*
φ_2 = *information_mortgages_needed*	φ_3 = *personal_loans_known*
φ_4 = *mortgages_known*	φ_5 = *available_loans_known*
φ_6 = *personal_loan_selected*	φ_7 = *mortgage_selected*
φ_8 = *personal_loan_application_completed*	φ_9 = *mortgage_application_completed*
φ_{10} = *applied_for_personal_loan*	φ_{11} = *applied_for_mortgage*
φ_{12} = *payment_options_clear*	φ_{13} = *loans_recommended*

The scenes and actions have already been named in Figure 1. Furthermore, the plot involves the Boolean conditions. (See Box A.)

As in the previous examples the names chosen for the propositional atoms should be self-explanatory, for example, $\varphi_0 = information\_loan\_types\_needed$ expresses that the user needs information about the available types of loans, while $\varphi_{12} = payment\_options\_clear$ indicates that the different payment options for mortgages are understood by the user.

User Roles: Deontic Logic for Web Information Systems

Users can be classified according to their roles, goals, and behavior. We use the term *actor* for such a group of users. The *role* of an actor indicates a particular purpose of the system. As such it is usually associated with obligations and rights, which lead to deontic integrity constraints.

Roles are used to classify actors according to their rights and obligations. For instance, in a Web-based conference system we may have roles for the program committee chairs, the program committee members, and for authors. In an online loan system we may distinguish between actors in the role of customers and those in the role of bank clerks. In most systems we may expect one default role that is taken on by any actors, whereas other roles require some form of identification or at least an active switch to this role.

Let us now look briefly at a more sophisticated way to express rights and obligations that depend on other actions. An *obligation* specifies what an actor in a particular role has to do. A *right* specifies what an actor in a particular role is permitted to do. Both obligations and rights together lead to complex deontic integrity constraints. We use the following logical language L for this purpose:

- All propositional atoms are also atoms of L
- If α is an action on scene s and r is a role associated with s, then $Odo(r,\alpha)$, $Pdo(r,\alpha)$ and $Fdo(r,\alpha)$ are atoms of L
- For $\varphi, \psi \in L$ we also have $\neg \varphi$, $\varphi \wedge \psi$, $\varphi \vee \psi$, $\varphi \rightarrow \psi$ and $\varphi \leftrightarrow \psi$ are also formulae in L

Here we use the more familiar notation for negation, conjunction, and disjunction than in the previous subsection. For the time being both approaches do not interfere with each other.

The interpretation is standard. In particular, $Odo(r,\alpha)$ means that an actor with role r is obliged to perform action α, $Pdo(r,\alpha)$ means that an actor with role r is permitted to perform action α, and $Fdo(r,\alpha)$ means that an actor with role r is forbidden to perform action α.

Example 4.

The online loan example plot from Example 3 only contains one role customer, thus all actions and scenes in this example are associated with these role. Nevertheless, we may express some deontic constraints using the logical language defined previously.

A customer has the obligation to leave details (action α_9), once a personal loan or a mortgage has been selected (condition φ_6 or φ_7), Furthermore, if a mortgage is selected (condition φ_7), the customer is obliged to describe securities (action α_{16}) and to enter obligations (action α_{17}), that is, we obtain the deontic constraints $\varphi_6 \vee \varphi_7 \rightarrow Odo(customer, \alpha_8)$ and $\varphi_7 \rightarrow Odo(customer, \alpha_{16}) \wedge Odo(customer, \alpha_{17})$. Furthermore, a customer is allowed to look at mortgage samples (action α_6), which is simply expressed by $Pdo(customer, \alpha_6)$.

We may of course extend the online loan system further by adding roles bank clerk and mortgage advisor and further deontic constraints.

User Profiles and Types

Modeling the behavior of an actor leads to *user profiles*, which can be modeled by giving values for various properties that characterize a user. Furthermore, each profile leads to preference rules that can again be expressed by constraints on the story space.

While roles classify actors according to their rights and obligations, *user profiles* and *user types* classify actors according to their behavior. That is, roles indicate a proactive approach to WIS modeling, whereas user profiling is reactive.

The general approach is to start with characterizing properties of users and to provide values for each of these properties. Each combination of such values defines a user profile. However, the behaviour for some of these profiles is usually the same. So we combine user profiles to user types.

Furthermore, each user profile or type leads to rules, in particular preference rules. According to the characterizing aspects of WISs we may distinguish between preferences concerning the content, the functionality, or the presentation. In the context of storyboarding such preferences can be expressed by constraints on the story space.

We will now discuss in more detail these user profiles and types. We start with a finite set Δ of *dimensions* capturing the properties of users. For each dimension $\delta \in \Delta$ we assume to be given a *domain dom*(δ). Some of these domains may be totally ordered, that is, there is a total order $\leq_\delta$ on *dom*(δ) usually, we drop the index. A totally ordered domain is also called a *scale* of the dimension.

As there are usually many dimensions, each of which has a domain with at least two elements, this gives us many ways to combine these values to obtain user profiles. In order to be able to manage the combinatorial explosion, we introduce user types.

If $\Delta = \{\delta_1, ..., \delta_n\}$ is a set of dimensions, then the set of *user profiles* (or the *user-grid*) over Δ is $gr(\Delta) = dom(\delta_1) \times ... \times dom(\delta_n)$. A user type over Δ is a subset $U \subseteq gr(\Delta)$.

This way of defining a user type as any subset of the user-grid leaves a lot of freedom to define a set $\{U_1, .., U_k\}$ of user-types for a particular story space. We must, of course, assure that this set of user types is *complete* in the sense that all user profiles are covered. That is, for each user profile $(v_1, .., v_n) \in gr(\Delta)$, that is, $v_i \in dom(\delta_i)$, there must exist at least one $j \in \{1, .., k\}$ with $(v_1, .., v_n) \in U_j$.

One might expect that user profiles that contribute to the same user type, do not differ too much in the values for the dimensions. For this consider cubes in the user-grid.

If $\Delta = \{\delta_1, .., \delta_n\}$ is a set of dimensions, then a subset $U \subseteq gr(\Delta)$ is a cube if it has the form $U = D_1, .., D_n$, such that for all $i = 1, ..., n$, for which $dom(\delta_i)$ is totally ordered scale, whenever $v_{i1}, v_{i2} \in D_i$ with $v_{i1} \leq_{\delta_i} v_{i2}$ holds, then also $v_i \in D_i$ for $v_{i1} \leq_{\delta_i} v_i \leq_{\delta_i} v_{i2}$. Thus, one common way of defining user types is to consider cubes in the user-grid. We call these user types *kiviat*, because they can be easily represented by Kiviat graphs. We expect that most user types will be kiviat.

The major purpose of introducing user types is to provide ways to customize the WIS to its users, that is, to personalize the system. In principle there are two ways of doing it. The first one would just introduce user-type-specific plots, whereas the second one would try to generate them out of preference rules and general rules about the story space. Therefore, it is a good idea to formulate preference rules. Even if user-specific plots are not derived but specified by WIS designers, the rules can be useful to quality check the customized plots.

In view of the algebraic constructors that were used to specify plots, we consider preference rules in connection with these constructors. This leads to the following definition.

A *preference rule* associated with a user type U is expressed through one of the following equations:

- An equation of the form $\varphi(\alpha+\beta)=\varphi\alpha$ expresses that a user conditionally prefers action α over action β, where the condition is expressed by φ. The special case $\varphi = true$ expresses an unconditional preference.

- An equation $p(p_1 + p_2)= pp_1$ expresses the conditional preference of the process p_1 over p_2 after the process p. The special case $p = 1$ expresses an unconditional preference.

- An equation $p_1 p_2 + p_2 p_1 = p_1 p_2$ expresses a preference of order, that is, if the processes p_1 and p_2 can be executed in arbitrary order, it is preferred to execute first p_1.

- An equation $p^* = pp^*$ expresses that in case of an iteration it will be executed at least once.

Story Space Customization

Let us now see how we can use preference rules to customize plots. For this, we exploit the fact that our story algebra carries the structure of a Kleene algebra with tests (KAT) as shown in Schewe and Thalheim (2005).

Kleene Algebras with Tests

As the set of processes P carries the structure of a Kleene algebra, the following conditions hold:

- $+$ and $\cdot$ are associative, that is, for all p, q, r we must have $p+(q+r)=(p+q)+r$ and $p(qr)=(pq)r$

- $+$ is commutative and idempotent with 0 as neutral element, that is, for all p, q we must have $p+q=q+p$, $p+p=p$ and $p+0=p$

- 1 is a neutral element for $\cdot$, that is, for all p we must have $p1=1p=p$

- for all p we have $p0=0p=0$

- $\cdot$ is distributive over $+$, that is, for all p, q, r we must have $p(q+r)=pq+pr$ and $(p+q)r=pr+qr$

- p^*q is the least solution x of $q + px \leq x$ and qp^* is the least solution of $q + xp \leq x$, using the partial order $x \leq y \equiv x + y = y$

In addition, the Boolean conditions involved in the processes, that is, the "tests," form a Boolean algebra. In order to exploit these equations for story space customization, we further take the preference equations into consideration, so we can start from equations in the following form:

- **Preferences:** An equation of the form $\varphi \, (\alpha+\beta)= \varphi \, \alpha$ expresses that a user conditionally prefers action α over action β, where the condition is expressed by φ. The special case $\varphi =1$ expresses an unconditional preference.

- **Precondition:** An equation of the form $\overline{\varphi} \, \alpha = 0$ (or equivalently $\alpha = \varphi\alpha$) expresses that the condition φ is a precondition for the action α.

- **Postcondition:** An equation of the form $\alpha \, \overline{\varphi} = 0$ (or equivalently $\alpha = \alpha\varphi$) expresses that the condition φ is a postcondition for the action α.

- **Invariance:** An equation of the form $\alpha\varphi = \varphi\alpha$, which is equivalent to $\overline{\varphi} \, \alpha = \alpha \, \overline{\varphi}$ and to $\varphi\alpha \, \overline{\varphi} + \overline{\varphi} \, \alpha\varphi = 0$, expresses that the condition φ (and so its negation φ) is invariant under the action α.

- **Exclusion:** An equation of the form $\varphi\psi=0$ expresses that the conditions φ and ψ exclude each other.

- **Parallelism:** An equation of the form $\alpha\beta= \beta\alpha$ expresses that the order of the actions α and β is irrelevant; hence they behave as if they were executed in parallel.

Then we can formalize the following optimization task, in which the minimality request refers to the order $\leq$ on processes, that is elements of the KAT, that was defined previously:

Given a process $p \in K$ that represents a plot of a story space, and a set Σ of equationson K that represents (among other constraints) user preferences and a postcondition ψ, we look for a minimal process p' such that $p\varphi = p'\varphi$ holds.

That is, the resulting process p' is a *personalization* of p according to the *user intention* formalized by ψ. We illustrate this kind of propositional reasoning with KATs by the following example.

Example 5.

Let us continue Example 3 and look at a user who is going to apply for a home loan. This can be expressed by the goal ϖ. Then we express application knowledge by the equations $\varphi_{10}\varphi_{11}=0$ (a user either applies for a home loan or a mortgage, not for both), $\varphi_{10}\varphi_9=0$ (a user applying for a home loan does not complete a mortgage application), and $\varphi_6\varphi_7=0$ (a user either selects a home loan or a mortgage, but not both).

Then we can simplify $p\varphi_{10}$ with the expression p from example 3 step by step. First we get $(\varphi_{10}+\varphi_{11})\varphi_{10}=\varphi_{10}$, which can then be used for:

$$(\varphi_6\alpha_8(\alpha_8+1)\alpha_9\alpha_{10}\alpha_{11}\alpha_{12}\varphi_8 + \varphi_7\alpha_8\alpha_8^*\alpha_{14}\alpha_{15}\alpha_{16}^*\alpha_{11}\alpha_{17}(\overline{\varphi}_{12}\alpha_{18}\alpha_{19})^*\varphi_{12}\alpha_{18}\varphi_9)\varphi_{10} =$$
$$\varphi_6\alpha_8(\alpha_8+1)\alpha_9\alpha_{10}\alpha_{11}\alpha_{12}\varphi_8\varphi_{10} + \varphi_7\alpha_8\alpha_8^*\alpha_{14}\alpha_{15}\alpha_{16}^*\alpha_{11}\alpha_{17}(\overline{\varphi}_{12}\alpha_{18}\alpha_{19})\varphi_{12}\alpha_{18}\varphi_9\varphi_{10} =$$
$$\varphi_6\alpha_8(\alpha_8+1)\alpha_9\alpha_{10}\alpha_{11}\alpha_{12}\varphi_8\varphi_{10}$$

Then finally we get:

$$(\alpha_7\varphi_6+\alpha_{13}\varphi_7)\varphi_6\alpha_8(\alpha_8+1)\alpha_9\alpha_{10}\alpha_{11}\alpha_{12}\varphi_8\varphi_{10} =$$
$$\alpha_7\varphi_6\varphi_6\alpha_8(\alpha_8+1)\alpha_9\alpha_{10}\alpha_{11}\alpha_{12}\varphi_8\varphi_{10}$$
$$+\alpha_{13}\varphi_7\varphi_6\alpha_8(\alpha_8+1)\alpha_9\alpha_{10}\alpha_{11}\alpha_{12}\varphi_8\varphi_{10} =$$
$$\alpha_7\varphi_6\alpha_8(\alpha_8+1)\alpha_9\alpha_{10}\alpha_{11}\alpha_{12}\varphi_8\varphi_{10}$$

This means that the story space can be simplified to:

$$\alpha_1((\varphi_0(\alpha_{21}\varphi_{13}+1)\alpha_2 + \varphi_1\alpha_3(\alpha_5+1)\varphi_3 + \varphi_2\alpha_4(\alpha_6+1)\varphi_4)^*\varphi_5)$$
$$\alpha_7\varphi_6\alpha_8(\alpha_8+1)\alpha_9\alpha_{10}\alpha_{11}\alpha_{12}\varphi_8\alpha_{20}\varphi_{10}$$

This simply means that for a user who is looking for a home loan application the part of the story space that deals with mortgage application will be cut out.

Decidability and Complexity

Let us now look at the personalization problem in the light of the theory of KATs. Our formalization in the previous section has led to an optimisation problem: we look for a minimal $p' \leq p$ with $\Sigma|=p'\psi=p\psi$. However, in the theory of KATs so far only completeness and the decidability of decision problems have been investigated. In other words, we only know about the decidability and complexity of problems of the form $\Sigma|=p=q$.

However, if the expression p that describes the story space is *-free, there will be only finitely many expressions p' with $p' \leq p$. In this case we can rephrase our problem by the following decision problem.

Given process p, $p' \in K$ such that p represents a story space and $p' \leq p$ holds, and a set Σ of equations on K that represents (among other constraints) user preferences and a postcondition $\psi \in B$, then decide, whether $\Sigma|=p\psi=p'\psi$ holds.

If p involves the *-operator, say we have a sub-expression q^*, it may be the case that replacing q^* by $(1+q+q^2+\cdots+q^n)$ leads to some p', for which $\Sigma|=p\psi=p'\psi$ holds. In this case adopt the following pragmatic strategy:

1.   Check whether for some n replacing q by $(1+q+q^2+\cdots+q^n)$ leads to some p' with $\Sigma|=p\psi=p'\psi$.

2.   If such an n exists, replace p by p', thus remove the occurrence of the *-operator.

3.   If such an n does not exist, leave the *-operator in p, and consider only those expressions $p' \leq p$, for which q^* is replaced by (q'^*) with $q' \leq q$.

While this strategy may miss out to find the optimal solution, it guarantees that we are able to reduce personalization to a decision problem.

For the equational theory of KATs we know from Kozen and Smith, 1996 that it is decidable, but PSPACE-complete. That is, we can decide in polynomial space, whether $p = q$ can be derived from the axioms of KATs. However, the decision problem we are dealing with is of the form $\Sigma|=p=q$ with a set of equations Σ, that is, in the Horn theory of KATs.

From Kozen(2002) we already know that such problems are undecidable in general. Even if we reduce ourselves to Kleene algebras instead of KATs, we already get Σ_1^0-completeness, that is, the problem is in general recursively enumerable hard.

However, the problem we deal with is not the general decision problem for the Horn theory, as in our case Σ only contains equations that have a particular form. From Kozen and Smith (1996) we know that we can reduce equations of the form $r = 0$-. These include equations obtained from pre and postconditions, exclusion conditions, and invariance equations – to the equational theory. Instead of showing $r = 0 \rightarrow p\psi=p'\psi$ we can equivalently show $p\psi + urn = p'\psi + urn$, where u is a "universal" process. That is $u = (\alpha_1+\cdots+\alpha_m)^*$, where the α_i are all the atomic actions that are not tests—it is easy to see (and crucial for the proof) that $p \leq u$ holds for all processes p. So we can remove all equations of the form $r = 0$ from Σ and enrich the equation that is to be derived instead.

This leaves us with only two kinds of equations: those arising from conditional preferences and those arising from parallelism. Recall that the former ones have the form $\varphi(\alpha+\beta) = \overline{\psi}_\alpha\alpha$. Here we apply a little trick and introduce exclusive postcondition ψ_α and ψ_β for α and β, respectively. Thus, we have the equations $\psi_\alpha\psi_\beta= 0$, $\overline{\psi}_\alpha\alpha = 0$ and $\overline{\psi}_\beta\beta = 0$. Then, we can replace the preference equation by $\varphi(\alpha+\beta)\psi_\beta = 0$. Hence, we get again equations of the form $r = 0$, which can be used to reduce the problem to a decision problem in the equational theory of KATs, which is PSPACE-complete.

Database Issues: The Power of Media Types

Each user of a WIS has information needs that have to be satisfied by the system. These information needs are usually not known in advance. Part of the needed information may depend on other parts, on decisions made while navigating through the WIS, and even on the information provided by the user. That is, the information portfolio of a user depends on the path through the WIS, that is, in our terminology on the story.

Media Types

Therefore, assuming that there is a database for the data content of the WIS with database schema S, the information need on a scene s definitely accounts for a *view* V_S over S. That is, we have another schema S_V and a computable transformation from databases over S to databases over S_V. Such a transformation is usually expressed by a query q_V.

This leads us to media types (Schewe & Thalheim, 2005). In principle, it is not important what kind of database we have as long as there exists a sufficiently powerful query mechanism that permits to define views. So assume to be given a database schema S, which itself is based on some underlying type system such as (using abstract syntax)

$$t = b \mid (\alpha_1 : t_1, ..., \alpha_n : t_n) \mid \{t\}.$$

Here b represents an arbitrary collection of *base types*, for example, *BOOL* for Boolean values T and F, **1** for a single value 1, *TEXT* for text, *PIC* for images, *MPIC* for video data, *CARD* and *INT* for numbers, *DATE* for dates, *ID* for object identifiers, *URL* for URLs, *MAIL* for e-mail addresses, and so forth. The constructors $(\cdot)$ and $\{\cdot\}$ are used for records and finite sets.

For each type $R \in S$ we have a representing type t_R. In a S-database db each type $R \in S$ gives rise to a finite set $db(R)$ consisting of pairs (i, v) with i of type *ID* and v of type t_R. Using this we may set up a powerful query language adapting a logic programming approach as in Abiteboul and Kanellakis (1989).

Thus, a query will be expressed as a set of rules (precisely: a sequence of such sets). Evaluating the rule body on a given database will result in bindings of variables, and the corresponding bindings for the head together with the creation of new identifiers for unbound variables results in an extension to the database. These extensions are iterated until a fixed point is reached.

In order to formalize this, assume to be given countable sets of variables V_t for each type t. These sets are to be pairwise disjoint. Variables and constants of type t are terms of that type. In addition, each $R \in S$ is a term of type $\{(ident: ID, value : t_R)\}$, and for each variable ι of type ID (and URL, respectively) there is a term $\hat{\iota}$ of some type $t(\iota)$. If $\tau_1, ..., \tau_k$ are terms of type t, then $\{\tau_1, ..., \tau_k\}$ is a term of type $\{t\}$, and if $\tau_1, ..., \tau_k$ are terms of type $\tau_1, ..., \tau_k$, respectively, then $(a_1 : \tau_1, ..., a_k : \tau_k)$ is a term of type $(a_1 : t_1, ..., a_k : t_k)$.

If τ_1, τ_2 are terms of type $\{t\}$ and t, respectively, then $\tau_1(\tau_2)$ is a positive literal (also called a fact) and $\neg\tau_1(\tau_2)$ is a negative literal. If τ_1, τ_2 are terms of the same type t, then $\tau_1 = \tau_2$ is a positive literal and $\tau_1 \neq \tau_2$ is a negative literal. A *ground fact* is a fact without variables.

A rule is an expression of the form $L_0 \leftarrow L_1, ..., L_k$ with a fact L_0 (called the head of the rule) and literals $L_1, ..., L_k$ (called the body of the rule), such that each variable in L_0 not appearing in the rule's body is of type ID or URL, respectively. A *logic program* is a sequence $P_1; ...; P_l$, in which each P_i is a set of rules.

Finally, a *query* Q on S is defined by a type t_Q and a logic program P_Q such that a variable *ans* of type $\{(url : URL, value : t_Q)\}$ is used in P_Q. A *Boolean query* can be described as a query Q with type $\mathbf{1}$. Alternatively, as we are not interested in creating a URL for the answer, we can simplify the approach and consider a logic program, in which a variable *ans* of type $BOOL = \{\mathbf{1}\}$ appears.

A logic program $P_1; ...; P_l$ is evaluated sequentially. Each set of rules is evaluated by computing an in *inflationary fixed point* as in inflationary DATALOG. That is, start with the set of ground facts given by the S-database *db*. Whenever variables in the body of a rule can be bound in a way that all resulting ground literals are satisfied, then the head fact is used to add a new ground fact. Whenever variables in the head cannot be bound in a way that they match an existing ground fact, the variables of type ID and URL will be bound to new identifiers or URLs, respectively.

Example 6.

Consider a query Q with type t_Q defined as:

(type : STRING, conditions : STRING, interest : STRING,

amount : CARD, disagio : RATIONAL, interest_rate : RATIONAL,

object : STRING, securities : {(value : RATIONAL, object : STRING,

type : STRING)}, customers : {(income :{(type : STRING,

amount : CARD, frequency : STRING)},

obligations : {(type : STRING, amount : CARD,

frequency : STRING)})})

Assume the database schema S contains (among others) the types *Loan_Type*, *Customer*, *Mortgage*, *Owes_Mortgage*, *Security*, *Income*, and *Obligation* with the following representing types:

t_{Loan_Type} = *(type : STRING, conditions : STRING, interest : STRING)*

$t_{Customer}$ = (customer_no : CARD, name : STRING, address : STRING,
        date_of_birth : DATE)

$t_{Mortgage}$ = (type : ID, mortgage no : CARD, amount : CARD,
        disagio : RATIONAL, interest rate : RATIONAL,
        begin : DATE, end : DATE, object : STRING)

$t_{Owes\_Mortgage}$ = (who : ID, what : ID, begin : DATE, end : DATE)

$t_{Security}$ = (whose : ID, for : ID, value : CARD, object : STRING,
        type : STRING)

t_{Income} = {who : ID, type : STRING, amount : RATIONAL,
        frequency : RATIONAL, account : CARD}

$t_{Obligation}$ = (who : ID, type : STRING, amount : RATIONAL,
        frequency : RATIONAL, account : CARD)

Then the following logic program P_Q will produce an anonymized set of mortgages:

$M_1(t,c,i,a,d,p,o,S,C,i\ ) \leftarrow Mortgage(i\ ,(i\ ,n,a,d,p,b,e,o)),$
$Loan\,Type(i\,(t,c,i));$
$\hat{S}(v,o,t') \leftarrow Security(i_s,(i_c,i_m,v,o,t')),M_1(t,c,i,a,d,\ p,o,S,C,i_m).$

$\hat{C}(I, O, i_c) \leftarrow Customer(i_c, (n', n, a, db)), Owes\_Mortgage(i_o, (i_c, i_m, b, e)),$
$M_1(t, c, i, a, d, p, o, S, C, i_m);$
$\hat{I}(t', a', f) \leftarrow \hat{C}(I, O, ic), M_1(t, c, i, a, d, p, o, S, C, i_m),$
$Income(i_m, (i_c, t', a', f, ac)).$
$\hat{O}(t', a', f) \leftarrow \hat{C}(I, O, i_c), M_1(t, c, i, a, d, p, o, S, C, i_m),$
$Obligation(i_o, (i_c, t', a', f, ac));$
$M_2(t, c, i, a, d, p, o, \hat{S}, D) M \leftarrow {}_1(t, c, i, a, d, p, o, S, C, i_m);$
$\hat{D}(\hat{I}, \hat{O}) \leftarrow \hat{C}(I, O, i_c), M_2(t, c, i, a, d, p, o, \hat{S}, D),$
$M_1(t, c, i, a, d, p, o, S, C, i_m);$
$Ans(u, (t, c, i, a, d, p, o, \hat{S}, \hat{D})) \leftarrow M2(t, c, i, a, d, p, o, \hat{S}, D).$

This logic program consists of a sequence of six sets of rules. In a nutshell, the fixed-point computed by the first set will contain the additional relation M_1, which collects information about mortgages including conditions and interest (from *Loan_Type*) and new identifiers S and C for the sets of securities and customers, respectively. The fixed-point computed by the next set of rules contains details for each of these sets. Furthermore, for the customers it creates new identifiers for sets of incomes and sets of obligations, the details of which are computed by the third set of rules. The last three sets of rules replace the identifiers for the sets of securities and customers, respectively, by the corresponding sets.

An *interaction type* has a name M and consists of a content data type *cont(M)* with the extension that the place of a base type may be occupied by a pair $l : M'$ with a label l and the name M' of an interaction type, a defining query q_M with type t_M, and a set of *operations*. Here t_M is the type arising from *cont(M)* by substitution of *URL* for all pairs $l : M'$.

Finite sets C of interaction types define *content schemata*. Then an S-database db and the defining queries determine finite sets $db(M)$ of pairs (u, v) with URLs u and values v of type t_M for each $M \in C0$. We use the notion presite for the extension of db to C. The pair (u,v) will be called an *interaction object* in the presite db. A Boolean query on $S \cup C$ defines a *condition* φ.

A *media type* extends an interaction type M together in two ways: It adds *adaptivity* and *hierarchies*, which can be formalized by a cohesion preorder $\preceq_M$ (or a set of proximity values) and a set of hierarchical versions $H(M)$, respectively. For our purposes here we concentrate on the operations that already come with the interaction types (for the extensions, see Schewe & Thalheim, 2005).

In general, an operation on a type R consists of a *signature* and a *body*. The *signature* consists of an operation name O, a set of input-parameter/type pairs $\iota_i : t_i$ and a set of output parameter/type pairs $o_j : t'_j$. The body is an *abstract program* using the following constructs:

- 1 and 0 are abstract programs meaning *skip* and *fail*, respectively.
- An *assignment x:=exp* with a variable x and an expression of the same type as x is an abstract program. The possible expressions are defined by the type system. In addition, we permit expressions $\{P\}$ with a logic program P, assuming that P contains a variable *ans*. The expression $\{P\}$ is interpreted as the result of the logic program bound to *ans*.
- If P, P_1 and P_2 are abstract programs, the same holds for the *iteration* P^*, the choice $P_1 + P_2$ and the sequence $P_1 \cdot P_2 = P_1 P_2$.
- If P is an abstract program and φ is a condition, then the *guarded program* φP and the postguarded program $P\varphi$ are also abstract programs.
- If x is a variable and P is an abstract program, then the *selection* $@x \bullet P$ is also an abstract program.

There are a few subtleties regarding variable scoping and restrictions to assignments that have to be taken into account for operations on interaction types (Schewe & Thalheim, 2005), but for our purposes here it is not relevant to discuss them.

With respect to the connection to the story space, the propositional conditions φ now have to be refined to conditions on $S \cup C$, while each action α on a scene s is refined by operations associated with the media type that supports s.

Correctness, Consistency, and Personalization

With the introduction of media types to support scenes we can no longer rely on simple equational reasoning using KATs. Therefore, we introduce a higher-order dynamic, where the order comes from the intrinsic use of the set constructor and the logic programs in queries. In fact, instead of using logic programs with a semantics defined by inflationary fixed-points, we could use directly higher-order logic enriched with a fixed-point operator.

As a consequence, we may consider a logic program P as a representative of a higher-order logical formula, say φ_P. If $\{P\}$ is used as the right-hand side of an assignment, then it will correspond to a term $\mathbf{I}ans.\varphi_P$ denoting the unique *ans* satisfying formula φ_P. That is, all conditions turn out to be formulae of a logic L, which happens to be a higher-order logic with an inflationary fixed-point operator. From the point of view of expressiveness the fixed-point operator is already subsumed by the order, but for convenience we do not emphasize this aspect here.

Furthermore, by adding terms of the form $\mathbf{I}x.\varphi$ with a formula φ and a variable x all assignments in operations are just "normal" assignments, where the left-hand side is a variable and the right-hand side is a term of L.

We now extend L to a dynamic logic by adding formulae of the form $[p]\varphi$ with an abstract program p and a formula φ of L. Informally, $[p]\varphi$ means that after the successful execution of p the formula φ necessarily holds (Harel et al., 2000). In addition, we use the shortcut $\langle p \rangle \varphi \equiv \neg[p]\neg\,\varphi$, so $\langle p \rangle \varphi$ means that after the successful execution of p it is possible that the formula φ holds.

Using our recursive definition of abstract programs the following rules apply to $[p]\varphi$ for a complex abstract program p:

$[1]\varphi \equiv \varphi$

$[0]\varphi \equiv 0\ [x := t]\ \psi \equiv \psi\ \{x/t\}$ (substitute all free occurrences of x in ψ by t)

$[p_1 p_2]\ \psi \equiv [p_1]\ [p_2]\psi$

$[p_1 + p_2]\psi \equiv [p_1]\psi \wedge [p_2]\psi$

$[p^*]\ \psi \equiv$ the weakest solution φ of $\varphi \leftrightarrow \psi[p]\varphi$

$[\varphi\ p]\ \psi \equiv \varphi \rightarrow [p]\ \psi$

$[p\ \varphi]\ \psi \equiv [\,p\,]\ (\varphi \rightarrow \psi)$

$[@x\cdot p]\ \psi \equiv \forall x[p]\ \psi$

The equivalence for the iteration operator refers to the implication order, that is, if $\varphi \models \psi$ holds, then ψ is called *weaker* than φ. Further rules looking also at the structure of ψ are given in Harel et al. (2000).

With these preparations we can rethink the reasoning about the story space. In the sequel we will discuss three applications of dynamic logic:

- We take a look at proof obligations for the operations that result from the specification of the story space.

- We take a look at proof obligations for the operations that arise from static and dynamic integrity constraints on the underlying database schema.

- We reconsider WIS personalization in the light of dynamic logic as opposed to KATs.

- *Story Space Proof Obligations.* Let p denote the KAT expression that represents the complete story space. If all conditions in p are replaced by conditions on the pre-site and all actions are replaced by the abstract programs defining the realizing operations, we obtain an abstract program, which by abuse of notation shall still be denoted p.

As a WIS has a general purpose, this can be formalized by some post-condition ψ. Thus, $[p]\psi$ describes the weakest condition, under which the purpose of the system can be achieved. If φ characterizes a precondition that should be sufficient for the achievability of the WIS purpose, then we obtain $\varphi \rightarrow [p]\psi$ as a *general story space proof obligation*. In most cases we should expect $\varphi \equiv 1$.

Similarly, we may concentrate on fragments p' of the story space expression of the form $\varphi p \psi$, which corresponds to a Hoare triplet $\{\varphi\}p\{\psi\}$ Hoare (1969) and thus gives rise to a *special story space proof obligation* $\varphi \rightarrow [p']\psi$.

- *Consistency Proof Obligations.* A *static constraint* on the underlying database schema S is a condition ζ, in which the free variables are among the $R \in S$. Such constraints give rise to the request that whenever an operation is started in a database satisfying ζ, then the database reached after successfully completing the execution of the operation, must necessarily satisfy ζ, too.

That is, for all operations p that are defined on a pre-site and all static constraints ζ we obtain a *static consistency proof obligation* $\zeta \to [p]\zeta$.

- A *dynamic constraint* on the underlying database schema $S = \{R_1,..., R_n\}$ is a condition ζ, in which the free variables are among in $S \cup S'$ with $S = \{R_1,..., R_n\}$ and each R_i' having the same type as R_i. The additional variables R_i' are used to distinguish between S-databases db, on which an operation p is started, and S'-databases db' resulting after p has been successfully executed.

Obviously, a dynamic constraint ξ has to be interpreted on a pair $\{db, db'\}$ of databases. Following a standard approach to dynamic consistency (Schewe, Thalheim, Schmidt, & Wetzel, 1992) we associate with ξ an abstract program:

$$p(\xi) = @\, R_1',\ldots,R_n' \bullet \xi R_1 := R_1' \ldots R_n := R_n'.$$

Then dynamic consistency of an operation p with respect to ξ means that p must "specialize" $p(\xi)$, that is, we require that $[p(\xi)]\psi \to [p]\varphi$ for all conditions ψ on S. Fortunately, this proof obligation can be rephrased using a renaming p' of $p(\xi)$ given by:

$$p' = @\, R_1',\ldots,R_n' \bullet \xi \{R_1 / R_1'',\ldots, R_n / R_n''\} R_1'' := R_1'' := R_1' \ldots R_n'' := R_n'.$$

Then the *dynamic consistency proof obligation* for p with respect to ξ becomes:

$$([p']\langle p \rangle (R_1 = R_1'' \wedge \cdots \wedge R_n = R_n''))\{R_1''/ R_1,\ldots, R_n'' / R_n\}.$$

Personalization Proof Obligations. The general approach to personalization that was outlined in the previous section is still the same, that is we can assume a set Σ containing general constraints on $S \cup C$ and specific constraints that refer to preferences of a particular user type. Examples of such preferences are the following:

- An equation $p_1 + p_2 = p_1$ expresses an unconditional preference of operation p_1 over p_2.

- An equation $\varphi(p_1 + p_2) = \varphi\, p_1$ expresses a conditional preference of operation p_1 over p_2 in case the condition φ is satisfied.

- Similarly, an equation $p(p_1 + p_2) = pp_1$ expresses another conditional preference of operation p_1 over p_2 after the operation p.

- An equation $p_1 p_2 + p_2 p_1 = p_1 p_2$ expresses a preference of order.

- An equation $p^* = pp^*$ expresses that in case of an iteration of operation p it will be executed at least once.

Furthermore, personalization assumes a postcondition χ that expresses the goals of the particular user. Then personalization of story space p aims at a simpler story space p' such that $[p]\chi \leftrightarrow [p']\chi$ holds.

Conclusion

In this chapter we formalized user preferences, obligations and rights and indicated how this formalization can be used to reason about the WIS specification. The work was done in the context of the Co-Design approach to WIS development (Schewe & Thalheim, 2005), but it seems to be not too difficult to adapt it to other methods such as ARANEUS (Atzeni, Gupta, & Sarawagi, 1998); OOHDM (Schwabe & Rossi, 1998); WebML (Ceri, Fraternali, Bongio, Brambilla, Comai, & Matera, 2003); HERA (Houben, Barna, Frasincar, & Vdovjak, 2003); or WSDM (De Troyer & Leune, 1998).

However, the formalization requires that the method contains models of users, user roles, actions, and logical conditions that bring these models together. These models are a central component of co-design, but they are only partially available in other methods. That is, the coupling of the work presented in this chapter with the other mentioned WIS development methods requires that these methods first take up directly or in a modified form the concept of storyboarding from the co-design approach.

We demonstrated that capturing preferences, obligations, and rights can be achieved on the basis of various logics. For the personalization of WISs according to preferences and goals we adopted propositional reasoning with

Kleene algebras with tests, which at the end amounts to a term rewriting approach. From this a new challenge arises that may allow us to dispense with explicitly modeling user types. In fact, the main purpose of user types is to associate preference rules with them, but these preferences may depend only on some of the characteristics of a user type. Thus, it may be advantageous to use conditional preference rules instead, and conditional term rewriting may turn out to be the key to personalization on a propositional storyboard level. This path of research will be explored in the future.

We also demonstrated that obligations and rights can be formalized in (propositional) deontic logic, but we were not yet able to take this approach beyond the first step of just capturing deontic constraints. For our future research we plan to investigate more deeply the application of deontic logic for reasoning purposes on WIS specifications.

The major challenge in dealing with preferences, obligations and rights, however, is the coupling of the approach with the detailed conceptual model of WISs that is given by media types, which are extended views on some underlying database schema. In logical terms this basically means that we leave the safe grounds of propositional reasoning, as actions are no longer atomic but refined by abstract programs, while propositional conditions are refined by conditions that can be evaluated on underlying databases. In this chapter we did not go further than indicating the use of higher-order dynamic logic to obtain proof obligations. In the same way we should expect proof obligations in higher-order deontic logic.

Thus, in dealing with preferences, obligations and rights we shift the focus of WISs from just conceptual modeling of particular data-intensive application systems to knowledge-intensive systems that require reasoning techniques in complex logics to be explored.

References

Abiteboul, S., & Kanellakis, P. (1989). Object identity as a query language primitive. In *SIGMOD (Special Interest Group on Management of Data) Record, 18*(2), 159-173. Retrieved from http://www.sigmod.org/sigmod/record/index.html

Antoniou, G., Billington, D., Governatori, G., & Maher, M. (2001). Representation results for defeasible logic. *ACM Transactions on Computational Logic, 2*(2), 255–287.

Atzeni, P., Gupta, A., & Sarawagi, S. (1998). Design and maintenance of data-intensive Websites. *Lecture Notes in Computer Science,* (Version 1377) 436-450. Springeer-Verlag. http://www.informatik.uni-trier.de/~ley/db/conf/edbt/AtzeniMM98.html

Broersen, J., Wieringa, R., & Meyer, J.-J.C. (2002). A fixed-point characterization of a deontic logic of regular action. *Fundamenta Informaticae, 49*(4), 107–128.

Ceri, S., Fraternali, P., Bongio, A., Brambilla, M., Comai, S., & Matera, M. (2003). *Designing data-intensive Web applications.* San Francisco: Morgan Kaufmann.

De Troyer, O., & Leune, C. (1998). WSDM: A user-centered design method for Web sites. In *Computer Networks and ISDN Systems-Proceedings of the 7ᵗʰ International WWW Conference* (pp. 85–94). Elsevier.

Dignum, F., Meyer, J.-J.C., Wieringa, R., & Kuiper, R. (1996). A modal approach to intentions, commitments and obligations: Intention plus commitment yields obligation. In M.A. Brown & J. Carmo (Eds.), *DEON 1996: Workshops in Computing* (pp. 80–97). SpringerVerlag, Berlin. http://citeseer.ist.psu.edu/dignum96modal.html

Eiter, T., & Subrahmanian, V.S. (1999). Deontic action programs. In T. Polle, T. Ripke, & K.D. Schewe (Eds.), *Fundamentals of information systems* (pp. 37–54). Kluwer Academic Publishers.

Elgesem, D. (1997). The modal logic of agency. *Nordic Journal of Philosophical Logic, 2*, 1–48.

Feyer, T., Schewe, K.-D., & Thalheim, B. (1998). Conceptual modeling and development of information services. In T. Ling & S. Ram (Eds.), *Conceptual modeling (ER'98)* (pp. 7–20). LNCS 1507. Berlin: Springer-Verlag.

Harel, D., Kozen, D., & Tiuryn, J. (2000). *Dynamic logic.* Cambridge: The MIT Press.

Hoare, C.A.R. (1969). An axiomatic basis for computer programming. *Communications of the ACM, 12*(10), 576–580.

Houben, G.-J., Barna, P., Frasincar, F., & Vdovjak, R. (2003). HERA: Development of semantic Web information systems. In *Proceedings of the Third International Conference on Web Engineering (ICWE 2003)* (LNCS 2722, pp. 529–538). Springer-Verlag.

Kaschek, R., Schewe, K.-D., Wallace, C., & Matthews, C. (2004). Story boarding for Web information systems. In D. Taniar & W. Rahayu (Eds.), *Web Information Systems* (pp. 1–33). Hershey, PA: Idea Group.

Kozen, D. (1997). Kleene algebra with tests. *ACM Transactions on Programming Languages and Systems, 19*(3), 427–443.

Kozen, D. (1999). On Hoare logic and Kleene algebra with tests. In *Proceedings of the Logic in Computer Science* (pp. 167–172).

Kozen, D. (2002). On the complexity of reasoning in Kleene algebra. *Information and Computation, 179*(2), 152–162.

Kozen, D., & Smith, F. (1996). Kleene algebra with tests: Completeness and decidability. In *Proceedings of the Computer Science Logic* (pp. 244–259).

Nute, D. (1997). *Defeasible deontic logic.* Kluwer Academic Publishers.

Schewe, K.-D. (2004). The power of media types. In *Proceedings of the WISE 2004: Web Information Systems Engineering.* LNCS. Springer-Verlag.

Schewe, K.-D., Kaschek, R., Wallace, C., & Matthews, C. (2005). Emphasizing the communication aspects for the successful development of electronic business systems. *Information Systems and E-Business Management, 3*(1), 71–100.

Schewe, K.-D., & Thalheim, B. (2004). Reasoning about Web information systems using story algebras. In *Proceedings of the ADBIS 2004*, Budapest, Hungary.

Schewe, K.-D., & Thalheim, B. (2005). Conceptual modeling of Web information systems. *Data and Knowledge Engineering, 54*(2), 147–188.

Schewe, K.-D., Thalheim, B., Binemann-Zdanowicz, A., Kaschek, R., Kuss, T., & Tschiedel, B. (2005). A conceptual view of electronic learning systems. *Education and Information Technologies, 10*(1-2), 83–110.

Schewe, K.-D., Thalheim, B., Schmidt, J.W., & Wetzel, I. (1992). Integrity enforcement in object-oriented databases. In *Proceedings of the Modeling Database Dynamics: Workshops in Computing* (pp. 174–195). Berlin: Springer-Verlag.http:www.informatik.uni-trier.de/~ley/db/conf/fmldo/fmldo92.html#ScheweTSW92

Schwabe, D., & Rossi, G. (1998). An object-oriented approach to Web-based application design. *TAPOS, 4*(4), 207–225.

Thalheim, B. (2000). *Entity-relationship modeling: Foundations of database technology.* Springer-Verlag.

Thalheim, B., & Düsterhöft, A. (2001). SiteLang: Conceptual modeling of Internet sites. In H.S. Kunii, S. Jajodia, & A. Sølvberg (Eds.), *Conceptual modeling (ER 2001)* (LNCS 2224, pp. 179–192). Berlin: Springer-Verlag.

Wieringa, R., & Meyer, J.-J.C. (1991). Actor-oriented specification of deontic integrity constraints. In B. Thalheim, J. Demetrovics, & H.D. Gerhardt (Eds.), *Mathematical Fundamentals of Database Systems (MFDBS 1991)* (LNCS 495, pp. 89–103). Springer-Verlag.

Wieringa, R., & Meyer, J.-J.C. (1993). Actors, actions, and initiative in normative system specification. *Annals of Mathematics and Artificial Intelligence, 7*(1-4), 289–346.

Section II

The Memetics
Approach to Assistance

Chapter VII

Building Intelligent Multimodal Assistants Based on Logic Programming in the Meme Media Architecture

Kimihito Ito, Hokkaido University, Japan

Abstract

This chapter introduces a software architecture to build intelligent multimodal assistants. The architecture consists of three basic components: a meme media system, an inference system, and an embodied interface agent system that makes multimodal presentations available to users. In an experimental implementation of the architecture, the author uses three components as the basic framework: IntelligentPad for a meme media system, Prolog for a logic programming system, and Multimodal Presentation Markup Language (MPML) for controlling an interface agent system. The experimental implementation shows how character agents are defined in a simple declarative manner using logic programming on meme media objects.

Introduction

Web applications, which are computer programs ported to the Web, allow end users to use various remote services and tools through their Web browsers. A Web application is a program that has an HTML-based front-end for users to utilize services provided by a remote HTTP server. There are an enormous number of Web applications on the Web, and they are becoming the basic infrastructure of everyday life.

In the article "Agents that Reduce Work and Information Overload" written in 1994, Maes (1994, p. 1) predicted the current situation of the Web as follows:

The "information highway" will present us with an explosion of new computer-based tasks and services, but the complexity of this new environment will demand a new style of human-computer interaction, where the computer becomes an intelligent, active and personalized collaborator.

This prediction has come true and we are facing the demand for computer-based intelligent assistants. *We have now* more than 10^9 pages on the Web and most of those pages are crawled by major search engines. Although we have seen remarkable developments in information retrieval technologies, such as ranking and clustering of Web pages (Joachims, 1998; Page, 1998), it still takes a lot of time to get satisfactory information by trying to retrieve documents from the Web. The more pages we have on the Web, the more time it will take for users to get satisfactory results from the Web.

In the last decade, technologies involving intelligent user interfaces (IUI) have evolved in the boundary areas between Human-Computer Interaction and Artificial Intelligence research (Lester, 2001). Lieberman (1997, p. 67) states, "An agent should display some [but perhaps not all] of the characteristics that we associate with human intelligence." Agents that provide active assistance to a user with computer tasks are called interface agents Maes (1994). Examples of today's successful interface agents include junk filtering functions implemented in e-mail client applications.

Embodied interface agents are interface agents that have a lifelike "body." By introducing a lifelike body to agents, interactions between agents and humans take on multimodality, including speech, facial expressions, and body gestures. Embodied interface agents are also applied in several e-learning systems (Graesser, VanLehn, Rosé, Jordan & Harter, 2001; Lester, Voerman, Towns & Callaway, 1999). We can already see the effectiveness of use of embodied agents (Höök, Persson & Sjölinder, 2000).

Embodied interface agents can be categorized into conversational agents and presentation agents. Embodied conversational agents interact with humans by having dialogues. Implementation systems of embodied conversational agents include Rea (Cassell, 2001), and Autotutor (Graesser et al., 2001). Presentation agents are designed to give attractive presentations to human users. PPP (André & Rist, 1996), virtual human presenter (Noma, Zhao, & Badler, 1997), and BYRNE (Binsted & Luke, 1999) are of this type of agent.

Some basic components of embodied interface agents are built into the Microsoft Windows operating system (Microsoft, 1999) and they can easily be used either in Visual Basic or in JavaScript. Despite their fundamental potential to present information to users, embodied interface agents are not yet used in many applications.

In this chapter, I propose an architecture for embodied interface agents which helps us to quickly obtain personalized information from the Web. I use three components as the basis of the framework: IntelligentPad, Logic Programming, and the MPML.

This chapter is organized as follows. In the next section, I describe the proposed architecture for building an intelligent multimodal assistant. In the third section, I summarize a meme media system IntelligentPad, and I introduce an inference mechanism to the IntelligentPad architecture in fourth section. In the fifth section, I describe a summary of Multimodal Presentation Markup Language that is used to define multimodal presentation. In the sixth section, I conclude this chapter with our future research plans.

Architecture

The architecture that I propose in this chapter consists of three components:

1. A framework to integrate independent Web application dynamically,
2. An inference mechanism to integrate Web applications based on declarative knowledge, and
3. An embodied interface agent which communicates to users with verbal and non-verbal modes of communication.

Figure 1. The architecture

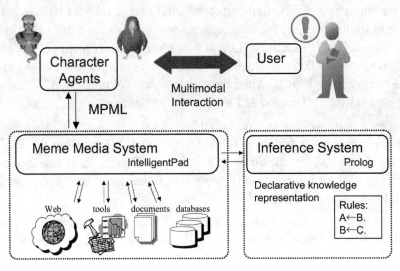

Figure 1 shows the architecture. In an experimental implementation of the architecture, the author uses three components as the basis of the framework: IntelligentPad for a meme media system, Prolog for a logic programming system, and Multimodal Presentation Markup Language (MPML) for controlling an interface agent system.

Meme media standardizes both user interface and connection interface of each media object in order to integrate them (Tanaka, 2003). IntelligentPad (Tanaka, 1989) is a meme media system that uses the metaphor of a sheet of chapter. Its application to the Web (Ito & Tanaka, 2003) provides a framework to reuse functions of existing Web application. This allows us to get around the implementation of both Agent and functions that existing Web applications already have.

Logic programming introduces logic to assistants. Logic programming is a style of programming based on deductive inference in the first-order logic. In this chapter, I use a Prolog interpreter for this purpose.

Multimodal Presentation Markup Language (Ishizuka, 2000) defines a scripting multimodal presentation with embodied character agents in the simple manner of XML. MPML provides embodied user interfaces for assistants.

Meme Media Technology and IntelligentPad

Meme media technologies (Tanaka, 2003) were proposed to enable people to reedit and redistribute intellectual resources and to accelerate the evolution of intellectual resources accumulated over the Web. The word "Meme Media" was coined by Y. Tanaka because meme media carry what R. Dawkins called "memes" (Dawkins, 1976).

IntelligentPad (Tanaka, 1989) is a meme media system that allows users to combine media objects (called "pads") through the metaphor of sheets of chapter. Media objects represented by pads vary widely. They range from multimedia documents to tools such as databases, charts, spreadsheets, and even Web applications. Figure 2 shows a screenshot of an IntelligentPad system.

Each pad has slots functioning as data I/O ports. Through "drag-and-drop" and "paste" operations, users can connect one pad to a slot of another pad.

Figure 2. A sreenshot of an IntelligentPad system

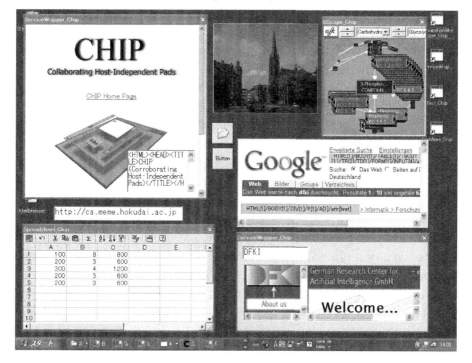

Figure 3. User-interface and connection interface. If a user pastes P_1 on P_2 with its connection to a slot of P_2, the primary slot of P_1 is connected to the slot of P_2.

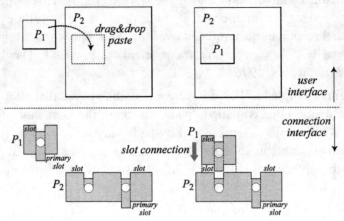

This operation simultaneously creates both a composite view and a functional linkage through a slot connection.

IntelligentPad represents each component as a pad, which is a sheet of chapter on the screen. A pad can be pasted on another pad to define both a physical containment relationship and a functional linkage between them. When a pad P1 is pasted on another pad P_2, the pad P_1 becomes a child of P_2, and P_2 becomes the parent of P_1. No pad may have more than one parent pad. Pads can be pasted together to define various multimedia documents and application tools. Unless otherwise specified, composite pads are always decomposable and re-editable.

In Figure 3, we show an abstract architecture of IntelligentPad. Each pad has both a standard user-interface and a standard connection interface. The user-interface of a pad has a card-like view on the screen and a standard set of operations like "move", "resize", "copy", "paste", and "peel". Users can easily replicate any pad, paste a pad onto another, and peel a pad off a composite pad. Pads are decomposable persistent objects. You can easily decompose any composite pad by simply peeling off a primitive or composite pad from its parent pad. As its connection interface, each pad has a list of slots that work like connection jacks of an AV-system component. A pad also has a single connection to a slot of its parent pad.

Table 1. A summary of three standard messages

Message	Summary
set *slotname value*	a child sets the specified value to its parent's slot
gimme *slotname*	a child requests its parent to return the value of its specified slot
Update	a parent notifies its children that some slot value has been changed

To set up data linkage between pads, IntelligentPad uses three standard messages, "set," "gimme," and "update." We show an outline of these three messages in Table 1.

A pad can be embedded in one parent at most. Each pad can have at most one connection to a slot of a parent pad. Connected pads form a tree structure. We do not restrict the maximum depth of the tree.

Each pad has one primary slot. When the value of the primary slot of a child is changed, the child sends a "set' message with the new slot value to its parent. Using this value, the parent changes its own slot values. Then, the parent pad notifies all of its children pads of its state change by sending an 'update" message. Each child that has received an "update" message sends a "gimme" message to the parent pad, changes its own slot values using the

Figure 4. Three standard messages, 'set', 'gimme' and 'update', between pads

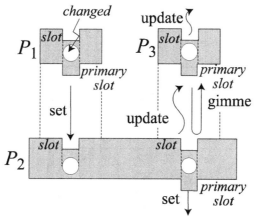

return value of this "gimme" message, and then sends an "update" message to each of its children. Using this mechanism, state changes are propagated from one pad to all the pads connected to it (Figure 4).

Wrapping Existing Web Applications with Pads

In this chapter, we use the verb "to wrap" in the sense of defining data I/O ports to input and to output data to and from an application to be wrapped.

In a previous chapter with Y. Tanaka, I proposed a framework that allows end-users to wrap an arbitrary Web application with a pad (Ito, 2003). Users can visually wrap Web applications with visual components, and visually combine them to define functional linkages among them. Users can also visually define functional linkages between wrapped Web applications and local tools in pad form such as chart drawing and spreadsheet tools to compose a single integrated tool pad.

We define a Web application as an application program that has an HTML-based front-end for the user to utilize some services provided by a remote HTTP server. Here, we summarize the proposed architecture for reusing existing Web applications.

Figure 5. Wrapping existing Web applications to be interoperable components. This framework was proposed in my previous paper with Y. Tanaka.

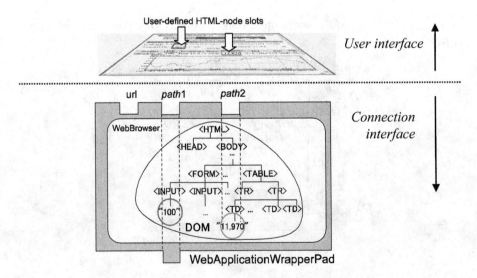

Figure 5 shows the architecture of Web Application Wrapping. A WebApplicationWrapperPad (WAWPad for short) consists of (1) a reference to the target Web Application and (2) references to the document portion to input/output data to and from a Web application. A URL is used to realize a reliable reference to the target Web Application. An XPath is used to realize a stable reference to the document portion to input and to output data to and from the Web application. An XPath expression identifies a set of HTML-nodes. For instance, we may specify an input form for a Web application with an XPath:

HTML[1]/BODY[1]/FORM[1]/INPUT[1]

The combination of a URL and an XPath allows us to define slots to input/output data to and from a Web application.

Figure 6 shows how users can wrap a Web application using our framework. Here, if the user clicks the right mouse button at some region that he or she wants to specify to work as a slot, a popup menu will be shown for a new slot corresponding to the specified HTML element.

Figure 6. Web application wrapping using only mouse operations

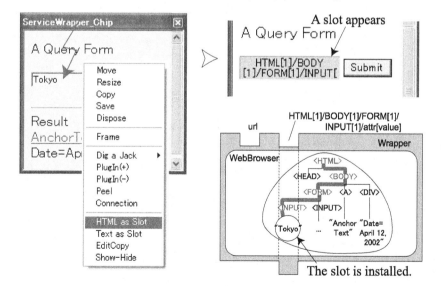

Agents Working on Meme Media

In this section, I introduce agents to the IntelligentPad environment. Pads in the IntelligentPad system are assumed to be linked to other pads through direct manipulation by users. This section introduces interface agents which manipulate pads on behalf of users. I make use of the inference mechanism of Prolog as the basis of the function of the agent. Figure 7 depicts a Prolog system functioning as an agent. The Prolog system manipulates pads by sending/receiving data through slots of pads. This approach is regarded as a "marionette strings" approach (Lieberman, 1998) because the agent uses a set of "strings" to control pads to make the pads work together. Each string corresponds one-to-one with a "set" and "gimme" function pair to each slot of a pad.

I will define several predicates that specify relations among the basic elements on IntelligentPad objects. We use the standard notation of logic programming (Lloyd, 1987).

We first define the predicate *pad(p)* to be true if *p* is a pad. The predicate *pad* allows us to construct a function which retrieves a set of all pad instances.

Figure 7. Two styles of functional Linkage between two pads

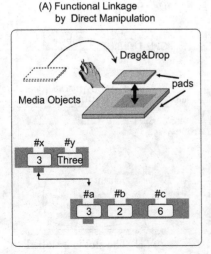
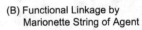
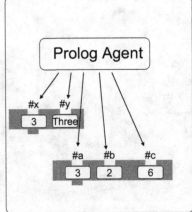

- **Definition 1:** An atomic formula *pad*(*p*) is true if *p* is a pad.

Example 1

Consider the set of pads shown in the Figure 8. The following five formulas are true.

- $pad(p_1)$
- $pad(p_2)$
- $pad(p_1) \wedge pad(p_2)$.
- $pad(p_1) \vee pad(p_2)$.
- $\leftarrow X\, pad(X)$.

With a Prolog interpreter which implements the predicate *pad*, the goal clause:

$$\leftarrow pad(X)$$

succeeds with one of the answer substitutions $\{X=p_1\}$ or $\{X=p_2\}$.

Next, we define the predicate *pad_slot*(*p*, *n*) that specifies the relation between pads and each of their slots. We also define the predicate *pad_slot_value*(*p*, *n*, *v*) to specify the relation among pads and their slots and each of their slot values.

- **Definition 2:** An atomic formula *pad_slot*(*p*, *n*) is true if *pad*(*p*) is true and *p* has a slot named *n*.

An atomic formula *pad_slot_value*(*p*, *n*, *v*) is true if *pad_slot*(*p*, *n*) is true and the slot *n* of *p* holds a value *v* as its slot value.

Example 2

Consider the set of pads shown in the Figure 8. All the following formulas are true.

Figure 8. A set of pads. Both p₁ and p₂ have slots #a, #b and #c. The slot values of #a, #b and #c in p₁ are 10, 2 and 12 respectively, while the slot values of #a, #b and #c in p₂ are 3, 2 and 6 respectively.

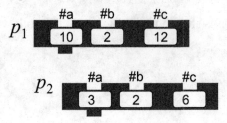

- *pad_slot(p_1, #a).*
- *pad_slot(p_1, #b).*
- *pad_slot(p_1, #c).*
- *pad_slot(p_2, #a).*
- *pad_slot(p_2, #b).*
- *pad_slot(p_2, #c).*
- *pad_slot_value(p_1, #a, 10).*
- *pad_slot_value(p_1, #b, 2).*
- *pad_slot_value(p_1, #c, 12).*
- *pad_slot_value(p_2, #a, 3).*
- *pad_slot_value(p_2, #b, 2).*
- *pad_slot_value(p_2, #c, 6).*
- *∃PN(pad_slot_value(P, N, 2)).*

The goal clause:

$$\leftarrow pad\_slot\_value(P, N, 2)$$

succeeds with either of the answer substitutions $\{P = p_1, N = \#b\}$ *or* $\{P = p_2, N = \#b\}$.

Prolog and Logic Programming use deductive inference. By introducing first-order definite clauses (rules), we build agents which use deductive inference on Meme Media objects. The following example uses the Web application wrapping technique shown in the second section.

Example 3

Consider the set of pads shown in Figure 9. Let p_1 be a WAWPad which wraps Lycos Finance. Suppose that we know that the wrapped Web application retrieves current stock quotes of companies on the New York Stock Exchange. Suppose that we also know that p_2 is a wrapper pad of Yahoo! Finance and the Web application converts currency from Japanese yen to U.S. dollars. We can describe the knowledge by the following two clauses:

C_1: *stock_quote_dollar(X, Y)←*
   pad_slot_value(p_1, #company, X)
   pad_slot_value(p_1, #quote, Y).

C_2: *currency_conversion(X, Y) ←*
   pad_slot_value (p_2, #dollar, X),
   pad_slot_value (p_2, #yen, Y).

C_3: *stock_quote_yen(X, Y) ←*
   stock_quote_dollar(X, Z),
   currency_conversion(Z, Y).

Suppose that the predicate *lives_in(X)* becomes true if the user lives in a country *X*. Lets consider the following clauses:

C_4: *stock_quote(X, Y) ←*
   lives_in(usa)
    stock_quote_dollar(X, Y)

C_5: *stock_quote(X, Y)←*
   lives_in(japan),
    stock_quote_yen(X, Y)

Clause C_4 states that a person who lives in the United States would want to know a stock quote price in dollars. On the other hand, C_5 assumes that a person who lives in Japan would want to know a stock quote price in Japanese yen.

The goal *stock_quote*(X, Y) will succeed and the user will get stock quote prices which are obtained by a foreign Web application.

Introducing Multimodal Agents

Web applications are provided in the form of documents. In other words, Web applications normally interact with users by sending HTML documents to users' Web browsers. In the previous section we developed a method to "attach" embodied interface agents to Web applications. In this section, we will introduce a "body" to Prolog agents to communicate with users through natural communication modalities.

Figure 9. Two wrapper pads. p_1 wraps Lycos Finance's Web application of stock quote retrieval. p_2 wraps Yahoo! Finance's Web application for currency conversion.

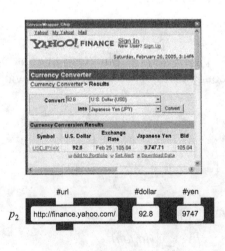

Multimodal Presentation Markup Language

We employ MPML (Multimodal Presentation Markup Language) (Ishizuka, Tsutsui, Saeyor, Dohi, Zong, & Prendinger, 2000) to offer users multimodal presentations using character agents. MPML was developed by Mitsuru Ishizuka in order to provide a metalevel description language commonly applicable to various multimodal presentation systems. MPML provides a simple scripting scheme for users to create a multimodal presentation in XML format.

In the major implementation of MPML, Microsoft Agent Microsoft (1999) is used to give presentations defined in a MPML. The package includes 2D cartoon-style character animation, speech recognition, and a Text-to-Speech (TTS) engine. Character agents in Microsoft Agent are also controlled through the use of the script language JavaScript. However, it is still difficult for non-programmers to write program code in JavaScript to control character agents.

The XML shown below is a sample MPML script to control character agents:

```
<mpml>
<head>
   <title>An Example of MPML</title>
   <agent char="Peedy" id="Peedy" x="100" y="400"/>
   <agent char="Genie" id="Genie" x="0" y="0"/>
</head>
<body>
<seq>
   <play id="Peedy" act="DoMagic1"/>
       <page ref="http://www.meme.hokudai.ac.jp" />
       <speak id="Peedy">
       Welcome to Meme Media Laboratory!
       </speak>
       <speak id="Peedy">
       Joining me now is Genie, who is tracking
       Meme Media research.
       </speak>
       <move id="Genie" x="500" y="400"/>
```

```
          <play id="Genie" act="Wave"/>
          <speak id="Genie" Hi!, I'm Genie.</speak>
        </seq>
    </body>
</mpml>
```

According to the script above, the character agents "Peedy" and "Genie" will talk in turns (Figure 10). The XML schema for MPML is provided at their MPML Home page.

As we have shown in the third section, Web applications can be instantaneously wrapped as IntelligentPad objects. Once a Web application is wrapped as a pad, it can be combined with other pads to compose a new integrated tool easily. For the attachment of a "body" to the Prolog agent that

Figure 10. A sample presentation using MPML. (1) At the beginning, character agents defined with <agent> appear on the screen. (2) The script instructs the browser to load an external Web page according to the <page> tag. (3) One of those agents is talking to the user according to the script written in the <speak> tag. (4) The other agent moves to the point specified in the <move> tag. (5) Finally, the agent moves his hand according to the <play act="Wave"> tag.

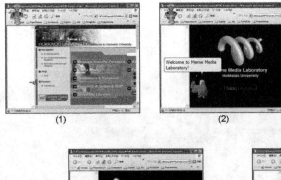

(1)   (2)   (3)

(4)   (5)

we introduced in the fourth section, we have developed a pad that controls character agents and gets them to give a multimodal presentation. This pad is the "MPMLPlayerPad."

The MPMLPlayerPad gives a multimodal presentation according to a given script written in MPML. Figure 11 shows a screenshot of it and an abstract of its connection interface. A character agent is shown with an MPMLPlayerPad on the user's desktop screen. An MPMLPlayerPad provides a slot named "MPML" as a "placeholder" for MPML script. When the MPML script, which is stored in the "MPML" slot, has been altered, the pad gives the presentation according to the updated MPML.

MPMLPlayerPad wraps the MPML 2.3a implementation, which was developed by Prof. Ishizuka's group at the University of Tokyo, to control character agents' behaviors.

MPML provides a simple scripting scheme for multimodal presentations in XML format. By converting information from external resources to MPML format, it is possible to generate a multimodal presentation from the external resources using computer programs such as XSLT.

Figure 11. User interface with the connection interface of MPMLPlayer-Pad

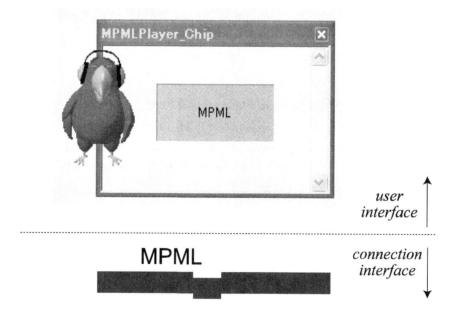

Now we have Web applications that are wrapped with meme media objects, an MPML player pad, and a logic programming environment on IntelligentPad. We will introduce intelligent multimodal assistants based on logic programming in the meme media architecture. Below, we give a simple example to indicate how inference works to give multimodal presentations.

Example 4

Consider the MPMLPlayerPad shown in Figure 11. The following clause C_6 defines a predicate $mpml\_play(Mpml)$ that gives presentation according to the given MPML.

$$C_6: \quad mpml\_play(Mpml) \leftarrow$$
$$pad\_slot\_value(p_3, \#mpml, Mpml).$$

Let m_1 be a MPML script given in the earlier part of this section; then the goal clause:

$$\leftarrow mpml\_play(m_1)$$

succeeds in showing the presentation shown in Figure 10.

Now let us consider a predicate which generates MPML script from a set of parameters.

Example 5

Consider the set of pads shown in Figure 8 and Figure 9.

The predicate $mpml\_for\_stock\_quote(C, Q, M)$ makes presentation scripts in MPML format. For a given company name and the stock quote price pair (c, q), the predicate makes an MPML script which contains c and q in its placeholder in an MPML template:

```
<mpml>
    <head>
        <title>Stock Quote Report </title>
        <agent char= "Peedy" id="Peedy" x="100" y="400"/>
    </head>
```

```
<body>
    <seq>
        <play id="Peedy" act="Search" />
        <speak id="Peedy"
        Today's stock quote price of c is q.
        </speak>
    </seq>
</body>
</mpml>
```

The following clauses of C_7 define the predicate *inform_stock_quote(C)*.

C_7:   *inform_stock_quote(C)←*
     stock_quote(C , Q),
     mpml_for_stock_quote(C, Q, M),
     mpml_play(M).

The goal clause:

←inform_stock_quote(C)

succeeds in giving a multimodal presentation. The presentation informs a user of the current stock quote price of the company *C* in either dollars or yen. The determination depends on the truth value of the predicate *lives_in(X)* that appears at the definition of stock_quote(*C*, *Q*). If the user lives in the U.S., the character agent will inform the user of the current stock quote price of the company *C* in dollars. Conversely, if the user lives in Japan, the stock quote is converted into Japanese yen automatically to be announced by the character agent.

Related Work

Lakshmanan, Sadri, and Subramanian (1996) have developed a logic called WebLog, which is a declarative system for Web querying and restructuring (Lakshmanan, et al., 1996). Rules to extract information from the Web can be described with WebLog. Users need to know the names of HTML tags which can be used to extract the information from the document. With the same motivation, several other query languages have been proposed for information extraction and integration of the Web. These are surveyed by Florescu, Levy, and Mendelzon (1998).

Bauer, Dengler, and Paul (2000) have introduced a PBD (Programming by Demonstration) method to train an information agent to identify and extract interesting pieces of information from the Web. They have implemented the method into InfoBeans (Bauer & Dengler, 1999). By accessing an InfoBox with an ordinary Web browser, users can wrap Web applications. By connecting channels among InfoBeans on the InfoBox, users can also functionally integrate them. The information shown in InfoBox is a set of document pieces copied from the original document. However, it is difficult for users to extend the system by introducing embodied character agents which give multimodal presentations to users.

Lieberman (1998) has developed ScriptAgent, which can be used to "attach" an interface agent to an existing Application. ScriptAgent and my proposed architecture share the same purpose. The difference is as follows. ScriptAgent captures sequences of user input events such as mouse operations and keyboard input, while agents in my proposal use data connection interface of slots by sending/getting data to and from the slots.

There are several studies on controlling embodied agent in a declarative way with logic programming. Figa and Tarau (2005) have proposed a Web based conversational agent architecture. The architecture is based on a distributed agent system called Jinni Agent (Tarau, 1998). Ruttkay, Huang, and Eliëns (2003) have proposed a Prolog-based architecture for 3D embodied agents that can interact with other agents in a 3D virtual world.

Letizia (Lieberman, 1995) assists Web browsing. Letizia recommends Web pages to its user. It proactively fetches links from the current pages that the user opens, and chooses those pages by learning past choices of the user.

Concluding Remarks

In this chapter, the author introduced architecture to build intelligent multimodal assistants based on logic programming in the meme media architecture.

We separate the assistants' tasks that support users into three basic components:

1.   A function to reuse functions of existing Web applications.
2.   A function for inferences.
3.   A function to interact with users with multimodal interaction.

In the experimental implementation of the architecture, the author uses three components as its basis: IntelligentPad, Prolog, and Multimodal Presentation Markup Language.

Prolog agents in the current implementation do not have the capability to learn. This is a highly necessary capability for agents to become intelligent personal assistants. Personal assistants should have knowledge about users by learning users' behavior. To have learning capabilities, we plan to use the framework of Inductive Logic Programming (ILP), which is a research area where various methods have been investigated for finding new rules from given examples and background knowledge (Muggleton, 1991).

The agents in the proposed system do not have the capability to communicate with each other either. Tarau has developed a Prolog-based scripting tool called Jinni for gluing together knowledge processing components (Tarau, 1998). Jinni uses a distributed blackboard model for communication among agents. Such communication among agents in this framework remains for future work.

References

André, E., & Rist, T. (1996). Coping with temporal constraints in multimedia presentation planning. In *Proceedings of the Thirteenth National Conference on Artificial Intelligence and Eighth Innovative Applications of Artificial Intelligence Conference* (pp. 142–147). The MIT Press.

Bauer, M., & Dengler, D. (1999). InfoBeans: Configuration of personalized information assistants. In *Proceedings of the 1999 International Conference on Intelligent User Interfaces* (pp. 153–156). ACM.

Bauer, M., Dengler, D., & Paul, G. (2000). Instructible information agents for Web mining. In *Proceedings of the 2000 International Conference on Intelligent User Interfaces* (pp. 21–28). ACM.

Binsted, K., & Luke, S. (1998). Character design for soccer commentary. *Robot Soccer World Cup II* (pp. 22–33). Lecture Notes in Computer Science 1604. Springer.

Cassell, J. (2001). Embodied conversational agents: Representation and intelligence in user interfaces. *AI Magazine, 22*(4), 67–84.

Dawkins, R. (1976). *The selfish gene.* Oxford University Press.

Figa, E., & Tarau, P. (2004). Conversational agents as Web services. In *Proceedings of the International Conference on Internet Computing* (pp. 773–782). CSREA Press.

Florescu, D., Levy, A.Y., & Mendelzon, A.O. (1998). Database techniques for the world-wide Web: A survey. *SIGMOD Record, 27*(3), 59–74.

Graesser, A.C., VanLehn, K., Rosé, C.P., Jordan, P.W., & Harter, D. (2001). Intelligent tutoring systems with conversational dialogue. *AI Magazine, 22*(4), 39–52.

Höök, K., Persson, P., & Sjölinder, M. (2000). Evaluating users' experience of a character-enhanced information space. *AI Communications, 13*(3), 195–212.

Ishizuka, M., Tsutsui, T., Saeyor, S., Dohi, H., Zong, Y., & Prendinger, H. (2000). MPML: A multimodal presentation markup language with character control functions. In *Proceedings of Agents2000 Workshop on Achieving Human-like Behavior in Interactive Animated Agents* (pp. 50–54).

Ito, K., & Tanaka, Y. (2003). A visual environment for Web application composition. In *Proceedings of the 14th ACM Conference on Hypertext and Hypermedia* (pp. 184–193). ACM.

Joachims, T., (1998). Text categorization with support vector machines: Learning with many relevant features. In *Proceedings of the Machine Learning: ECML-98, 10th European Conference on Machine Learning* (pp. 137–142). Lecture Notes in Computer Science 1398. Springer.

Lakshmanan, L.S.V., Sadri, F., & Subramanian, I.N. (1996). A declarative language for querying and restructuring the WEB. In *Proceedings of the Sixth International Workshop on Research Issues in Data Engineering: Interoperability of Nontraditional Database Systems* (pp. 12–21).

Lester, J.C. (2001). Introduction to the special issue on intelligent user interfaces. *AI Magazine, 22*(4), 13–14.

Lester, J.C., Voerman, J.L., Towns, S.G., & Callaway, C.B. (1999). Deictic believability: Coordinated gesture, locomotion, and speech in lifelike pedagogical agents. *Applied Artificial Intelligence, 13*(4-5), 383–414.

Lieberman, H. (1995). Letizia: An agent that assists Web browsing. In *Proceedings of the Fourteenth International Joint Conference on Artificial Intelligence* (pp. 924–929). Morgan Kaufmann.

Lieberman, H. (1997). Autonomous Interface Agents. In *CHI 97 Conference Proceedings* (pp. 67–74). ACM

Lieberman, H. (1998). Integrating user interface agents with conventional applications. In *Proceedings of the 1998 International Conference on Intelligent User Interfaces* (pp. 39–46). ACM.

Lloyd, J. W., (1987). *Foundations of logic programming*. Springer.

Maes, P. (1994). Agents that reduce work and information overload. *Communications of the ACM 37*(7), 30–40.

Microsoft. (1999). *Microsoft Agent: Software development kit*. Microsoft Press.

Muggleton, S. (1991). Inductive logic programming. *New Generation Computing, 8*(4), 295–318.

Noma, T., Zhao, L., & Badler, N.I. (2000). Design of a virtual human presenter. *IEEE Computer Graphics and Applications, 20*(4), 79–85.

Page, L., Brin, S., Motwani, R., & Winograd, T. (1998). *The PageRank citation ranking: Bringing order to the Web*. Stanford Digital Library Technologies Project.

Ruttkay, Z., Huang, Z., & Eliëns, A. (2003), Gestures for embodied agents with logic programming. *Recent Advances in Constraints, Joint ERCIM/CoLogNET International Workshop on Constraint Solving and Constraint Logic Programming* (pp. 266–284). Lecture Notes in Computer Science 3010. Springer.

Tanaka, Y. (2003). *Meme media and meme market architectures: Knowledge media for editing, distributing, and managing intellectual resources.* IEEE Press, John Wiley & Sons.

Tanaka, Y., & Imataki, T. (1989). IntelligentPad: A hypermedia system allowing functional composition of active media objects through direct manipulations. In *Proceedings of the IFIP 11th World Computer Congress* (pp. 541–546).

Tarau, P. (1998). Jinni: A lightweight Java-based logic engernet. In *Proceedings of the International Workshop on Implementation Technology for Programming Languages Based on Logic* (pp. 1–15).

Chapter VIII

From Planning Tools to Intelligent Assistants:
Meme Media and Logic Programming Technologies

Nataliya Lamonova, Hokkaido University, Japan

Kimihito Ito, Hokkaido University, Japan

Yuzura Tanaka, Hokkaido University, Japan

Abstract

This chapter introduces an approach for creating Web application capable of operating in complex environments is introduced. The approach shows how Meme Media technologies combined with other technologies can be used for solving deferent kinds of problems in particular related to Therapy Planning in clinical trials. Combination of logic programming and fuzzy logic for creating Web applications is also introduced.

Introduction and Motivation

Nowadays a large variety of Web technologies enable end users easily to use various services through their Web browsers. At the same time the evolution of these technologies causes various difficulties and makes high demands on software developers to create not only a static repository of hypertext information and graphics but also software that have intellectuality and mobility and that respond dynamically to user input.

Creating Web-based agents is one more step towards creating sites having artificial intelligence. One of the most interesting and promising approaches to programming agents is **logic programming** of agents (Davison, 2001). This approach has good prospects, because the ideology and principles of logic programming are very convenient for searching, recognition, and analysing unstructured, poorly structured, and hypertext information.

This chapter proposes an approach for creating and using **agent system**s in Web applications through their Web browsers (Ito & Tanaka, 2003; Tanaka, 2003). The approach allows users to manipulate pads in the **IntelligentPad** environment by using remote http servers as the Prolog Server and the MATLAB Web server.

Agent-System for IntelligentPad Environment

IntelligentPad architecture allows users to combine media objects (called pads) through their view integration (Ito & Tanaka, 2003; Tanaka; 2003; Tanaka, Fujima, & Sugibuchi, 2000).

Figure 1 shows an agent systems that combine media objects on behalf of users. Implementation of the system consists of two dependent parts:

*   An HTTP-based Prolog Server, and
*   Coordination of **Meme Media** objects through Prolog.

The Prolog server is a Web application that evaluates Prolog goals given by client programs such as Web browsers. HTML-based Web interface provides an input form for the goal clause to be sent to the server. The server evaluates

Figure 1. An HTTP-based Prolog server

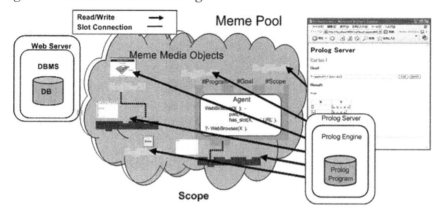

the submitted goal clause and returns its result to users in the HTML format. Users and/or programs can use computation resource of remote computers through **logic programming** language **Prolog**. Client programs can also upload Prolog programs to the server. Since the Prolog server is a Web application, Prolog server can be wrapped by a WebApplicationWrapperPad. For the details of the WebApplicationWrapperPad, we refer the reader to our previous work (Ito & Tanaka, 2003).

Prolog server wrapped as a pad is called AgentPad. An AgentPad has coordinates pads in a meme pool, on behalf of users.

Coordination of Meme Media Objects

Our task was to create an **agent system** (AgentPad) that automatically monitors Web application environments and, because it has learning abilities, can also maintain a set of the last *n* results. This data can then be used to condition new task structures.

For details of elementary predicates that coordinate pads, we refer to our previous work (Ito, 2005).

Definition of a Scope A Scope is defined by the predicate "in scope." The following clause defines a scope in which the drawing area of each pad is contained in the drawing area of PrologPad.

in_scope(P):-

pad(P),prolog_pad(P1),pad_bounds(P1,X,Y,W,H),

pad_contained(P,X,Y,W,H).

The role of the agent pad in the IntelligentPad environment is to operate on pads in its scope. The agent pad is a program written in Prolog and consists of predicates that define media objects like pads, their relationships and functional linkages between them.

The following predicates indicate the basic principles of predicate-building in the definition of media objects.

serviceWrapper(X):-

pad(X),pad_slot(X,'URL').

pad(PadURL):-

padlist(List),member(PadURL,List).

By this mechanism the functionality of the agent pad is defined by the operations:

- obtaining a list of pads in the scope,
- a list of slots of specified pads,
- the values of specified slot,
- paste operation,
- slot connection,
- Web application wrapping,
- query servicing, and
- pad constraint checking.

As an interface the agent pad uses of Prolog server's interface as it is shown on the Figure 2. It uses a priori described predicates (http-server, chipcordinator) as well.

Figure 2. Coordination of pads with HTTP-based Prolog server

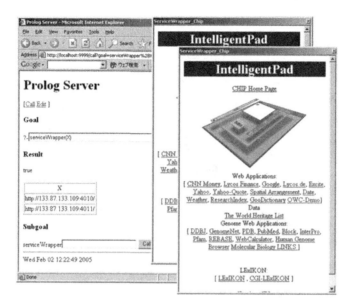

Agent-System for the Tasks of Therapy Planning

The past few years have witnessed a rapid growth in the number and variety of applications of **fuzzy logic** (Tsoukalas & Uhrig, 1997; Zadeh, 1965). The applications range from consumer products such as cameras, washing machines to industrial process control, medical instrumentation, and decision-making systems. Planning is a central task of artificial intelligence and its application to **therapy planning** has been much discussed (Arnold & Jantke, 1995, 1997; Dötsch, Ito & Jantke, 2005). Our system is one way of solving the problem of planning in this field. Problems like whether particular therapy protocol B should be included in, or excluded from, clinical trials for treatment of highly malignant non-hodgkin-lymphomas (NHL). Patients can be included into therapy protocol if all criteria are true or excluded if they are false. We examined the solution of this problem by applying a very powerful concept based on fuzzy logic. We combined the fuzzy system with a Web interface that allowed us to use it as a component of IntelligentPad applications.

Figure 3. Fuzzy inference system

Figure 3 shows graphical user interface (GUI) tools from the Fuzzy Logic Toolbox which is provided by **MATLAB**.

The process of fuzzy inference involves membership functions, fuzzy logic operators, and if-then rules.

We chose membership functions (4), (5), logic operations and defined 6 if-then rules (1), (2), which allowed us to realize our fuzzy inference system (3) on the basis of the Sugeno-type system.

Sugeno-Type Fuzzy Inference System

In this kind of fuzzy system output membership functions are either linear or constant. This makes the output model more simple that is, defuzzification is unnecessary.

Our six rules have the following form:

if x_1 is A_1 and x_2 is A_2 and … and x_n is A_n,

then $y = f(x_1, x_2, \ldots, x_n)$

(1)

or in the vector form

if x is A then $y = f(x_1, x_2, \ldots, x_n)$,

(2)

where $y = f(x_1, x_2, \ldots, x_n)$ – fuzzy function.

The output of the system can be described as:

$$y = \frac{\sum_{i=1}^{M} \varpi_i y_i}{\sum_{j=1}^{M} \varpi_i},$$

(3)

where ϖ_i – weight multipliers,

y – general output of the system,

y_i – output of i-th rule,

M – number of rules.

For our zero-order Sugeno model, the output level y is a constant (inclusion or exclusion of the NHL-B therapy protocol).

Figure 4. Membership functions (MF)

We chose two forms of membership function. The first was the simplest triangular membership function ([4] and Figure 4a).

$$\mu_A(x) = \begin{cases} 1 - \dfrac{|x-c|}{d}, & \text{for } x \in [c-d, c+d] \\ 0, & \text{in other cases.} \end{cases} \tag{4}$$

This straight line membership function has the advantage of simplicity. The other membership function that we used was a simple Gaussian curve (Figure 4b). with the deferent parameters c and σ.

$$\mu_A(x) = \exp\left[-\left(\frac{x-c}{\sigma}\right)^2\right], \tag{5}$$

where x – input signal,

c – centers of functions,

σ – width.

These membership functions specify our fuzzy sets which describe vague concepts (for example "state of patient"), and admits the possibility of partial membership ("state of patient" is "rather better"). The degree an object belongs to a fuzzy set is denoted by a membership value between 0 and 1 (inclusion or exclusion NHL-B protocol is to the degree 0.8). A membership function associated with a given fuzzy set maps an input value to its appropriate membership value. As logic operators for NHL-B protocol criteria are used the boolean operator *AND* (min) in the case of inclusion and *AND NOT* (1 - *A*) for exclusion.

Implementation of Agent for NHL-B Protocol

Figure 5 shows an implementation of the fuzzy logic system for inclusion or exclusion of the NHL-B therapy protocol in clinical trials. The fuzzy system is realized as a MATLAB Web server application and consists of M-files

(files native to MATLAB), Hypertext Markup Language (HTML form). The application involves the following documents:

- An HTML input document for date submission to MATLAB. Service-Wrapper-Chip with run HTML submission of Therapy Protocol NHL-B form is used for it.
- A MATLAB M-files and FIS-file with fuzzy inference system to process input data and compute results.
- An HTML output document for display of MATLAB's computation.

The various interacting platforms are integrated and organised in a cascade mechanism in the following way. First the Web application "Therapy Protocol NHL-B" is loaded by means of the ServiceWrapper-Chip or just using standard Web-browsers on a client workstation. Then the completed HTML form is sent to **MATLAB** using *matweb*. *Matweb* is a TCP/IP client of the **MATLAB** Server.

The mechanism of loading the client is implemented by code:

```
<html>
<form action="/cgi-bin/matweb.exe"
method="POST" target="outputwindow">
<input type="hidden" name="mlmfile"
value="webchip"><p>
<head>
<title>Therapy protocol NHL-B</title>
</head>
```

The first line of the code

```
<form action="/cgi-bin/matweb.exe"
method="POST" target="outputwindow">
```

calls *matweb*, the entry point to the MATLAB Web Server. *matweb*.exe is the Microsoft Windows NT name of the program uses the Common Gateway Interface (CGI) and used by MATLAB Web Server to extract the following data from HTML form function **retstr=webchip(instruct,outfile):**

...
instruct.Age

instruct.LDH

instruct.Disease

instruct.Diagnosis

instruct.Thrombozyten

instruct.Leukozyten

instruct.PatientState

instruct.Treatment

instruct.Bone

instruct.Signature

The line:

```
<input type="hidden" name="mlmfile"

value="webchip">
```

provides the name of the MATLAB M-file (*mlmfile*) named *webchip* to run. The program *matweb* runs MATLAB with the fuzzy system, which receives the data, analyzes them, and generates responses, which may include graphics. It then places the output data into the MATLAB structure and calls *htmlrep* to place the output data into HTML output form. Following code shows this process:

```
% M-file
templatefile = which('webchip2.html');
if (nargin == 1)
retstr = htmlrep(outstruct, templatefile);
elseif (nargin == 2)
retstr = htmlrep(outstruct, templatefile,

outfile)
```

The main advantage of the system is that it uses remote resources. It is not necessary to have all portions of the system on the same machine. Indeed, MATLAB, the MATLAB Web Server, and the Web server daemon (httpd), all run on a remote server (5).

Figure 5. Web application for NHL-B therapy protocol (Copyright by The Math Works, Inc. Reprinted with permission.)

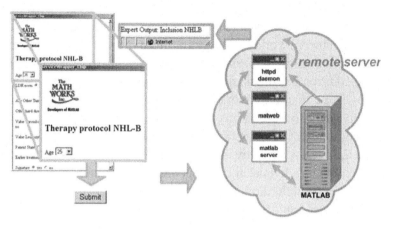

Summary and Conclusion

An approach is introduced for creating an agent-based systems technology that combines principles of **logic programming** and **fuzzy logic**. One part of this chapter is based on the **IntelligentPad** architecture that organizes and controls the system. Another part of the system is based on fuzzy theory. This part provides decision values based on received data. In this particular case the fuzzy inference system was created using the Sugeno-type system. This was chosen because it works well with linear techniques, optimization, and adaptive techniques. It has guaranteed continuity of the output surface and is well-suited to mathematical analysis. Such fuzzy logic systems have great utility for obtaining and explaining results. They are, however, unable to learn from the knowledge gained during this process.

The system was implemented as a **MATLAB** Web Server application. It is software developed by The MathWorks and allows the easy deployment of any MATLAB based applications via the World Wide Web. The Web Server is an ideal deployment tool for a quick, inexpensive, and secure way to share applications. MATLAB applications running on the MATLAB Web Server can be run on any machine with Internet access using a Netscape or Microsoft Web browser. As a result, users of the applications are not required to learn MATLAB, and MATLAB need not be running or installed on the client machine. The MATLAB application resides only on the server machine controlled by the developer. This means that applications running on the Web Server can be updated centrally without concern for revision control. In the near future it will be possible to develop a hybrid net which combines the advantages of fuzzy systems and artificial neural networks. Indeed, this is a major focus of current work. In systems of this more advanced kind the inferences are still made on the basis of the apparatus of fuzzy logic. However, in a crucial additional process, the corresponding membership functions are adjusted by using neural network learning algorithms. Such a system uses not only *a priori* information but can also obtain new knowledge from the dynamic environment. The work of the immediate future will therefore be to improve the agent-system by implementing control strategies that support dynamic recursive redefinition of subgoals. In other words, to create self-learning systems which allow the modification of logical reasoning during and after the operation of the logic program by adjusting it to information newly arriving from outside.

References

Arnold, O., & Jantke, K. P. (1995). Anwendung einer Logik der Constraints in der operativen Prozeßführung in Logik in der Informatik.(Using contstraints, logic in the active processes.) In P.H. Schmitt (Ed.), *3 Jahrestagung der GIFachgruppe 0.1.6* (pp. 13–27). (In: Schmitt, P. H. (Ed.). *Logic in Information Science. 3* pp. 13–27). Universität Karlsruhe, Fakultät für Informatik, Bericht 23/95. (University Karlsruhe, Information Science Department, Return 23/95.)

Arnold, O., & Jantke, K.P. (1997). Inductive program synthesis for therapy plan generation. *New Generation Computing, 15*(1), 27–58.

Davison, A. (2001). *Logic programming languages for the Internet.* In A. Kakas & F. Sadri (Eds.), *From logic programming into the future.* Retrieved June 2, 2006, from http://fivedots.coe.psu.ac.th/~ad/papers/summBob.ps.gz

Dötsch, V., Ito, K., & Jantke, K.P. (2005, March 1-5). Human-agent co-operation in accessing and communicating knowledge media: A case in medical therapy planning. In G. Grieser & Y. Tanaka (Eds.), *International Workshop on Intuitive Human Interface for Organizing and Accessing Intellectual Assets 2004* (pp. 68–87). Dagstuhl Castle, Germany. Lecture Notes in Artificial Intelligence 3359. Springer-Verlag.

Ito, K. (2005). Meme media and logic programming approach for intelligent media systems. In *Proceedings of the 2005 International Conference on Active Media Technology*, Kagawa, Japan.

Ito, K., & Tanaka, Y. (2003). A visual environment for Web application composition. In *Proceedings of the Fourteenth ACM Conference on Hypertext and Hypermedia* (pp.184–193). Nottingham, UK.

Tanaka, Y. (2003). Meme media and meme market architectures: Knowledge media for editing, distributing, and managing intellectual resources. In *Proceedings of the 2005 International Conference on Active Media Technology* (pp. 611–616). Kagawa, Japan.

Tanaka, Y., Fujima, J., & Sugibuchi, T. (2000). Meme media and meme pools for re-editing and redistributing intellectual assets. In *Proceedings of the Kyoto International Conference on Digital Libraries: Research and Practice* (pp. 208–216), Kyoto, Japan.

Tsoukalas, L.H., & Uhrig, R.E. (1997). *Fuzzy and neural approaches in engineering.* New York: John Wiley & Sons.

Zadeh, L.A. (1965). Fuzzy sets. *Information and Control, 8*, 338–353.

Chapter IX

Memetic Approach to the Location-Based Ad Hoc Federation of Intelligent Resources

Yuzura Tanaka, Hokkaido University, Japan

Abstract

The current Web is a mine of tools and services and the gate to ubiquitous computing environments with a huge number of highly distributed mobile and embedded intelligent resources. Their advanced reuse in assistance systems that support whole processes of our tasks requires federation of resources, that is, both discovery of appropriate resources from a certain scope of resources, and their interoperation and coordination for the required demand. Such a scope and the demand may dynamically change. This chapter focuses on such cases in which both change dynamically, and the change of demand cannot be predicted. Assistance systems for such cases must be able to support us to instantaneously perform federation of Web resources in an ad hoc way. They require new technologies for ad hoc federation of Web resources, and for restricting the scope of discovery in accordance with dynamically changing situations. This paper proposes the use of meme media technologies for ad hoc federation of intelligent resources over the Web. It also proposes the Wiki piazza architecture that works as a repository and lookup service, and combines this service with a location reference service to propose a way of restricting the scope of discovery using location-dependent contexts. These technologies enable location-based ad hoc federation of intelligent resources over the Web and ubiquitous computing environments.

Introduction

During the last decade, the Web has become a very rich gigantic mine of all kinds of multimedia documents on almost any kinds of topics and subjects, varieties of ready-to-run application tools, and almost any kinds of services. These services include information and database reference services, simulation services, map services, data conversion and analysis services, e-learning services, and metainformation services such as search engines. Today, you can mine the Web to obtain almost whatever information items, application tools, or services you may think of. The Web is becoming the primary source of information resources and intelligent resources including tools and services for assisting a huge variety of our tasks.

However, in practice, we are not yet able to fully utilize the rich variety of these resources over the Web in our daily tasks. A task in general consists of a set of subtasks among which a flow of information is defined. A task may change its information flow among subtasks depending on the input and output of each subtask. A task is atomic if it cannot be decomposed into subtasks. A task that can be performed by a tool or a service is an example of an atomic task. Tools and services can perform some atomic tasks for us. However, non atomic tasks cannot be performed by any tools or any services. Each non atomic task requires coordinated use of more than one tool or service. We need an assistance system to coordinate not only the access of more than one tool or service, but also the user's interaction, to perform a task.

We are not yet able to fully utilize the rich variety of Web resources for **assistance systems**. There are three main difficulties in their reuse for assistance systems. First, it is not always easy to find out an available resource reusable for each atomic subtask. One reason lies in the fact that it is generally difficult to quantify the functionality of the resources reusable for a specific subtask. Without quantifying the functionality of each resource, it is not possible to search for resources with a desired function. This is the difficulty of functional quantification. Another reason is the difficulty to quantify resources in terms of the compatibility of their interface to their reuse environment. This is the difficulty of interface quantification. Second, it is not always possible to reuse the found resource in its **interoperation** with other resources for the required assistance. Generally, such a reuse requires some modification of the resource interface to make it interoperate with other resources. This is the difficulty of interoperation. Third, it is not easy to coordinate interoperable resources for the required assistance. This is the difficulty of **coordination**.

Solutions to these difficulties somehow require another level of assistance, that is, assistance for the discovery, interoperation, and coordination of tools and services for the required assistance. As a solution to the first difficulty, we have already search engines and metasearch engines, which fully index and rank Web pages analyzing their textual contents and links, and use such indices and ranks to retrieve appropriate Web pages for arbitrarily specified keywords. However, such indices are not sufficient to quantify either the functionality or the interface of each embedded tool or service.

As a solution to the second difficulty, that is, the difficulty of interoperation, we may use **Web service** technologies together with SOAP protocol. However, this solution cannot be applied to the interoperation among **Web applications**, nor to the interoperation between a Web application and a Web service. As tools for atomic subtasks, we are already using various Web applications whose functions are not yet provided as Web services. We know that some functional combinations of more than one Web application may perform significantly useful tasks for assisting some of our jobs. For example, in the bioinformatics research field, it is said that more than 3000 Web applications are already available. Some perform homology search for a given DNA sequence to find out candidate genes with similar sequences. Some provide a reference service about the details of each known gene. These two Web applications are themselves tools for atomic subtasks in bioinformatics. The combined usage of these two Web applications will work as a new composite tool. However, in order to obtain the detail information about a single candidate gene, they need to make a copy of the accession number of this gene in the search result of the homology search, and to paste this copy in the input form of the second Web application. In order to obtain the details of the first 30 candidate genes, they need to repeat the above mentioned manual procedure for 30 times. We need a new method to compose a new service by combining more than one Web application.

As a solution to the third difficulty, that is, the difficulty of coordination, some proposals were already made for the coordination of Web services (Gudgin, 2004; Tai, Khalaf & Mikalsen, 2004; Terai, Izumi & Yamaguchi; Tai, Khalaf & Mikalsen, 2004). Such coordination is also called **orchestration** (Tsalgatidou & Pilioura, 2002; Zirpins, Lamersdorf & Baier, 2004) or **choreography** (Foster, Uchitel, Magee & Kramer, 2004) of Web services.

There may be three different ways of defining functional combinations and coordination of available Web applications and/or Web services, i.e., static definition, dynamic definition, and ad hoc definition. Each of them selects some intelligent resources out of a certain scope of resources, makes them interoperate with each other, and coordinate them to satisfy given demands. For a static demand and a static scope of resources, the selection, interoperation, and coordination of intelligent resources can be also statically defined. If either of the demand or the scope of resources may dynamically change, the selection, interoperation, and coordination of intelligent resources need to be defined either dynamically or in an ad hoc way. If the demand is static or its dynamic change can be predicted and a priori specified, we can use dynamic definition of selection, interoperation, and coordination. If the demand cannot be predicted, we need ad hoc definition of selection, interoperation, and coordination.

Pervasive computing denotes an open system of intelligent resources in which users can dynamically select, interoperate, and coordinate some of these intelligent resources to perform their jobs satisfying their dynamically changing demands. Pervasive computing assumes the wide distribution of such intelligent resources, not only over the Web, but also over ubiquitous computing environments. In pervasive computing, the definition and/or execution of selection, interoperation, and coordination of intelligent resources are called **federation**. While the integration denotes interoperation and coordination of intelligent resources with a priori designed standard interoperation interfaces, federation denotes interoperation and coordination of intelligent resources without a priori designed interoperation interfaces. As mentioned, there may be three different types of federations, that is, static federations, dynamic federations, and ad hoc federations.

A static federation uses a static description to relate each component of a new composition with the component of some available resource that may be explicitly specified or semantically quantified. **Semantic Web** (Berners-Lee, Hendler & Lassila, 2001) technologies such as RDF (Brickley & Guha, 2000) were introduced for this purpose. Composition with existing Web documents using RDF defines a portal site, but cannot make more than one Web application interoperate with each other through parameter bindings. Semantic Web technologies can define parameter bindings only among Web services through an agent program. This technology is called **Semantic Web Service**.

The Semantic Web Service technology (Benbernou, 2005; Howard & Kerschberg, 2004; McIlraith, Son & Zeng, 2001) aims to enable a wide variety of agent technologies for automated Web service discovery, execution, composition, and interoperation. It is based on both Semantic Web technologies and agent technologies over the Web such as the Web agent technology (Waldinger, 2001) and the sofbot (Etzioni & Weld, 1994). The Semantic Web service framework enables us to program an agent for a dynamic federation of more than one Web service.

Dynamic federations based on the Semantic Web service framework uses an agent program for the discovery, execution, composition, interoperation, and coordination of Web services. Therefore, both the quantification conditions for discovery, and the way of interoperation must be predictable for us to program them in the agent. Dynamic federation is different from ad hoc federation. The latter deals with the case in which the quantification conditions for discovery, and the way of interoperation are not predictable, and cannot be programmed.

Dynamic federation technology, however, cannot enable us to combine two Web applications that we come across to find it useful to combine for assisting our current task. Even if the same two functions are also provided as Web services, we need to develop an agent for their interoperation before we can utilize the composite function. This is not only time consuming as well as cost inefficient, but also troublesome since it breaks the continuity of our thought in our current task. We need a new technology for instantaneous federation that can be defined in an ad hoc way.

Ad hoc federation denotes such instantaneous federation of resources that is defined on site, at any time, and at any place, by a non-programmer user without writing any programs. Ad hoc federation of intelligent resources is attracting the attention for on-site instantaneous analysis, strategic planning, and immediate action with the maximum use of accessible resources for assistance, especially in risk management such as disaster relief and zoonosis control, financial analysis and planning, user-customizable security and management system for office and home, strategic business analysis and management, customizable control of sensor or actuator networks, user-customizable monitor and control of home electronic appliances, and so forth. Ad hoc federation of intelligent resources requires ad hoc definability of interoperation, coordination, and an interactive easy way of finding appropriate resources and getting their proxies to utilize their functions.

This chapter focuses on ad hoc federation of intelligent resources embedded in Web applications, and proposes two enabling technologies based on the **meme media** technologies developed by our group. The first technology aims at ad hoc definition and execution of interoperation and coordination of resources embedded in either Web applications or Web services, while the second technology aims at interactive discovery of appropriate resources and acquisition of their proxies.

Easy and interactive discovery of resources in ad hoc situations requires some ways of automatically restricting the search scope in accordance with dynamically changing situations. Otherwise, the scope is too large to find the appropriate ones instantaneously. We may use the user's current context such as the time, the location, and the people in the same location to narrow down the search scope for the discovery of appropriate resources. In ubiquitous computing environments, some intelligent resources are available only around specific locations. Such examples include a slide projection service available in a specific room, a nearby restaurant and hotel reference service at a terminal or an airport, and an explanation service around each article on exhibition. These services are location-dependent. The discovery for location-dependent services can automatically narrow down the scope of discovery to those resources available at the current location. This paper proposes a location-based **repository and lookup service** system, which can be also instantaneously constructed as an example application of our ad hoc federation technology to both a Wiki service Web application and another Web application for a location reference service.

Federation is location-based if its scope of resources depends on the physical location where it is defined. **Location-based federation** can use a location-based repository and lookup service for interactive discovery of resources. This chapter focuses on location-based ad hoc federation of Web resources for assistance, and proposes its enabling technologies in the framework of meme media technologies.

We will first propose a generic solution to ad hoc federation over the Web and ubiquitous computing environments. We assume that intelligent resources are accessible directly or indirectly through the Web, namely either through Web applications or through Web services. Then we will apply this solution to location-based ad hoc federation of intelligent resources. We use meme media technologies as enabling technologies. **Meme media** technologies are media technologies for reediting and redistributing not only multimedia contents but also application tools and services (Tanaka, 2003). When applied to the Web, meme media technologies allow us to extract arbitrary HTML nodes including input forms and output contents from Web pages, and to define interoperation among them, only through direct manipulation, which works as an ad hoc federation technology. We will apply this ad hoc federation technology to a **Wiki service** system, make it work as a repository and lookup service of meme media objects, and then combine this with a location reference service to propose a location-based repository and lookup service for location-based ad hoc federation of intelligent resources.

Meme Media as Enabling Technologies

IntelligentPad is a two-dimensional representation version of the **meme-media** architecture. Its architecture can be roughly summarized as follows for our current purpose. Instead of directly dealing with component objects, IntelligentPad wraps each object with a standard pad wrapper, that is, a software module with a standard visual representation and a standard functional linkage interface, and treats it as a media object called a pad. Each pad has both a standard user interface and a standard connection interface. The user interface of every pad has a card like view on the screen and a standard set of operations like "move," "resize," "copy," "paste," and "peel." As a connection interface, every pad provides a list of slots that works as IO ports, and a standard set of messages "set ," "gimme," and "update." Each pad defines one of its slots as its primary slot. Most pads allow users to change their primary slot assignments.

You may paste a pad on another pad to define a parent-child relationship between these two pads. The former becomes a child of the latter. When you paste a pad on another, you can select one of the slots provided by the parent pad, and connect the child pad to this selected slot. The selected slot is called the connection slot. Using a "set" message, each child pad can set the value of its primary slot to the connection slot of its parent pad. Using a "gimme" message, each child pad can read the connection slot value of its parent pad, and update its primary slot with this value. Whenever a pad has a state change, it sends an "update" message to each of its child pads to notify that there was a state change. Whenever a pad receives an "update" message, it sends a "gimme" message to its parent pad to read the recent value of the slot it is connected. For each slot connection, you can independently enable or disable each of the three standard messages, "set," "gimme," and "update." By pasting pads on another pad and specifying slot connections, you may easily define both a compound-document's layout design and functional linkages among these pads. Further details on its architecture, its applications, and its extension to the three dimensional representation version of meme media can be found in Tanaka (2003).

Clipping and Connecting WEB Resources for Federation

C3W Framework for the Federation of Web Applications

The Web is becoming a rich source of information resources and intelligent resources including texts, multimedia contents, tools, and services that are open for public use. Here we will show the **C3W framework** we have developed for the clipping and the connecting of fragments of Web resources. Figure 1 shows, at its bottom right corner, a Web page by U.S. Naval Observatory showing day and night over the earth. This Naval Observatory Web application allows us to specify any time in GST, and displays the day and night over the earth at this time. The left object in this figure is a composite pad showing the difference of day and night over the earth at a given time of a day in arbitrarily chosen two different seasons, for example, on summer solstice and on winter solstice. This composite pad was constructed by clipping out the time and date input forms and the simulated visual result as pads from the Naval Observatory Web pages, and pasting these clips on a special pad called C3WsheetPad. The time and date input forms include the year, the month, the day, the hour and the minute input forms. These pads clipped out from the same Web application that may possibly change pages

Figure 1. Construction of a new intelligent resource, using contents extracted from Web pages as meme media objects

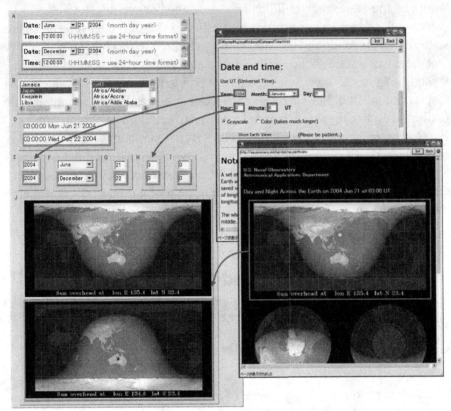

keep their input and output relationship in the original Web application. This relationship among the clips is maintained by the base C3WsheetPad. When a clipped-out pad is pasted on a C3WsheetPad, it is given a unique cell name like 'A,' 'B,'…, 'A1,' 'B1,' … on this C3WsheetPad.

Four more pads are clipped out from a time-conversion Web application, and pasted on the same C3WsheetPad. They also keep the input and output relationship in the original time-conversion Web application. Therefore, these four pads with cell names 'A,' 'B,' 'C,' and 'D,' perform a conversion from an input local time to the corresponding GST. The cell A accepts a local time input. The cell B is for the selection of a local time zone. The cell C is used to specify London to obtain the GST in the cell D. This GST corresponds to the local time that is input to the cell A.

Using the spreadsheet-like function of C3WsheetPad, you can specify an equation between the cell D and the cells E, F, G, H, and I to set the year, the month, the day, the hour, and the minute of the GST time in cell D to the cells E, F, G, H, and I extracted from Naval Observatory page. For example, you can specify the expression "<--*year*(D) " in cell E to use the last four numeric characters of the output of cell D as the input to cell E. Such a linkage definition using expressions makes these two sets of clips extracted from the two independent Web applications interoperate with each other. In Figure 1, we further applied the multiplexing to the input cell A to obtain multiple outputs in the output cells D, E, F, G, H, I, and J.

All these operations are performed through direct manipulation of pads. For browsing the original Web page, we use a Web browser pad, which dynamically frames different extractable document portions for different mouse locations so that its user may move the mouse cursor around to see every extractable document portion. When it frames a desired object, you can just drag the mouse to clip out this object as a pad. All the pads thus clipped-out from the same Web application keep their original functional relationship even after their arrangement on the same C3WsheetPad. Whenever you input a new date to the extracted date input form, the corresponding extracted output pad showing a simulated result will change its display. This simulation is performed by the server for the Web application from which all these pads are clipped out. Such a direct manipulation process enables us to easily customize and interoperate existing information resources and intelligent resources published by a huge variety of Web applications.

The multiplexer pad, when inserted between the base C3WsheetPad and the local time input clip of cell A, automatically inserts another multiplexer pad between the base C3WsheetPad and every clip whose value may depend on the input to this local time input clip. If you make a copy of the local time input clip on the multiplexer pad at cell A, then each of the dependent multiplexer pads automatically makes a copy of its child pad. Mutually related multiplexer pads maintain the relationship among the copies of their child pads. The original copies, the second copies, and the third copies on the mutually related multiplexer pads respectively form independent tuples of clips. Each of these tuples maintains input and output relationship among its constituent clips. In Figure 1, two simulation results are obtained for two different local times. This mechanism can be used for the intercomparison of more than one case.

Mechanism of the C3W Framework

Web documents are defined in HTML format. An HTML view denotes an arbitrary HTML document portion represented in the HTML document format. The pad wrapper to wrap an arbitrary portion of a Web document is capable of both specifying an arbitrary HTML view and rendering any HTML document. We call this pad wrapper HTMLviewPad. Its rendering function is implemented by wrapping a legacy Web browser, Internet Explorer. The specification of an arbitrary HTML view over a given HTML document requires the capability of specifying an arbitrary substructure of the internal representation of HTML documents, namely, the DOM tree. HTMLviewPad specifies its HTML view by specifying the DOM tree node that is the root of the subtree representing this HTML view. The DOM tree representation allows us to identify any of its nodes with its HTML path expression such as /HTML[0]/BODY[0]/TABLE[0]/TR[1]/TD[1].

The definition of an HTML view consists of a source document specification, and a sequence of view editing operations. A source document specification uses the document URL. Its retrieval is performed by a function "GETHTML" in such a way as

```
url = 'http://www.abc.com/index.html';
doc = url.GETHTML();
```

The retrieved document is kept in DOM format. The editing of an HTML view is a sequence of DOM tree manipulation operations selected out of the followings:

- **CLIP(*node*):**
  To delete all the nodes other than the subtree with the specified node as its root.
- **DELETE(*node*):**
  To delete the subtree with the specified node as its root.

An HTML view is specified as follows:

defined-view = source-view.DOM-tree-operation(node),

where *source-view* may be a Web document or another HTML document, and *node* is specified by its path expression. This code is called the view editing code of the HTML view. The following is an example view definition code.

```
view1 = doc
    .CLIP('/HTML/BODY/TABLE[1]')
    .CLIP('/TABLE[1]/TR[1]')
    .DELETE('/TR[1]/TD[2]');
```

After the first CLIP operation, the node /TABLE[1]/TR[1] corresponds to the node /HTML/BODY/TABLE[1]/TR[1] of the original document doc. The former path expression /TABLE[1]/TR[1] is called the relative path expression.

An HTMLviewPad with a view editing code can execute this code to recover the edit result when necessary. Its loading from a server or a local disk to a desktop is such a case.

Instead of specifying a relative path expression to identify a DOM tree node, we will make the HTMLviewPad to dynamically frame different extractable document portions for different mouse locations so that its user can move the mouse cursor around to see every extractable document portion. When the HTMLviewPad frames what you want to clip out, you can drag the mouse to create another HTMLviewPad with this clipped-out document portion. The new HTMLviewPad renders the clipped-out DOM tree on itself. Figure 2a shows an example clip operation, which internally generates the following view editing code.

```
url = 'http://www.abc.com/index.html';
view = url.GETHTML()
        .CLIP('/HTML/BODY/TABLE[1]');
```

Figure 2. Direct manipulations for extracting and removing views

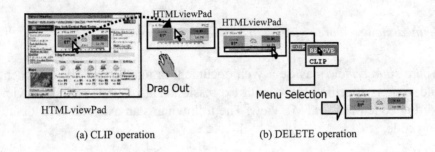

(a) CLIP operation (b) DELETE operation

The HTMLviewPad provides a pop-up menu of view-editing operations in-cluding CLIP and DELETE. After you select an arbitrary portion, you may select either CLIP or DELETE. Figure 2b shows an example delete operation, which generates the following code.

```
url = 'http://www.abc.com/index.html';
view = url.GETHTML()
      .CLIP('/HTML/BODY/TABLE[1]')
      .DELETE('/TABLE[1]/TR[2]');
```

Here we consider the clipping of more than one HTML node from more than one Web page visited through a single navigation, and their functional recom-bination based on the functional linkage relationship among these nodes in this navigation. Figure 3 shows a Google Web page, and the clipping of the keyword input form, and the first search result through a search navigation with "IntelligentPad" as a search keyword. The Web browser used here is also an HTMLviewPad. We can use its node specification mode to clip out HTML nodes only through mouse operation. The HTMLviewPad internally holds a sequence of such operations as a view editing code including event operations. Event operations include the following three operations:

- **CLICK*(anchor_node)*:** to return the destination Web page of this an-chor

- **SET***(form_node, input)***:** to set an input value to the specified form input node
- **SUBMIT***(submit_node)***:** to return the output page by sending the corresponding server a query specified by the current input-form values.

In this example, we first clipped out the keyword input form, and the search area selector as two new HTMLviewPads from the Google home page.

These clips have the following view editing codes:

- **Clip 1:** view = url.GETHTML()

  .CLIP(π);

- **Clip 2:** view = url.GETHTML()

  .CLIP(π1);

Figure 3. Clips extracted from a single navigation and their recombination on a ClipboardPad

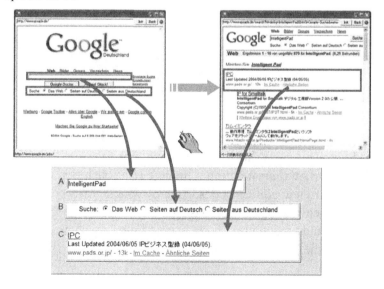

After these clips are clipped out, the HTMLviewPad Clip 0 showing the Google home page has the following view editing code:

- **Clip 0:** view = url.GETHTML();

Then we input a search keyword "IntelligentPad" on this Google home page, set a selector, and click the search button to obtain the first search result page. This changes the view editing code of Clip0 as:

- **Clip 0:** view = url.GETHTML()
  .SET(π, 'IntelligentPad')
  .SET(π1, *)

  .SUBMIT(π2);

where .SET(π1, *) denotes that the current HTML view at node π1 is set to the node π1. This substitution may seem to be redundant. However, in the later discussion, this parameter value is connected to the Clip 2, and is updated by a set message from this clip that may have changed its HTML view through user's interaction.

Now the Clip 0 shows the second page. From this page, we clipped out the first search result as another new HTMLviewPad Clip 3.

- **Clip 3:** view = url.GETHTML()
  .SET(π, 'IntelligentPad')
  .SET(π1, *)
  .SUBMIT(π2)
  .CLIP(π3);

Each of these clips is pasted on the same C3WsheetPad immediately after it is clipped out. This C3WsheetPad is used to make these clips operate with each other based on their functional linkage relationship in the navigation. It holds a list of view editing codes, each of which corresponds to a single navigation. When we clip out and paste Clip 1 on a C3WsheetPad, it creates a new entry in the view editing code list, and puts the view editing code of Clip 0 at this time. This entry value becomes as follows:

view = url.GETHTML();

The C3WsheetPad associates this clip a new cell name 'A', creates a corresponding slot #A, and connects Clip 1 to this slot. It associate the slot #A with the node π. This adds one more operation .CELL ('A'π) at the end of the above code using the following new operation:

- **CELL*(cell_name, node)*:** To associate the specified cell with the specified node, and to return the same HTML view as the recipient.

When we paste Clip 2 on the same C3WsheetPad, it searches the list for an entry with such a code that is a prefix of the view editing code σ of Clip 0 at this time. This comparison neglects all the CELL operations in the code stored in each entry of the code list. The C3WsheetPad updates this entry with the code σ, inserts all the CELL operations in the old entry code at the same positions in σ, and adds one more CELL operation to associate the node $\pi1$ with the new cell 'B.' This entry value becomes as follows:

```
view = url.GETHTML()
        .CELL('A', π)
        .CELL('B', π1);
```

The C3WsheetPad connects Clip 2 to the slot #B.

The code in the entry created by the preceding clips in the same single navigation, when all the cell defining actions being neglected, must always be a prefix of the current view editing code of Clip 0. If there is no entry with such a code in the list, it means that a new navigation has just started. This case will be detailed later.

When we finally paste Clip 3, the same entry of the code list becomes as follows:

```
view = url.GETHTML()
        .CELL('A', π)
        .CELL('B', π1)
        .SET(π, 'IntelligentPad')
        .SET(π1, *)
```

```
.SUBMIT(π2)

.CELL('C', π3);
```

The C3WsheetPad connects Clip 3 to the slot #C.

When we input some keyword on Clip 1, it sends a set massage to the slot #A with this new input keyword as a parameter value. The C3WsheetPad scans CELL operations for the slot #A, finds the associated node π, searches for a SET operation with π as its first parameter, replaces its second parameter with the input keyword, and executes this view editing code. When we select an item on Clip 2, it sends a set message to the slot #B with its updated HTML view as a parameter value. This value is used to rewrite the second parameter of SET($\pi 1$, *). Then this C3WsheetPad executes the view editing code.

Whenever the C3WsheetPad executes a view editing code, it sends update messages to all the clips working as output devices. Each of these clips sends a gimme message to its connection slot. The C3WsheetPad searches for the node associated with this connection slot, and returns the HTML view of this node. Each recipient clip will change its HTML view to this new value.

These mechanisms allow clips obtained during a single navigation to interoperate with each other based on their original functional relationships in the navigation.

When we start a new navigation and paste the first clipped-out pad on the C3WsheetPad, it groups the slots defined in the preceding navigation, and associates this group with its latest list entry storing a view editing code to maintain the relationship among these slots. For the new navigation process, the C3WsheetPad creates a new entry to keep updating a new view editing code for maintaining the relationship among slots to be newly created.

C3WsheetPad allows us to define equations among their cells. The equation $<\!\!-\!\!f(C_1, C_2, \ldots C_n)$ defined for a cell C_0 means that the value of the function f evaluated using the values of the cells $C_1, C_2, \ldots C_n$ should be used as the input value of the cell C_0. The value of each of the right hand side cells is evaluated by reexecuting the stored view editing code that relates these cells.

As mentioned above, some cell values are HTML views. However, for simple HTML views such as text strings or text input forms, it is more convenient to treat them as non-HTML text strings. Clips with such simple values actually work as follows. When a new input is given, such an input form clip sends only the input value to the slot of the base C3WsheetPad. It holds the path expression to specify only this input-value portion, instead of the one specifying the clipped-out input form. The C3WsheetPad also uses this path expression to replace only the input item with the current slot value in the reexecution of its corresponding view editing code. For each clip that works as an textual output from a C3WsheetPad, the clip holds the path expression to specify only this textual output portion, instead of the one specifying the clipped-out HTML node. The base C3WsheeetPad uses this path expression to output only the specified text portion to the corresponding slot in the reexecution of the corresponding view editing code. The clip uses this slot value to replace the specified text portion of its latest HTML view and to render the result. These modifications enable such simple clips to define text value slots, instead of HTML-view value slots.

Embedding Clips in MS Word and Excel Documents

Recently, we have extended our C3W framework so that Web clips can be embedded as objects in MS Word and Excel documents. We developed a special pad object MSPad that can be treated as an MS Word object or an MS Excel object, and can be embedded into MS Word and MS Excel documents. MSPads that have been independently embedded in the same Word document work as shared copies of the same MSPad. MSPads also work as C3WsheetPads. In order to embed Web clips in a word document, you can first embed an MSPad in the word document for each Web clip, and paste this clip on this MSPad. You may also define an appropriate slot, namely a cell, on an embedded MSPad with its relationship to another cell created for a Web clip, and paste a text pad with its connection to this slot. This allows you to use text pads instead of HTMLviewPads. You may also hide the pad borderline to make the embedded contents look naturally as if they are parts of the ordinary Word documents. Figure 4 shows an example Word document with several embedded Web clips interoperating with each other.

Each MSPad can be also embedded in any Excel cell. It keeps the value of its slot to which its child pad is connected always equal to the Excel cell value. MSPads embedded in the same Excel sheet work as shared copies of the same MSPad, however each of them may have a different child pad and a different slot. They only share the code list. Figure 5 shows an example Excel sheet with several embedded Web clips interoperating with each other.

Figure 4. An MS Word document with six interoperable embedded Web clips extracted from CNN Money Stock Quote pages

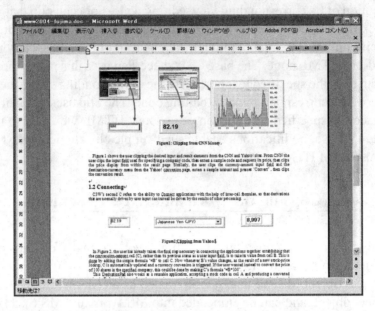

Figure 5. An MS Excel sheet with interoperable embedded Web clips extracted from CNN Money Stock Quote pages

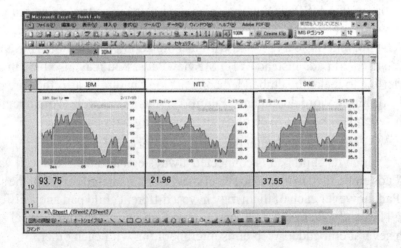

Proxy Pads for Reusing Legacy Systems and Web Services

Figure 6 shows a form interface framework for relational databases. A form interface is a visual interface that provides users with an office-form view of retrieved records. IntelligentPad works as a form-construction kit for relational databases. The base pad in this figure works as an interface to a legacy database management system. Such a pad that works as a **proxy object**, or an interface object, of some external system is called a proxy pad. Examples of such external systems include industrial-plant control systems, database management systems, computer-controlled devices, numerical computation programs running on supercomputers, and all kinds of Web services.

A database proxy pad DBProxyPad performs all the details necessary to access a database. It has slots including the #query slot, the #search slot, the #insert slot, the #delete slot, the #previousCandidate slot, the #nextCandidate slot, the #result slot, and the #currentRecord slot. The whole set of pads available in IntelligentPad works as a form construction kit for the visual interface of this database. A RecordPad is a blank-sheet pad. When it receives an "update" message, it reads out a record-type value, i.e., an association list, from its parent pad and holds this record. A RecordPad allows us to add an arbitrary number of special slots called attribute slots. It also allows us to remove a specified slot from its list of attribute slots. Each attribute slot, when requested to send back its value, reads out the stored record and gets the value of the attribute having the same name as this attribute-slot name. If the record does not have the same attribute name, this attribute slot returns the value "nil." When a RecordPad is pasted on the DBProxyPad with its

Figure 6. A form interface framework using pads

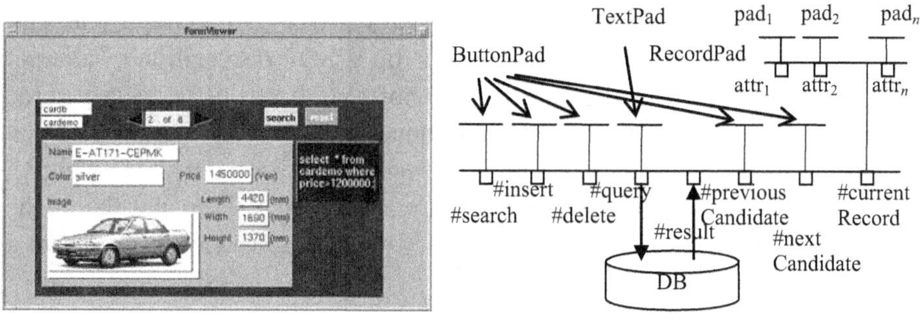

connection to the #currentRecord slot of this proxy pad, it works as a base pad to define a form representation of each record that will be retrieved from the DBProxyPad (Figure 6).

The pad pad$_i$ in Figure 6 is a display pad that shows the value of the attribute attr$_i$ of a record stored in the RecordPad. Some examples of such a display pad are TextPad, ImagePad, MoviePad, and BarMeterPad. A mouse click of the ButtonPad connected to the #search slot invokes a search of the database. A click of the ButtonPad connected to the nextCandidate slot advances the record cursor to the next candidate record in the list of retrieved records stored in the #result slot. In its typical use on a DBProxyPad, a RecordPad divides each retrieved record into a set of attribute-value pairs. Each attribute value is set to the slot with the same name as its attribute name. Depending on the value type of each attribute slot, you may connect a text viewer pad, an image viewer pad, a drawing viewer pad, or a video viewer pad to this slot. You may arbitrarily design the layout of these viewer pads on the RecordPad. A DBProxyPad with a RecordPad pasted with some viewer pads is called a form-based DB viewer, or a form interface to a database.

For specifying a query in the #query slot of a DBProxyPad, you can simply use a text pad. An SQL query written on this text pad is sent to the #query slot of the proxy pad. When the #search slot is accessed by a set message, DBProxyPad issues the query stored in its #query slot to the corresponding database, and sets the retrieved set of records in its #result slot. It has a cursor to point one of the records in the #result slot. The pointed record is kept in the #currentRecord slot. The cursor can be moved forward or backward respectively when the #nextCandidate slot or the #previousCandidate slot is accessed by a set message.

The development of a proxy pad for a **legacy application** requires programming. If the legacy has its own graphical user interface, the development task becomes difficult in general.

For **Web services** with WSDL descriptions on their interfaces, however, we can semi-automate the development of their proxy pads. Our framework for wrapping Web services first analyzes the WSDL description of a target Web service to show us the list of all IO ports, and asks us to specify some of them to work as slots. Then it can automatically develop a proxy pad that communicates with this Web service using SOAP protocol. For example, a proxy pad for a database Web service may have the same slot list as the mentioned DBProxyPad, and can be used in the same way to construct a form interface. However, it accesses a remote database Web service instead of a local database system.

Proxy pads can be combined with other types of pads including C3Wsheet-Pads with some clips from Web applications. Such a combination defines an ad hoc federation among a huge variety of resources that are published either as Web applications or as Web services.

Wrapping WiKi Service to a Repository and Lookup Service

Our clipping-and-connecting framework can be also applied to a **Wiki service** to make it work as a worldwide repository of pads for sharing and exchanging them. Such a repository is useful for interactive discovery of appropriate resources and reusable compositions for assisting our tasks. Wiki is a piece of server software that allows users to freely create and edit Web page content using any Web browser (Cunningham, 2003). Wiki supports hyperlinks, and has simple text syntax for creating new pages and crosslinks between internal pages on the fly.

In order to construct a pad repository system from Wiki, you first need to access a Wiki page, and to clip out the four items, that is, the URL input, the

Figure 7. A pad repository system Piazza constructed using a Wiki service

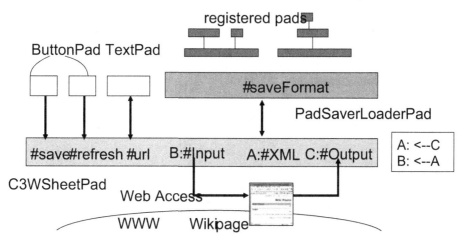

HTML input form, refresh button, and the output page, as pads. Then you need to paste these clips on a C3WsheetPad (Figure 7). You further need to paste a PadSaverLoaderPad on the same C3WsheetPad, and to relate its input and output respectively to the clipped-out input form and the clipped-out output page. PadSaverLoaderPad makes bilateral conversion between pads on itself and a list of their save format representations in XHTML. Suppose that the PadSaverLoaderPad, the input form clip, and the output page clip are given cell names 'A,' 'B,', and 'C.' The interoperation among them can be specified by two equations among these cells, i.e., an assignment statement '<—C' for cell A, and another statement '<—A' for cell B.

People can access any page specifying its URL, drag-and-drop arbitrary composite pads to and from the PadSaverLoaderPad in this composition to upload and download them to and from the corresponding Wiki server. Each page is shown by the PadSaverLoaderPad. This pad repository system is called **Wiki Piazza**. Figure 8 shows a Wiki Piazza system. Users may manipulate and/or edit some pads on an arbitrary Wiki Piazza page to update their states. They can complete such an update by clicking the save button to

Figure 8. A worldwide repository of pads developed by applying meme media technologies to Wiki

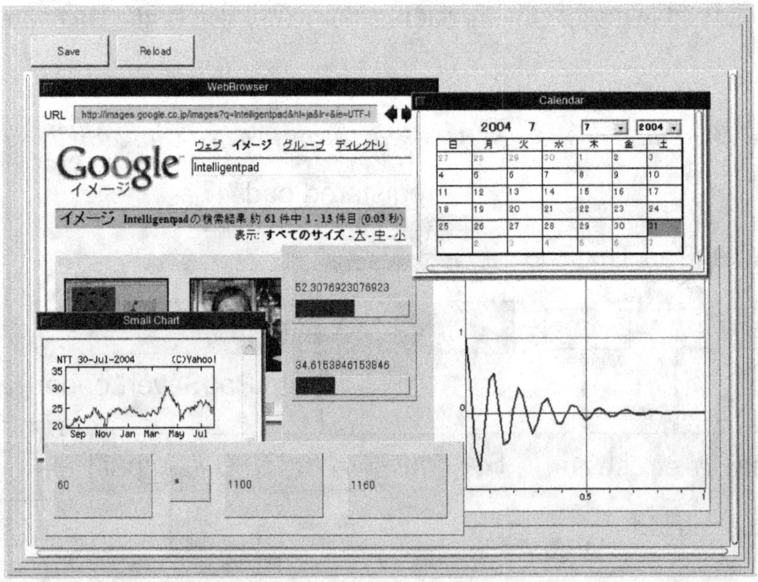

upload the page update to the corresponding server. Another user accessing the same page can share the updated pads by just clicking the reload button to retrieve the latest version of this page from the corresponding server. For a jump from a page to another page in a Wiki Piazza system, we can use an anchor pad that can be pasted on a Wiki Piazza page. This anchor pad holds a URL that can be set through its #refURL slot. When clicked, it sets this URL to the #url slot of the Wiki Piazza system, that is, to the #url slot of the base C3WsheetPad.

A Wiki Piazza system allows people not only to publish and share pads, but also to compose new pads by combining components of those pads already published on some of its pages, and to publish these newly composed pads. The collaborative reediting and redistribution of intellectual resources represented as pads in a shared publishing repository by a community or a society of people will accelerate the memetic evolution of resources in this repository, and make it work as a meme pool. Such a meme pool is especially useful in the community of people sharing an interest in a specific area of assistance. A Wiki Piazza system enables such a community to share not only tools and services, but also combined reuses of them, namely, expertise on how to federate some of them for different specific purposes.

Pervasive Computing and Location-Based Ad Hoc Federation

Pervasive computing is an open system of intelligent resources, and requires both a **repository service** and a **lookup service**. The repository service is used to register available intelligent resources. A lookup service is used to find out a desired intelligent resource from a repository of available intelligent resources, and to get its reference as a proxy object as well as a method to access it through the proxy. In addition, pervasive computing needs to allow users to define interoperation among intelligent resources and/or their **proxy objects** in an ad hoc way to perform their jobs.

We assume that all the intelligent resources of our concern including embedded and mobile resources in ubiquitous computing environments are published as Web applications or Web services. Some of them are open to the public, while others are available only to closed user communities. Web applications and Web services of the latter type may use Web-based security control technologies such as the password-based access control to restrict their access. Web applications and Web services execute intelligent resources in their servers. When accessing Web applications or Web services, client systems execute only the Web browser code with some plug-in codes or service invocation codes using SOAP. Application codes are executed by the corresponding servers. Client systems need not execute codes of object classes unknown to them. Therefore, federation among Web applications and Web services requires no object migration across networks, and causes no class migration problem.

The meme media technologies for extracting Web resources and for reediting them to compose new resources allow us to dynamically define ad hoc federation among intelligent resources published as Web applications or Web services. Such a composite pad composed of pads extracted from the same Web application works as a proxy of this Web application. A composite pad composed of pads extracted from Web applications, or proxy pads of Web services, as well as other pads, defines, and performs ad hoc federation of these intelligent resources.

For a repository service, we may use a Wiki Piazza system both for resource providers to register new intelligent resources, and for resource consumers or users to look up and to reuse available resources. Its pages can be a priori categorized for different usages and/or different contexts. Proxy pads of intelligent resources can be also a priori categorized for different usages or different contexts into groups. Proxy pads in the same group may be published on the same Wiki Piazza page. Some page may provide proxy pads for some specific task, for example, proxy pads of Web applications for stock-market information-service, while some other may provide proxy pads available at some specific location, for example, proxy pads of a printing service and a slide-projection service.

Figure 9 shows a Wiki Piazza page of the latter type. It provides proxy pads of services available in a meeting room. This Wiki Piazza page is automatically accessed by the following mechanism. In our laboratory building, each room is equipped with an independent access point for wireless network connection. Each access point can detect which wireless-connection PC card enters and leaves its covering area. Our laboratory installs a location reference server to manage and to provide information about the current location of each wireless-connection PC. When you carry your own PC and enter a room for a slide presentation, you can just click a special pad, which automatically opens the Wiki Piazza page corresponding to this room. When clicked, this special pad on the desktop first accesses the location reference server to know the current room number, and then accesses a room URI reference server to know the URI of the Wiki Piazza page corresponding to this room. Then it invokes a Wiki Piazza system with this URI. The automatically accessed page in Figure 9 contains three service proxy icon pads. One of them is a proxy icon pad of a slide-projection service. You can click this icon pad to open the proxy pad, which is shown on the right in the lower left window in Figure 9. This proxy pad has a file input pad, and two buttons to get the next or the previous slide. You can drag and drop your local PowerPoint file icon into this file input pad, and immediately start your slide presentation using the projector in this room without setting any cable connections. Such a mechanism provides a location-based repository service for users to get proxies of location-dependent services, and enables users to define federation of some of them with other resources in an ad hoc manner.

Since our system architectures and frameworks use generic meme media technologies and Web technologies, all the above mentioned functions can be applied in an ad hoc way to any intelliegnt resources in any open environments accessible through the Web. They can be also applied to intelligent

Figure 9. A Wiki Piazza page with proxy icons of services available in this room, and the use of a slide projection service proxy to project a local presentation file to a large screen

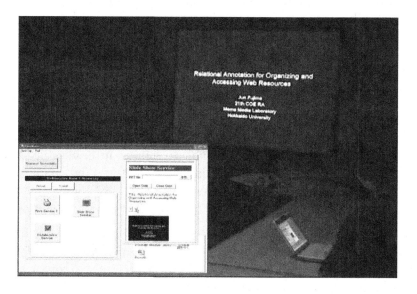

resources over any closed intranetworks, and furthermore to any combination of open resources over the Web and proprietary resources over a closed intra-network environment. From the view point of assistance, our location-based Wiki Piazza technology enables us to publish and to share location-dependent assistance tools and services for their repository and lookup, and to make some of them instantaneously interoperate with each other for new assistance in an ad hoc way.

Conclusion

The current Web is a mine of tools and services and the gate to ubiquitous computing environments with a huge number of highly distributed mobile and embedded intelligent resources. Their advanced reuse in assistance systems that support whole processes of our tasks requires enabling technologies for federation of resources, i.e., both the discovery of appropriate resources from a certain scope of resources, and their interoperation and coordination for the required demand. Such a scope and the demand may dynamically change.

For such cases in which they are both static, Semantic Web technologies can be used to relate each component of a new composition with the component of some available resource that may be explicitly specified or semantically quantified. Composition with existing Web documents by RDF defines a portal site, but cannot make more than one Web application interoperate with each other through parameter bindings. Semantic Web technologies can define parameter bindings only among Web services through an agent program. This technology is called Semantic Web service.

For cases in which the demand is predictable, Semantic Web service technologies can be used for federation among Web services.

This chapter focused on such cases in which both the scope and the demand change dynamically, and the change of demand cannot be predicted. Assistance systems for such cases must be able to support us to instantaneously perform federation of Web resources in an ad hoc way. They require new technologies for ad hoc federation of Web resources, and for restricting the scope of discovery in accordance with dynamically changing situations.

This paper proposed the use of meme media technologies for ad hoc federation of intelligent resources over the Web. It also proposed the Wiki piazza architecture that works as a repository and lookup service, and combined this service with a location reference service to propose a way of restricting the scope of discovery using location-dependent contexts. These technologies have enabled location-based ad hoc federation of intelligent resources over the Web and ubiquitous computing environments.

The use of meme media technologies as the basic architecture has made our ad hoc federation technologies applicable not only to HTML nodes in Web applications, but also to proxies of Web services and local legacy applications. However, our ad hoc federation technology is not robust against any style change of source Web applications, since the extraction of clips uses path expressions as their node identifiers. Our technology has another important problem to consider, which is whether it may cause any copyright violation. This is not only a technological problem, but also a social problem. We need new consensus and a new law. From the technological point of view, we can introduce a special mark for the author of each Web page to declare permission to the clipping of page contents, and restrict the applicability of the clipping operation only to those pages with such permission.

References

Benbernou, S., & Hacid, M.S. (2005). Resolution and constraint propagation for Semantic Web services discovery. *Distributed and Parallel Databases, 18*(1), 65–81.

Berners-Lee, T., Hendler, J., & Lassila, O. (2001). The Semantic Web. *Scientific American, 284*(5), 34–43.

Brickley, D., & Guha, R.V. (Eds.). (2000). *Resource description framework (RDF) schema specification* (1.0). CR, W3C. Retrieved June 2, 2006, from http://www.w3.org/TR/2000/CR-rdf-schema-20000327

Cunningham, W. (2003, November 27). *Wiki design principles*. Portland Pattern Repository, 27 November 2003.

Etzioni, O., & Weld, D. (1994). A softbot-based interface to the Internet. *Communications of the ACM, 37*(7), 72–76.

Foster, H., Uchitel, S., Magee, J., & Kramer, J. (2004). Compatibility verification for Web service choreography. In *Proceedings of the IEEE International Conference on Web Services (ICWS'04)* (p. 738). IEEE Computer Society.

Gudgin, M. (2004). Web services: Secure, reliable, transacted. Innovation in Web services architecture. In *Proceedings of the 2004 ACM SIGMOD International Conference on Management of Data* (pp. 879–880). ACM.

Howard, R., & Kerschberg, L. (2004). Brokering semantic Web services via intelligent middleware agents within a knowledge-based framework. In *Proceedings of the Intelligent Agent Technology, IEEE/WIC/ACM International Conference on (IAT'04).*

McIlraith, S.H., Son, T.C., & Zeng, H. (2001). Semantic Web services. *IEEE Intelligent Systems, 16*(2), 46–53.

Tai, S., Khalaf, R., & Mikalsen, T. (2004). Web services: Composition, integration, and interoperability: Composition of coordinated Web services. In *Proceedings of the 5th ACM/IFIP/USENIX International Conference on Middleware* (pp. 294–310). ACM.

Tanaka, Y. (2003). *Meme media and meme market architectures: Knowledge media for editing, distributing, and managing intellectual resources.* New York: IEEE Press, Wiley-Interscience.

Terai, K., Izumi, N., & Yamaguchi, T. (2003). Coordinating Web services based on business models. In *Proceedings of the 5th International Conference on Electronic Commerce ICEC '03* (pp. 473–478). ACM.

Tsalgatidou, A., & Pilioura, A. (2002). An overview of standards and related technology in Web services. *Distributed and Parallel Databases, 12*(2/3), 135–162.

Waldinger, R. (2001). Deductive composition of Web software agents, In *Proceedings of NASA Goddard Workshop Formal Approaches to Agent-Based Systems.* Lecture Notes in Computer Science, 1871. Springer-Verlag.

Zirpins, C., Lamersdorf, W., & Baier, T. (2004). Service composition: Flexible coordination of service interaction patterns. In *Proceedings of the 2nd International Conference on Service Oriented Computing* (pp. 49–56). ACM.

Section III

Applications

Chapter X

From E-Learning Tools to Assistants by Learner Modelling and Adaptive Behavior

Klaus Jantke,
Research Institute for Information Technologies Leipzig, Germany

Christoph Igel, Universität des Saarlandes, Germany

Roberta Sturm, Universität des Saarlandes, Germany

Abstract

Humans need assistance in learning. This is particularly true when learning is supported by modern information and communication technologies. Most current IT systems appear as more or less complex tools. The more ambitious the problems in the application domain are, the more complex are the tools. This is one of the key obstacles to a wider acceptance of technology enhanced learning approaches (e-learning, for short). In computer science, in general, and in e-learning, in particular, we do need a paradigmatic shift from tools of a growing complexity to intelligent assistants to the human user. Computerized assistants that are able to adapt to their human users' needs and desires need some ability to learn. In e-learning, in particular, they need to learn about the learner and to build an internal model of the learner as a basis of adaptive system behavior. Steps toward assistance in e-learning are systematically illustrated by means of the authors' e-learning projects and systems eBuT and DaMiT. These steps are summarized in some process model proposed to the e-learning community.

Technology Enhanced Learning: Pros and Cons

Technology has always been changing humans' lives, and the impact of science and technology has frequently been even deeper and longer lasting than expected at the beginning of a change. We are currently experiencing substantial changes driven by information and communication technologies, in general, and by the Internet pervading work places and private homes, in particular.

In the area of education ranging from elementary schools through universities to continuing education and life-long learning, information and communication technologies are paving the road for fundamentally new learning experiences.

The pros of e-learning are discussed in many publications, sometimes even organized toward formation of a strategy as in Igel and Daugs (2002), for example. There are convincing summaries of the benefits of technology enhanced learning for the industries. Tom Kelly, CISCO's vice president of worldwide training, circumscribes it as follows:

E-learning is not the answer to every question, but it needs to be applied as broadly as possible. The classroom simply cannot address business issues. If you have to teach 100 people about one topic, you can train 25 people in a classroom at a time and repeat the course four times. But if you have to train 3,000 people every 60 days on a new product, or on a new technology, or on a new market—there's no way that the classroom can work. There's no way to scale. There's no way to have an impact on the company. It is doomed to fail.

(http://fastcompany.com/magazine/39/quickstudy.html)

Motivations to get engaged in e-learning are expectations of added value of new media and added value of information and communication technologies like, for instance, independence of time and place—learning anytime, anywhere (Igel & Daugs, 2002).

From a didactic point of view, there are options for new concepts as situated learning and exploratory learning. Strategic options are ways to address wider audiences, off campus vs. on campus, bridging the gap from the academia to distance education and life long learning and, last but not least, new approaches to controlling in education through the exploitation of learning histories and technology-supported cost analysis.

There is an obvious convergence of technologies and media (computers and computer networks, television, audio communication), promising connections of online and off-line media, and emerging mobility in IT services.

In contrast to the pros, there are plenty of cons as well. Who properly works in the area of e-learning, not only as a "technology provider" (This word sounds like an excuse for scientists and engineers who do not care about how to wield the tools they are producing.), but employing e-learning in regular use, rapidly learns about a variety of difficulties. If you do so, you are also facing learners' frustration for several reasons.

Learners' most frequent complaints refer to missing or inappropriate feedback. Learners feel *misunderstood* by computers. In fact, nowadays all human learners *are misunderstood* by their computers, as computers are far from understanding anything—there is no need for a Chinese Room argument (Searle, 1980) to clarify this.

Here, a brief explanation seems to be necessary, as one of the reviewers of this chapter claimed that "the reference to a Chinese Room Argument is irrelevant, because the chapter deals with what current technology can deliver, while the work of Searle deals with the philosophical limits of computers." What a misunderstanding!

The present chapter does *not* deal with current technology, that is, tools in e-learning, but with steps towards future assistant technologies, thereby touching the rather philosophical question for the computers' potentials or limitations *to understand human learners*.

Human teachers are bringing in a virtually infinite background of implicit knowledge and skills when taking care of their students (Damasio, 1999).

The teacher's care is highly appreciated especially in difficult learning situations—when there are too many choices and one is lost in the content, when repeatedly reading, watching or listening does not lead to a satisfying result, when something does not work as expected, when the learner's solution to an exercise is wrong, but the learner does not know why, or when it simply gets boring.

What we do need are e-learning computer systems that react appropriately, that is, adaptively to the learner's general needs, to the learner's current problems and to the specific context.

Figure 1. Inspection of a learner model in eBuT containing bookkeeping and recommendations

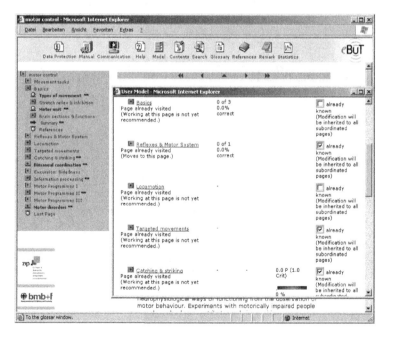

Adaptivity and System's Assistance at Work

Adaptivity to the learner's needs and desires is the ultimate aim of the authors' work toward a paradigmatic shift from e-learning tools to e-learning assistants. The authors' work relies on their own experience in designing, implementing and using e-learning systems for higher education. The systems DaMiT (http://damit.dfki.de) and eBuT (http://www.bewegung-und-training.de) are in daily use (see descriptions in Igel & Daugs, 2003a, 2003b; Igel & Sturm, 2003; Jantke, Grieser & Memmel, 2004; Jantke, Lange, Grieser, Grigoriev, Thalheim & Tschiedel, 2004a, 2004b).

DaMiT is a system for the domain of *knowledge discovery and data mining* mostly used for studies in computer science and business administration systems. The domain of eBuT is *human movement and training sciences* used in studies of sports science, kinesiology, or medicine. Both systems have been

Figure 2. Navigation advice in eBuT adapted to the state of the learner model

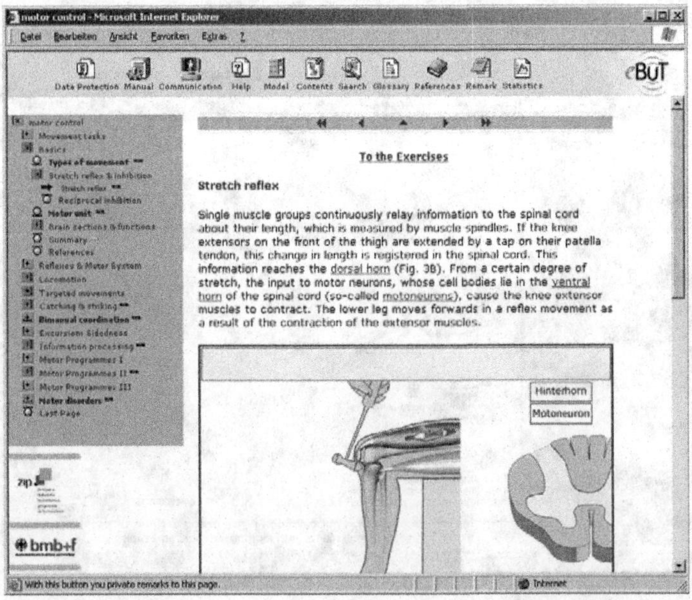

developed independently. They enjoy mutually different strengths and have both their individual peculiarities. The authors' common interest is in their systems' adaptivity as laid out in Jantke (2005), for example. The systems' adaptivity currently available is setting the stage for a transformation from e-learning tools into intelligent learning assistants.

The backbone of any system's adaptivity is its knowledge about the user, that is, the learner. The learner model of eBuT (see Figure 1) has been designed as a multilevel overlay model following Weber (2005). In contrast, the DaMiT learner model is flat in structure, but enjoys a particular feature: expressive learning goals. These fundamentals are not discussed in detail.

Instead, we are going to illustrate the systems' adaptivity at work. Concerning adaptivity, the authors rely on systematic approaches as developed in Specht (1998) and Weber, Kuhl, and Weibelzahl (2001), among others.

Figure 3. Navigation advice in eBuT adapted to the state of the learner model

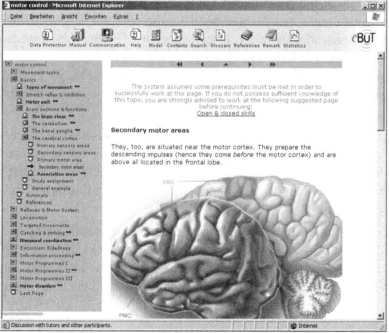

A first appearance of an e-learning system's adaptivity is guiding the learner's navigation through the system's content. In eBuT, this is based upon the top level information of the multilevel overlay model.

The navigation overview on the left hand side informs the learner about pages already visited (bracket on the left side as in "[+", e.g.) and those not yet seen (annotated like "+]"). The arrow is pointing to the present page "Stretch reflex." Derived from the learner model, there does appear some link To the Exercises on top of the page understood as a suggestion to the learner.

The DaMiT system is offering a different version of assistance on the level of navigation. Learners may have preferences of more or less succinct presentations. Those who prefer more examples and illustrations and are willing to spend more time with their studies get extra pages offered. There are additional case studies as well as animated illustrations, for example. To say it in terms of the book metaphor, the content offered to learners who prefer a more succinct presentation contains less pages. However, the learner has always the freedom to chance the presentation style from what is called *example-oriented* to *theory-oriented* and vice versa.

Figure 3, displaying another screenshot from the eBuT system, there appears a warning (in red). From the system's analysis of the learner model's top level entries, it derives the "belief" that the learner might have a lack of prerequisites. The system's assistance consists in directing the learner straight to suitable background material. A closer inspection of Figure 3 exhibits that the learner has left out several topics preceding the one currently visited. Those are shown as red icons (in black and white print identifiable by the bracket on the right as in "+]") above the arrow pointing to the page displayed. This system reacts accordingly.

The reader may easily recognize that the assistant system has to rely on hypothetical knowledge about its human user. Leaving out some learning material does not necessarily mean that one is not sufficiently familiar with the content. However, the system has to make its guesses that may be revised later, if necessary.

So far, the system's adaptivity consists in guiding the learner's navigation according to the system's knowledge about the learner and, derived from this knowledge, the system's belief about the learner's needs and desires. Taking into account that the system may be mistaken, the final decision about the navigation is left to the human user.

Figure 4. A definition within the DaMiT system in formal and informal presentation

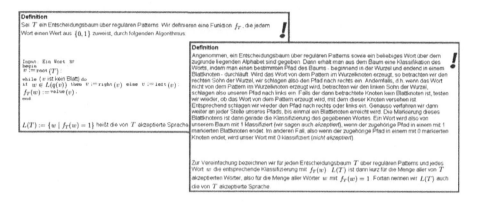

Another functionality of an e-learning system's assistance may be to offer one and the same content in different forms according to the learner's preference or even to the learner's mood.

The authors' experience has shown that a larger number of learners enjoy changing the views at learning content. Reading some definition in a strictly mathematical form and in another more explanatory formulation, for instance, frequently leads to a deeper understanding.

In the DaMiT system, a large amount of material is available in different variants enabling the learner to view it from different perspectives.

Figure 4 is displaying two cutouts from two dual presentation pages showing a certain definition in its formal variant (left cutout) and in its informal variant (right cutout). It is worth to be mentioned that the cutouts shown are not complete pages of the DaMiT presentation. In DaMiT, a page that appears on the learner's screen usually consists of several smaller units. Modularity is crucial to the systems ability to assemble slightly varying presentations dynamically.

It is already known for decades (Hull, 1943; Thorndike, 1913) that the effect of exercising depends substantially on the feedback provided to the learner. Responding to a learner's efforts in solving an exercise is a key assistance functionality.

The eBuT system is offering a variety of feedback forms. The screenshot on the left displays the systems explanation why the learner's answers are incorrect. The screenshot on the right shows an even more elaborate attempt of the eBuT system to assist the human learner. Background information is offered.

There is an obvious problem with offering variants of system's response to the learners' input in dependence on internally stored knowledge. The varying learning paths have to be anticipated at system design and content development time. The authors favor didactic design through storyboarding as outlined in Jantke and Knauf (2005).

The examples drawn from DaMiT and eBuT sketched in the present chapter may be seen as first steps toward intelligent systems' assistance. In fact, they are only representing features of adaptive tools. The stage is set for more system intelligence. It is an exciting task to transform the current state of the art into the next generation of e-learning systems—*intelligent assistants*.

Figure 5. Variants of system's response to forced-choice questions in eBuT

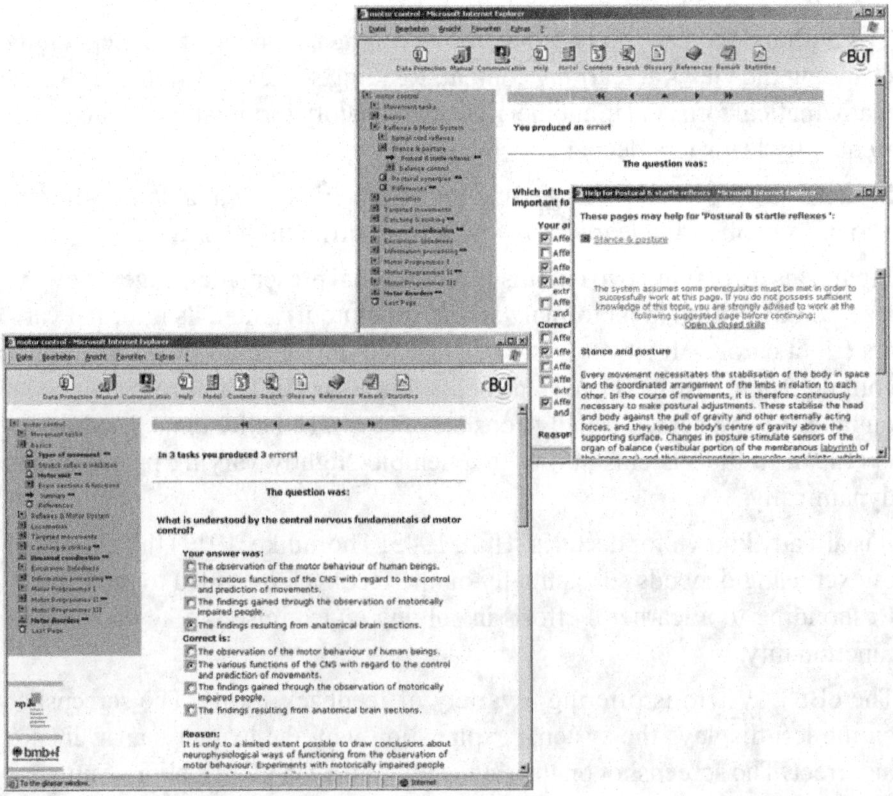

Technologies for Systems' Adaptivity and Assistance

After we have seen adaptivity in e-learning at work, it is worth to ask for the technologies behind this systems' behavior. The problem to be investigated later on is how to use and to extend these technologies for the transformation to systems' assistance. Another problem is whether one may need new technologies.

It is obviously fundamental to equip an e-learning system with knowledge about the learner. Database and user modeling technologies are invoked. A crucial conceptual question is what to model about a human learner, which properties to ascribe to a learner and how to acquire the necessary information during the learner's interaction with the computer system. There are some novelties. In certain domains, one may exploit additional knowledge as demonstrated in Nébel (2005), where the author exploits the fact that the learners he is addressing are also patients within a particular medical treatment. In Jantke, Grieser, and Lange (2004), the authors develop query scenarios for learner modeling without the learner's awareness of being modeled.

If expressive learner models are available and the learner's current situation is reasonably reflected by the e-learning system, one may ask how to assist the learner. The problem area begins with didactic issues beyond technologies. But didactics and technologies cannot be completely separated. The eBuT system demonstrates how concepts from media didactics Weber (2005) are related to and implemented by representational decisions (Igel & Daugs, 2003b).

Adaptivity means—as illustrated in some detail previously—to present the system's content in varying order and form and to approach the learner with different opportunities to act. For doing so, the right digitalized material must be found in the right moment to be presented in the right way.

Whatever "learning objects" are (there does not exist any consensus in the community), they have to be annotated suitably. Annotations require decisions about metadata concepts. Which metadata are required depends very much on the intended functionality. XML provides the technology of choice. After the conceptual decisions about (hierarchies of) learning objects and metadata, one may represent the learning content. (Discussion about authorship, digital rights, getting students involved, integrating research and e-learning content and the like are suppressed here.) accordingly and store it in some relational data base, for example. The decision about the underlying data base schema is another issue.

The crux beyond all the technicalities discussed so far is that variants of presentation require available variants of material. When a human teacher—on the fly—in response to the students' needs (perhaps, recognizing that they are getting tired or bored) effortlessly decides to change some presentation, for instance, by repeating a certain explanation in other words, this relies on competencies and so-called soft skills acquired and trained over years.

For a computerized assistant, this requires (1) to have the different material available (two or more variants must be prepared) and (2) to have some control implemented to change the presentation dynamically. The crux is to develop those variants with a certain vision of their use under some particular didactics in mind.

Systems' Intelligence in E-Learning: Pros and Cons

It is the authors' strong belief that so-called *systems' intelligence* is, to some extent, an ultimate criterion of success for technology enhanced learning. Learners do need care and are usually frustrated when being treated inappropriately. The learners' mood is a substantial factor of the learning success (Bransford, Brown, & Cocking, 2003; Davis, Sumara, & Luce-Kapler, 2000). There is no more need to argue in favor of intelligent assistance to human learners.

The crux is that machine intelligence is expensive (Jantke, 2004b). Both the DaMiT project and the eBuT project, though not yet resulting in intelligent computerized assistants, let the developers to the limits. For illustration, consider variants of content as shown in Figure 4. To offer those alternatives requires to design, produce, and integrate multiple variants of learning objects. The DaMiT system does contain hundreds of units in multiple forms.

The next inevitable step is to develop strategies for the system's adaptive behavior and to implement them. Evaluation is another inevitable issue not discussed here in more detail. To stick to the issue of designing the systems behavior, one has to take into account that an intelligent assistant for e-learning is more than just an IT system. The high level design of such a system requires to anticipate the intended human-machine interactions. The first author's recent approaches to attack the high level design problem in e-learning lead to some storyboard concept (Jantke & Knauf, 2005). Storyboards are understood as representations of a community of learners' potential learning experiences. As such, they go beyond the limits of conventional software engineering.

Needless to mention that not only multiple content production is expensive, storyboarding is an ambitious and time-consuming process as well.

The cons briefly mentioned above are possibly not that much surprising. As a consequence of the present chapter's discussion, the authors suggest to develop a program for gradually introducing intelligent systems' assistance into e-learning. Such a program has to cover a large variety of issues, needs competencies from different disciplines, and should be attacked within a concerted endeavor of a sufficiently strong community.

Transformation Steps from Learning Tools to Assistants

The area of e-learning is still having its teething troubles. Notions and notations are under development. There is not much agreement about what should be accepted as an e-learning system and what should not. A large number of developers decided to begin with simple approaches and to offer elementary services with the intention to go first steps, at least. The reluctance to employment of top level technologies has many good reasons. Among them, the missing standards and the insufficient support by development tools are two prominent arguments.

When discussing the paradigmatic shift from e-learning tools to e-learning assistants, one has to take into account the remarkable number of simpler systems that have just been invented. Besides introducing innovative assistants, we have to think about transformation strategies leading from tools to assistants.

Transformation processes like the one under consideration may be, at least, seen from two different perspectives: top-down and bottom-up. It is not easy to say which way is more promising. Stanislaw Lem when pondering about the development of Artificial Intelligence in his book *Die Technologiefalle* circumscribed the problem with the following words: "Die Möglichkeiten sind so weit wie der Ozean, und wir haben weder einen ordentlichen Kompaß noch eine Karte" (p. 261), roughly saying, *the space of possibilities is as wide as the ocean, but we neither have a compass nor a map.*

Especially when going to develop a new e-learning solution from scratch, a top-down approach that starts with some carefully developed storyboard seems highly desirable. But this shall not be the focus of the present chapter. An in-depth discussion of the authors' perspectives at (or dreams of) a new development from scratch had to begin with intensive investigations of storyboard concepts and technologies (Jantke & Knauf, 2005). This is left to another publication.

The present chapter, instead, is intended to lay out some process model toward a bottom-up introduction of intelligent systems' assistance into e-learning (see Figure 6). The paradigmatic shift announced will take place, but slowly step by step.

Figure 6. Top level of the transformation process model

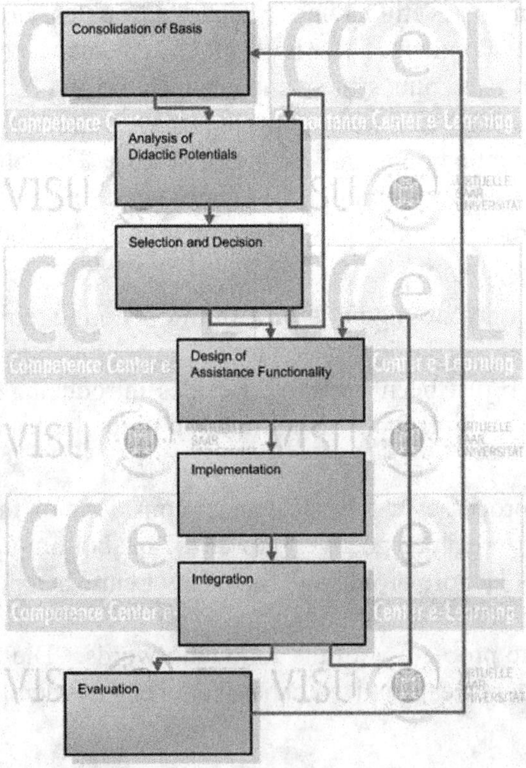

This is a rough process model which may be completed, refined and extended. A future version might fill pages and may be accompanied by its manual. Several aspects are obviously left out. For instance, there is no reasoning about available resources and the related resource allocation is suppressed. Curricular aspects are completely missing in this first approach.

The authors confine themselves to a brief discussion of the core steps. As said earlier, both systems eBuT and DaMiT are not yet assistant systems. They are both quite successfully used in technology enhanced learning and enjoy didactically driven learner adaptivity, to some extent. But they still need to be transformed from tools into assistants.

- **Consolidation of basis** means to summarize what you have available for advancing your system and service. This is a point badly underestimated in the academia. Universities suffer from a continuous loss of competency when students are finishing their studies and leaving the institute. It might be that you have great applets, but the sources are gone, for example.

- **Analysis of didactic potentials** addresses the question where to begin. Which are the points that promise most valuable improvements? In DaMiT, for instance, one of these points is surely using the expressive learning goals to better serve learners with different intentions adaptively.

- **Selection and decision** is an inevitable administrative step because the transformation of tools into programs may be performed in literally innumerably many ways.

- **Design of assistance functionality** is the crucial creative step from tool functionality to system assistance. In DaMiT, for instance, we have very expressive interactive applets for exploratory learning. One of the applets allows the learner to pose data mining problems to the computer system which in turn tries to solve the learning task. The goal is to enable learners to develop a feeling for the complexity of learning tasks. Currently, this applet does not adapt to the human's learning goal. Some learner not interest in in-depth studies, but in getting an overview, might better be served by an illustrative case study than by her/his own time-consuming exploration.

- **Implementation** is an obviously essential and complex task in performing the transformation.

- **Integration** means to relate the novel functionality to the learning environment. It means much more than just plugging in some implementation. Among other aspects, new possibilities of user interaction may provide new potentials of learner modeling and, thus, lead to some additional procedures of feeding the learner model.

- **Evaluation** is widely accepted to be inevitable. However, there are several problems with the evaluation of e-learning systems. In particular, when taking an incremental approach as sketched by the present process model, it remains unclear to which granularity of system and service changes evaluation activities should be applied.

To sum up, the present process model comprises the authors' approach to make eBuT and DaMiT true assistant systems. This will be a laborious process, but it will lead us to the next generation of e-learning systems.

Summary and Conclusion

The authors admit that several aspects of the problem under consideration have been simply left out. The field ranges from role concepts, role adaptivity, and rights management through presentation generation technologies like the stored procedures of the DaMiT system to concerns on privacy issues and data security.

Other issues like storyboarding and metadata, which are deemed to be of a particular importance, are discussed in some detail, but not truly worked out.

Storyboarding—at least in its ambitious form favoured by the authors—is not yet mature enough. When submitting this chapter, the source, Jantke and Knauf (2005), has been just about one month old.

An area of research and development in its own right is established by the vision of assistant systems that are able to practice didactics for the benefit of human learners. A deeper discussion is beyond the limits of the present chapter.

As said above, among the many prerequisites of intelligent systems' assistance in e-learning, there are metadata concepts to annotate learning objects. A basic problem is that the community's agreement about metadata and the development of standards is far behind the needs. The authors experienced the necessity to extend available standards for required applications in DaMiT and eBuT. For illustration, the DaMiT system has an integrated e-payment, but none of the existing metadata standards for e-learning has concepts for the representation of payment information. One can take it for granted that the transformation from e-learning tools to e-learning assistants will bring with it further needs to extend current metadata standards.

Beyond all those topics in technology enhanced learning left out or discussed only in a brief, the authors have put most emphasis on some process model for introducing intelligent systems' assistance into e-learning. Well-prepared by means of the state of the art report, the reader—hopefully—should have got an impression of how to apply this process model to the authors' systems and services DaMiT and eBuT. In some sense, the authors advocate an evolutionary process towards more system assistance in technology enhanced learning.

Next steps of research and development will be (1) a completion and more explicit representation of the process model and (2) an application of the process model to DaMiT and eBuT.

In such a way, the transformation from e-learning tools to intelligent systems' assistants will be exemplified. Both steps shall be deeply dovetailed. The authors' application efforts will help to evaluate and revise the process model. In turn, the applications may benefit again.

Acknowledgments

The authors gracefully acknowledge several years of an enjoyable and fruitful cooperation with many colleagues and friends within the joint e-learning projects (1) DaMiT: http://damit.dfki.de, and (2) eBuT: http://www.bewegung-und-training.de. Readers are invited to pay a visit to these service pages in the Internet.

References

Bransford, J. D., Brown, A. L., & Cocking, R. R. (Eds.). (2003). *How people learn: Brain, mind, experience, and school.* National Academy Press.

Damasio, A. (1999). *The feeling of what happens: Body and emotion in the making of consciousness.* Hartcourt.

Davis, B., Sumara, D., & Luce-Kapler, R. (2000). *Engaging minds: Learning and teaching in a complex world.* Lawrence Erlbaum Associates.

Flechsig, K.-H. (1996). *Kleines Handbuch didaktischer Modelle (Small manual of didactical models).* Eichenzell: Neuland.

Hull, C. L. (1943). *Principles of behavior.* New York: Appleton-Century-Crofts.

Igel, C., & Daugs, R. (2002). Mehrwertpotenziale Internetbasierter Lehre (Added value capabilities of Internet-based teaching). In K. P. Jantke, W. S. Wittig, & J. Herrmann (Eds.), *Vom e-Learning bis e-Payment: Das Internet als sicherer Marktplatz (From e-learning to e-payment: The Internet as a safe marketplace)* (pp. 8–19). Berlin: infix.

Igel, C., & Daugs, R. (2003a). eLearning in der Bewegungs- und Trainingswissenschaft: Das Engineering des BMBF-Projektes "eBuT" (eLearning in movement and training science: The engineering of the project eBut backed by the Federal Ministry of Education and Resarch). *dvs Informationen, 18*(3), 5–8.

Igel, C., & Daugs, R. (2003b). Zur Individualisierung Internetbasierter Lehr-Lern-Prozesse: Didaktische Überlegungen und technologische Entwicklungen im BMBF-Projekt "eBuT" (Individualization of Internet-based teaching-learning processes: Didactical considerations and technological developments in the eBUT). In U. Beck & V. Sommer (Eds.), *Learntec 2003: 11. Europäischer Kongress und Fachmesse für Bildungs- und Informationstechnologie* (pp. 253–258). Karlsruhe: Holler Verlag.

Igel, C., & Daugs, R. (Eds.). (2005). *eLearning in der Sportwissenschaft: Strategien, Konzeptionen, Perspektiven (eLearning in sports science: Strategies, conceptual design, prospects).* Schorndorf: Hofmann.

Igel, C., & Sturm, R. (2003). Server-Architektur, Autorensystem, Datenbanken, Assets: Die Informationsinfrastruktur des Projektes "eBuT" (Server architecture, authoring tool, databases, assets: The information infrastructure of the eBut). *dvs Informationen, 18*(3), 9–13.

Jank, W., & Meyer, H. (2002). *Didaktische Modelle (Didactical models)*. Frankfurt a.M.: Cornelsen.

Jantke, K. P. (2003, June 13). Knowledge discovery & data mining: Lehren und Lernen im Internet (Knowledge discovery & dat mining: Teaching and learning in the Internet). In *Köthener Informatik-Tag*. Köthen: FH Anhalt.

Jantke, K. P. (2004a, June 3-4). Neue Technologien: Potentiale und Probleme illustriert an Anwendungen des e-Learning (eingeladener Hauptvortrag) (New technologies: Potentials and problems illustrated on eLearning applications – invited speech). In *Wismarer Wirtschaftsinformatik-Tage, WIWITA 2004*.

Jantke, K. P. (2004b, June 3-4). ROI: Das unlösbare Problem des e-Learning (ROI: The unsolvable problem of eLearning). In *Wismarer Wirtschaftsinformatik-Tage, WIWITA 2004*.

Jantke, K. P. (2005). Informatik und Künstliche Intelligenz: Beiträge zur Adaptivität einer kommenden Generation intelligenter eLearning-Systeme (Information technology and artificial intelligence: Contributions on adptivity of a coming generation of intelligent eLearning systems). In C. Igel & R. Daugs (Eds.), *eLearning in der Sportwissenschaft: Strategien, Konzeptionen, Perspektiven (eLearning in sports science: Strategies, conceptual design, prospects)* (pp. 49–70). Schorndorf: Hofmann.

Jantke, K. P., Degel, G., Grieser, G., Memmel, M., Rostanin, O., & Tschiedel, B. (2004, September 29 - October 1). Technology enhanced dimensions in e-learning. In M.E. Auer & U. Auer (Eds.), *International Conference on Interactive Computer Aided Learning, ICL 2004* (CD). Villach, Austria.

Jantke, K. P., Grieser, G., & Lange, S. (2004, September 29 - October 1). Adaptation to the learners' needs and desires by induction and negotiation of hypotheses. In M.E. Auer & U. Auer (Eds.), *International Conference on Interactive Computer Aided Learning, ICL 2004* (CD), Villach, Austria.

Jantke, K. P., Grieser, G., & Memmel, M. (2004, October 4-6). DaMiT: Data Mining lernen und lehren (Learning and teaching data mining). In *Lernen, Wissensentdeckung und Adaptivität (Learning, Knowledge detection and adaptivity)* (LWA-2004), Fachgruppentreffen Maschinelles Lernen (FGML). Berlin.

Jantke, K. P., & Knauf, R. (2005, January 3-6). Didactic design through storyboarding: Standard concepts for standard tools. In *Proceedings of the First International Workshop on Dissemination of E-Learning Technologies and Applications,* Cape Town, South Africa.

Jantke, K. P., Lange, S., Grieser, G., Grigoriev, P., Thalheim, B., & Tschiedel, B. (2004a, April 14-17). Learning by doing and learning when doing. In I. Seruca, J. Filipe, S. Hammoudi, & J. Cordeiro (Eds.), *Proceedings of the International Conference on Enterprise Information Systems* (Vol. 5, pp. 238–241), Porto, Portugal. INSTICC.

Jantke, K. P., Lange, S., Grieser, G., Grigoriev, P., Thalheim, B., & Tschiedel, B. (2004b, September 27-30). Work-integrated e-learning: The DaMiT approach. In O. Sawodny & P. Scharff (Eds.), *Proceedings of the 49 Internationales Wissenschaftliches Kolloquium, TU* (Vol. 2, pp. 333–339). Shaker Verlag.

Jantke, K. P., & Lunzer, A. (2005). Search, comparison and evaluation in exploratory e-learning with subjunctive interfaces. In *Proceedings of the 3rd Conference on Professional Knowledge Management, 1st Workshop on Learner-Oriented Knowledge Management and KM-Oriented E-Learning,* Kaiserslautern, Germany.

Jantke, K. P., Memmel, M., Rostanin, O., & Rudolf, B. (2004, November 1-5). Media and service integration for professional e-learning. In *Proceedings of the E-Learn 2004, World Conference on E-Learning in Corporate, Government, Healthcare & Higher Education,* Washington, DC.

Jantke, K. P., Memmel, M., Rostanin, O., Thalheim, B., & Tschiedel, B. (2003). Decision support by learning-on-demand. In *CAiSE Workshop 2003*, Klagenfurt, Österreich.

Klein, B., & Weber, G. (2002, March 3-5). Die Realisierung von Adaptivität mit dem Internet-Autorensystem NetCoach (The realization of adaptivity with the Internet authoring tool NetCoach). In U. Rinn & J. Wedekind (Eds.), *Referenzmodelle netzbasierten Lehrens und Lernens (Models of reference on net-based teaching and learning)* (pp. 101–118). Münster: Waxmann.

Nébel, I.-T. (2005). Patient and learner adaptation in e-learning by induction based on medical context. In R. Kaschek (Ed.), *Perspectives of Intelligent Systems' Assistance, International Workshop,* Palmerston North, New Zealand.

Rothwell, W. J., & Kazanas, H. C. (2004). *Mastering the instructional design process: A systematic approach* (3rd ed.). Pfeiffer.

Searle, J. R. (1980). *Mind, brains, and programs: Vol. 3 of The Behavioral and Brain Sciences*. Cambridge University Press.

Specht, M. (1998). *Adaptive Methoden in computerbasierten Lehr/Lernsystemen (Adaptive methods in computer-based teaching-learning systems)*. Doctoral thesis, Universität Trier, FB Psychologie.

Tergan, S.-O., & Schenkel, P. (Eds.). (2004). *Was macht E-Learning erfolgreich? Grundlagen und Instrumente der Qualitätsbeurteilung (How does eLearning become successful? Basics and tools of quality-assessment)*. Springer.

Thorndike, E. L. (1913). *Educational psychology* (Vol. 1 & 2). New York: Columbia University Press.

Weber, G. (1996). Episodic learner modelling. *Cognitive Science, 20*, 195–236.

Weber, G. (1999). Adaptive learning systems in the World Wide Web. In *User Modeling; Proceedings of the Seventh International Conference UM'99* (pp. 371–378). Springer.

Weber, G. (2005). Mediendidaktik: Varianten virtueller Lehr-/Lernformen (Versions of virtual teaching-learning forms). In C. Igel & R. Daugs (Eds.), *eLearning in der Sportwissenschaft: Strategien, Konzeptionen, Perspektiven (eLearning in sports science: Strategies, conceptual design, prospects)* (pp. 71-98). Schorndorf: Hofmann.

Weber, G., Kuhl, H.-C., & Weibelzahl, S. (2001). Developing adaptive Internet based courses with the authoring system NetCoach. In S. Reich, M.M. Tzagarakis, & P.M.E. De Bra (Eds.), *Hypermedia: Openness, structural awareness and adaptivity* (pp. 226–238). Springer.

Chapter XI

Mathematics in Virtual Knowledge Spaces:
User Adaptation by Intelligent Assistants

Sabina Jeschke, Berlin University of Technology, Germany

Thomas Richter, Berlin University of Technology, Germany

Abstract

The workplace of scientists and engineers is about to change: even though numerical software and computer algebra systems remove the burden of routine calculation, it becomes more important than ever to get familiar with new concepts and methods quickly. Given the rapid growth of knowledge in today's sciences, traditional "learning on supply" (i.e., defining the learning goal as the accumulation of knowledge) is no longer applicable; instead, adequate learning and teaching methods have to be established to guide learners towards efficient self-controlled learning.

Traditional methods of teaching can only satisfy this demand partially: lectures provide elementary base knowledge, but do not encourage active independent deliberation in the matter. Classical hands-on training in laboratories on the other hand requires additional human resources and is often constrained by the financial possibilities of the involved institutions.

We do not aim to replace the mentioned classical forms of teaching; rather, we want to show how the application of New Media and New Technology presents a turning point in the educational system by providing tools that close the gap between passive document retrieval systems on the one hand and practical courses in laboratories on the other hand.

The value added by the New Technology is the ability to enrich traditional methods of education—teacher centered teaching, literature research, homework training, and laboratory experiments—by some limited form of "intelligence" and by suitable interfaces to allow closer integration of these areas to improve the learning process. Thus, tools are proposed that are not only able to adapt to the learning process of the student, but are also smart enough to point towards additional background information and thus actively support the learner beyond what has been possible before.

Four areas of the application of New Media are presented: the presentation of mathematical content, intelligent lexicon toolkits that are able to learn from natural language texts, homework training courses that are able to break up assignments into elementary subproblems as needed by the learner, and Virtual Laboratories that are able to provide courses that adapt to the errors of the learner, but are still rich enough to be used in research problems.

Introduction: Why Intelligent Assistants?

Mathematics is the key technology of the 21st century: besides being a research field of its own, it is the key ingredient for studies in engineering sciences, physics, computer science and many other fields. Teaching mathematics therefore means teaching a very broad, heterogeneous audience with varying fields of interest; teaching at the Berlin University of Technology in particular means having to handle increasing student numbers with decreasing funding. Luckily, mathematics is a highly structured field using a very precise, formalized language. Its internal structure is built on well-developed entities, for example, fields, vector spaces, linear mappings, all integrated into a well-accepted ontology. Given that more and more of the computational tasks are solved by the computer today, the demand for *understanding the concepts* and *interpreting the results* of the electronically performed operations becomes a major task of the mathematical education. Therefore, the structure and workings of mathematics has to be understood by students—and can thus be exploited to aid the design of electronic tools supporting the learning process.

To achieve this however, we must *go beyond* the first generation of e-learning (Jeschke & Keil-Slawik, 2004) which was rarely more than computer assisted document management. We therefore need technology that provides enough flexibility to adapt to the requirements of the field and the learning process of the student.

If our goal is contributing to multiple learning scenarios *and* providing a scientific broadness at the same time, the complexity of the user interfaces is likely to rise. This is of course undesirable for our purpose; therefore, e-learning environments have to evolve from complex toolkits to systems that contain a certain amount of autonomy, enough to support human operation processes by a degree of artificial intelligence, since students should *learn the subject matter, not how to use the software*.

In short: we need *intelligent assistants*. Therefore, the concepts which have been recently developed in the field of Artificial Intelligence have to be adapted to Virtual Knowledge Spaces and their components. The impact of intelligent assistants reaches from adaptivity to specific usage patterns up to actively supporting the learning or research process itself by applying the analytic capabilities of computer systems to perform mathematics.

Background: E-Learning at the Berlin University of Technology

The Berlin University of Technology is one of the three universities in Berlin, focused mainly on the fields of engineering and applied sciences; it also offers studies in mathematics, physics and even studies in humanities. With over 30,000 enrolled students, it is one of the major universities of Germany. Undergraduate courses in mathematics for engineers typically have around 1,500 to 2,000 participants, taught by up to five lecturers in parallel. These courses are organised and maintained by the Institute of Mathematics and Natural Sciences.

To improve the education for this audience, the institute has established the Multimedia Center for e-learning, e-teaching and e-research, or MuLF (MuLF), for short, which is within the tradition of many earlier third-party funded research projects from the area of electronic learning, for example, Mumie (Mumie), Moses (Moses), Nemesis (Nemesis), BeLearning (BeLearning), and the Virtual Laboratories Project located at the DFG Research Center, Matheon (Matheon). All these projects focus on the mathematics education of engineers, computer scientists, physicists and mathematicians; the teaching level here ranges from undergraduate mathematics up to graduate studies in mathematics and physics.

The research foci of the e-learning group of the faculty range from pedagogical aspects in electronic learning down to technical aspects that need to be solved to implement these goals. The pedagogical aspects cover the development of concepts for intelligent training environments, the design of explorative learning environments and models for user adaptivity. Concepts for distributed teaching and learning in the spirit of eBologna (EU, 1999) are also researched.

All mentioned aspects require background knowledge from a broad variety of other disciplines that are also under research; we deal with problems of semantic encoding, analysis of mathematical language and specific matter ontology, with the design of semantic retrieval systems and aspects of automatic validation of mathematical solutions, down to some computer science problems like constructing integration technologies for open e-learning environments and the design of distributed systems for cooperative learning.

Classification of E-Learning

In the following, a classification of e-learning support into four categories is presented, always keeping in mind that these have to be understood as intertwined and entangled with each other (Figure 1): the *content area*, presenting matter in a structured way as it is typically taught in lectures and courses. The *training area* provides a framework for homework assignments and hands-on training, the *semantic retrieval area* parses natural language texts into a knowledge-network and answers individual requests on relations within this

Figure 1. Categories of e-learning and their basic properties

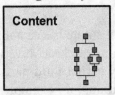

Content

* Courses from granular elements of knowledge
* Composition with the CourseCreator tool
* Interactive multimedia elements
* Nonlinear navigation

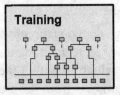

Training

* Exercises, combined into exercise paths
* Interactive, constructive environment
* Embedded in an exercise network
* Intelligent input & control mechanisms

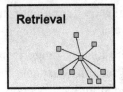

Retrieval

* User-driven information retrieval system
* Knowledge networks
* User defined constructions
* Includes an "encyclopaedia"

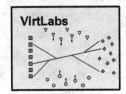

VirtLabs

* Combinable experiments
* Explorative learning and research
* Experiments integrating CAS & Num. Tools
* Intelligent input & control mechanisms

network, forming an intelligent encyclopaedia. Last but not least the *Virtual Lab area* allows self-controlled learning by providing the infrastructure for experiments and hands-on training.

All four areas are going to be introduced in detail, describing their state of implementation and giving prospects for intelligent assistants within each area.

E-Learning Equipment at the Berlin University of Technology

The e-learning initiative of the Berlin University of Technology started with the BMBF (i.e., German Ministry for Education and Research)-funded project, MUMIE (Mumie) (Dahlmann, Jeschke, Seiler & Sinha, 2003) which aims at enriching classical undergraduate math lectures with multimedial content. MUMIE has been designed from ground up to support students in more than one way in their studies: it should not only present the material taught in lectures and make it available for pre or postlearning by allowing nonlinear navigation, it would also contain the exercises and homework assignments for independent study. Thus, the design of the "content area" and the "training area" as two approaches to support learners within one common e-Learning framework existed right from the start. The content area currently contains material for an undergraduate course on linear algebra for engineers. It includes references to exercises in the training area that allow students to intensify their knowledge on the topics which were introduced and presented in the course. Vice versa, the homework assignments stated in the training area refer to the corresponding topics of the course. Details are given in the "Content Area" and "Training Area" sections.

Not much later, the idea was born to enlarge this concept by an encyclopaedia making the material more accessible. By extending this idea, the conception of a knowledge base (Beierle & Kern-Isberner, 2000; Görz, Rollinger & Schneeberger, 2000; Haun, 2002) for mathematics was considered, plus the requirement to fill this knowledge base with existing material as found in textbooks. Due to the lack of resources, we had the hope to automatize this process to a good degree. This concept evolved into the "retrieval area" introduced above, and induced the dissertation of one member of our research group Natho (2005). Even though there is no retrieval front-end for its knowledge data base yet, the current codebase is already able to extract the linguistic structure from natural language texts, that is, syntactical relations between words and their function within a sentence. It has been found (Natho, 2005) that this structure often allows programs to extract mathematical relations between terms, which is mainly due to the very formalized way in which language is used in mathematical context. This project will become part of the Mumie framework soon, allowing students not only to look up words as in a dictionary, but also allowing them to find relations between topics and chapters of a course, see the "Retrieval Area" section. This integration work is currently under development. We plan to integrate this project into the Mumie framework soon.

The "Virtual Lab" area is the youngest member of the Mumie family. Even though the idea of using cellular automata—see the "Virtual Lab" and "VideoEasel" sections—to implement models of statistical mechanics is not new (Toffoli & Margolus, 1987). The author (Richter, n.d.) has been playing with the idea to exploit this for educational purposes for a while until he had been given the chance to implement the software as project G4 of the MATH-

EON Research Center at the Berlin University of Technology. The resulting virtual laboratory VIDEOEASEL, which will be described in its own section in more detail, has now been already deployed for the course Mathematical Physics II—Statistical Mechanics—at the University of Technology, and at the Heinrich Hertz School in Berlin. Although being the youngest component of MUMIE, it is the first project that has been equipped with assistant technology, to be described in "Intelligent Assistants" section.

Efforts to enrich the training and the content area are currently running, and our concepts for doing so are described in the following sections in more detail.

Content Area

The content area is the electronic representation of the content of a specific course or lecture. In order to aid the lecturer and the student, the topic of a course is separated into minimal knowledge atoms following a specific matter ontology. A knowledge atom is the smallest presentable unit in a mathematics course, that is: a specific definition of a mathematical object, a theorem describing the properties of an object, a single motivation for a definition, an example out of several examples for a mathematical statement, or an algorithm. The content area may contain several knowledge atoms targeting at presenting the same mathematical property, that is, several versions of a proof or a theorem might, or even should, exist. The ontology on which this classification is based should not be confused with the ontology of mathematical objects (sets, tuples, maps, etc.) but is rather the ontology used to *present* and *organize* mathematics in books and lectures.

These atoms are enriched by interactive applets (Figure 2), and composed to courses. This concept on the one hand allows efficient re-use of existing atoms and their recomposition to new courses, thus simplify the task of the lecturer, while on the other hand it also allows non-linear navigation for students to either follow courses or refresh their knowledge in exam preparation. It is here again important to note that authors have to be encouraged to provide several equivalent, but different presentations of the underlying mathematical ideas to gain the flexibility required to adapt courses to various audiences.

The course content is presented as a network, shown on the left-hand side of Figure 2, allowing students to browse freely within the matter while showing the relations and dependencies between the atoms. The atoms themselves are required to be context-free or almost context-free to be read and recombined independently. The "red thread" (illustrated by a broad line in Figure 2) indicates the recommended course order. It represents one possible lecture through the material; alternative routes are available simply by selecting the desired atoms.

In its current form, created to a major extent by S. Jeschke, R. Seiler, and co-workers of the MUMIE-project (Mumie), it consists of a database providing the knowledge atoms, an application server delivering the contents as HTML data, and a course creator tool that defines the linkage of the atoms—as vertices in a graph—to a complete topic, see Figure 2.

In the left frame the course and the corresponding knowledge atoms of this applet are displayed. The "red thread" indicates the recommended course schedule. In the main frame an exercise is shown, which prompts the learner to construct a line parallel to the x-axis in a distance 2 from the origin.

Clearly, this design allows reusing existing material easily to adapt courses to changing requirements. The prospects for intelligent assistants in the content

Figure 2. A course in the MUMIE-platform, showing a sample application of linear algebra

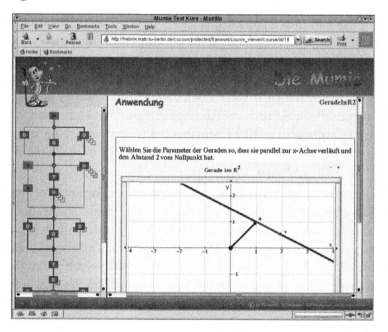

area are plentiful: they would observe the usage patterns of both the lecturer creating and the student using a course and thus would allow adapting the presented material to the corresponding user. Looking at the vertices of the course-graph, an assistant would be able to select the proper presentation style of the content that fits the learner's style best, for example, textual representation vs. visualisation (see also the "Intelligent Assistants" section for a discussion of user types). In Figure 2, an assistant would be able to select an alternative route through the material, not following the suggested red thread if the usage patterns of a student indicate that this would be more beneficial for presenting the material.

But assistants could also help lecturers to combine the atoms to courses given the demands of the audience and the author at hand, and thus act on the edges of the course-graph as well; the tool developed for this process is the so-called *Course Creator*. Even though the Course Creator is currently just a graphical composition toolkit without own intelligence, given the dependencies between the atoms and the preferences and demands of the lecturer and the audience an assistant would be able to propose a full course.

Semantic Retrieval Area

While the content area requires that the content provided to students and teachers is already integrated into a network of knowledge atoms, the main focus of the semantic retrieval area is to construct these networks from mathematical texts formulated in natural language. The mentioned texts could be taken from a mathematical textbook or lecture notes; while we do not believe that it is possible to entirely extract the contents automatically from these raw materials, we are confident that a semiautomatic approach requiring manual interaction gains enough information from the source to make the usage of the tool worthwhile (Natho, 2005).

The resulting knowledge networks represent connections between terms as well as dependencies between mathematical statements. Even though this front-end is not implemented yet, the resulting network could be visualised by a retrieval system, making the connections between terms and statements accessible and attractive to the student—providing a valuable tool for exam preparation or homework assignments. Alternatively, the network would prove useful for the authors of lectures as well as it helps to build up an electronic lecture from printed "traditional" material.

In its current form, mainly developed by N. Natho as part of the MUMIE-environment (Natho, 2005), (Mumie), the software "mArachna" implements a semi-automatic natural language parser that analyses mathematical texts for their linguistic structure; that is, starting from the syntactical linkage of words into sentences, mArachna builds up graphs of objects and relations between these objects.

Figure 3. The architecture of the tool. A converter analyzes the mathematical content given in LATEX form, identifying theorems, definitions, and other mathematical entities and separating them from non-parsable contents, for example, images, applets, graphs and similar non-textual sources of information. (Rather: hard to parse content. While technology might be in development to allow even semantic analysis of images or applet code (Dahlmann, Jeschke, Seiler & Wilke, 2005), those attempts are not considered here; the emphasis of this project aims at parsing of natural language texts.) Since

Figure 3. Architecture of the semantic retrieval tool, showing the information flow through its modules, from top to bottom

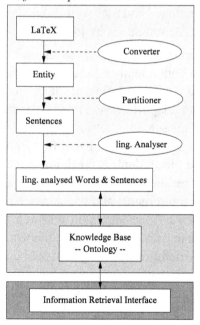

LATEX requires or at least encourages authors to already tag mathematical entities, this parsing process is greatly simplified

The *partitioner* breaks up these entities to identify their internal structure by means of a simple pattern matching algorithm that already requires a basic morphological analysis of the sentences.

A full *linguistic analysis* of the sentences based on Chomsky's transformational grammar is applied in the next step, segmenting sentences into phrases and identifying their syntactic function within them.

The *semantic analysis* detects relations between these phrases, groups them into objects and builds triples of object pairs and relations, thus assigning a semantic to the phrases. These object triples are used to build up semantic networks within the *knowledge base*, allowing an *information retrieval* front-end to gain access to it. A knowledge base is a data base system that contains graphs whose nodes are terms, in our case mathematical entities like "group" or "determinant," and whose edges represent relations between these terms, for example, whether one term is a specialisation of another or contains another, and so forth.

Semantic analysis of natural language is an active research field and as such many problems are still open. Restriction to mathematical texts simplifies this task to a major degree: the texts are to be supplied in LATEX, already providing a very simple form of semantic annotation. Additionally, mathematical language is highly formalized and uses well-defined phrases, simplifying the process of identifying the semantics by identifying these phrases.

Even though this system already qualifies as an intelligent assistant by itself, especially its retrieval component could be enhanced by making use of assistants that try to find a representation of the contents suitable for a given user profile, and thus to adapt the answers of the system to its user. Clearly, another application of the semantic retrieval system would be the initial step of reverse-fitting an existing lecture in paper form into the content area, thus aiding the lecturer and the student. A third, inner-mathematical application of the semantic analyzer might be to identify similarities within the internal structure, that is, requirements and conclusions of theorems to build up cross-relations between ad hoc unrelated research fields, thus supporting mathematical research to gain insight into the metastructure of mathematics. For example, given the definition of the gcd in elementary number theory, an assistant might point out that its requirements, namely a ring with division algorithm and without zero divisors, apply also to polynomial rings, and thus a gcd can be defined there as well.

Training Area

The training area provides students with highly structured exercises to delve into the subject of a course to a higher degree than by just following the lecture. The keywords here as in all other fields discussed so far are *granularity & structure* of the exercises. Thus, a given assignment is structured into sub-problems to be solved by the student so that a corresponding easier exercise can be given to focus on trouble points in case the student gets stuck. In other words, the training area is designed around a hierarchically structured graph of exercises providing individual learning units.

This type of adjustment enables learners to gradually enhance their competencies in self-directed problem solving.

Here an excerpt from a course on linear algebra, showing graph-like dependencies. Basic exercises in the bottom row.

Figure 4 shows an excerpt of a training network containing exercises of a course on linear algebra. For example, to solve a linear differential equation

Figure 4. Training network of exercises

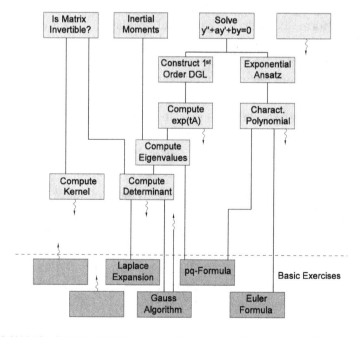

with constant coefficients, one could allow the user to pick either the exponential ansatz, that is, insert $y(t) := \exp(\lambda t)$ or to transform this equation into a vector-valued first-order equation and solve this system by means of the matrix exponential function. As one can observe already in this tiny example, training networks are typically no trees. They are true graphs and may contain same nodes even on different levels in the hierarchical network, as the position of a node depends on the context where the exercise represented by it is needed. In the given example, the Gauss Algorithm as a basic exercise could also be stated as an initial problem to solve for.

Cross-links to the corresponding chapters in a lecture, available in the content area provide the necessary background to solve the assignments; providing several ways to master an exercise allows the student to keep his personal style or allows the teacher to setup an exercise network which sets relevant foci for the course.

The training area concept in its current state, developed chiefly by S. Jeschke and R. Seiler (Mumie), is mainly based on Java applets that state classical exercises in the field of undergraduate linear algebra, allowing the student to gain the required score to be admitted to the final exams. Figure 5 demonstrates a typical homework assignment within the training network. In the example shown, the user is asked to answer an assignment on matrix multiplication, kernel, and image of a linear mapping.

One of the major challenges in developing multimedia-based learning and teaching platforms is to drive dynamical validation forwards, that is, using internal or external tools that are able to validate the correctness of a statement *dynamically* and *on the fly*. As far as the field of mathematics is concerned, computer algebra systems, automatic proving—if available—as well as specific numerical software have been used. The possibilities made available by linking external tools to training environments are currently not well exploited. A central reason for this unnecessary restriction is the lack of proper interface definitions—or even the total lack of any interface at all—at both the training tools as well as the external software.

Intelligent validation tools are characterized by their tolerance towards various notations and formulations of the same subject. To achieve this tolerance, it is not only necessary to encode exercises semantically instead of just providing a textual formulation, but also to use and interpret the same semantic correctly within the validation toolkit. The semantic coding of scientific content is, therefore, an important research challenge (Caprotti & Carlisle, n.d.; Saarland Universität, n.d.; W3C, n.d.).

Figure 5. A typical homework assignment in the MUMIE-Platform

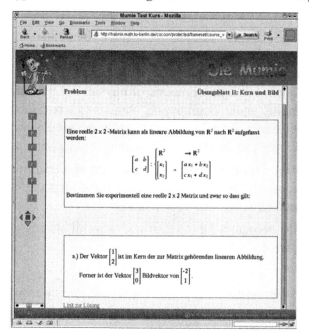

Here the reader is required to compute a 2×2 matrix such that (1,2)T is in its kernel and (3,0)T is the image of (-2,1)T. Matrix multiplication is defined atop. On the left, the navigator through the exercise graph, which is a straight line here, is shown.

The prospects for intelligent assistants in this field are manifold, and the functionality provided by them is in most cases imperative to make learning within the training area fruitful. As discussed above, user input must be validated and qualified—let it be automatic or semiautomatic—and if weaknesses show up, intelligent feedback in the form of hints or reinforcing exercises must be generated. Additionally, intelligent feedback must be given to the learner as to why his exercise might have failed and which matter to study or repeat. Intelligent tutoring will help the training area tools to provide exercises that both adapt to the learning process of the student as well as to the preferred presentation form of the contents—for example students might either prefer a mathematically exact definition or a hand waving demonstration that appeals to intuition. By observing the user's behavior, an intelligent tutoring system would then be able to offer a suitable exercise to train the student in the subtasks in which significant deficiencies have been identified.

Virtual Laboratory Area

Virtual Laboratories use the metaphor of a scientific laboratory as guiding line for the design of the software. That is, similar to real laboratories, they provide the framework and equipment to setup and run experiments, that is, qualitative and quantitative explorations of physical or mathematical phenomena of the model under examination. Similar to a real laboratory, it is not the primary goal of a Virtual Laboratory to define the experiments or the learning goals: it is left to the lecturer or organiser of a course to do so.

Applications of laboratories range from experiments for traditional lectures, homework assignments, and practical training for students up to aiding researchers in experimentation and visualization.

That is, a Virtual Laboratory has to deal with several classes of user types and deployment areas:

- **Demonstration setup:** To address lecturers, it must be easy to setup and perform experiments, optimally by graphically combining the required components or loading readily-setup experiments from a data pool.

- **Training and tutorials:** The main field of application for Virtual Laboratories as e-learning software of the second generation (Jeschke & Keil-Slawik, 2004) lies in the implementation of autonomous exercises, projects, and training that are supported by a member of teaching staff. Sophisticated user's guidance is decisive in shortening the adjustment period to the laboratory's interface. Partially pre-prepared experiments can circumvent the access obstacles and encourage further experiments. However, the interface has to provide full access to all functionalities.

An important aspect for practical training courses is that a given problem has to be solved within the interaction of a group of learners. It is reasonable to demand the support for cooperative learning scenarios as an important feature of this concept of Virtual Laboratories. Last but not least, to make a Virtual Laboratory applicable to real-life research problems, its flexibility and proper integration of well-accepted computer algebra systems is imperative. The pedagogical profile for Virtual Laboratories is defined in detail in section "Towards a pedagogical profile."

- **Self-study, homework, preparation for exams:** These fields of application require completely autonomous work from the students in order to train self-guided learning. Opposite to the previously mentioned introduction in training and tutorials, there is no support from the teaching staff, working hours and place of work are totally independent of the university. However, in this application, it is similarly desirable for the laboratory to be available to multiple users, thus supporting cooperation within homework groups, even outside the physical framework of the university.

- **Implementation in research:** Here is where flexibility and, more importantly, the integration and interconnection of the laboratories with other software elements and existing infrastructures are highly required. While a good tutorial and intuitive user interface is indeed always helpful and highly desirable, this scenario can require a higher degree of previous knowledge and—where applicable—a certain adjustment period. The complexity and specific quality of the algorithms is decisive, as they define how appropriate the given laboratory is to the modelling of relevant problems.

A Virtual Laboratory should ideally address all the above-mentioned purposes. The given demands have consequences on the architecture of the software design under consideration: to offer interfaces that are adapted to the corresponding group of users, Virtual Laboratories are separated into kernels, user interfaces and a third interconnecting layer allowing the combination of various labs into larger experiments, see the subsection on "Consequences for the Software Design."

In its current form, mainly developed by Th. Richter, the existing Virtual Lab VIDEOEASEL (Richter, n.d.) focuses on the field of statistical physics and statistical mechanics, described in detail in the VIDEOEASEL section. This field was chosen because it ideally combines mathematical research and its applications to important problems of natural science, engineering and economy: elementary mathematics is often sufficient to construct interesting models in this area, and thus the construction of models is very accessible to students. However, highly nontrivial phenomena can be observed and measured due to the interaction of the atomic components that are, even today, only partially understood and still under research. These components might be the molecules of a gas, spins of a ferromagnet, and so forth. To give just one example: phase transitions as an everyday phenomenon in large physical systems are complex phenomena; however, exact proofs exist only for the most elementary models, for example, the Ising model (Ising, 1925; Onsager, 1944).

Within VIDEOEASEL, probability, analysis, dynamical systems, and cellular automata are the important mathematical disciplines which can be brought to action in an environment of interesting applications like image data compression and de-noising, phase transitions, transmission from microscopic reversibility to macroscopic irreversibility for large numbers of atomic components (Jeschke, Richter & Seiler, 2005).

Towards a Pedagogical Profile

One of the defining principles of a Virtual Laboratory is that it does not define "learning units"—instead, it defines "learning spaces" for virtual experiments. The definition of learning goals remains to be given by the lecturer or the leader of the seminar or training course. Virtual Laboratories are tools to achieve a high-quality education *within* a course by providing virtual devices, algorithms, and so forth. The goal is rather to allow students to develop skills in problem solving and self-controlled learning that are required for their future professional work. Especially laboratories should provide enough freedom for individual or unusual experiments outside the limitations set by the curriculum (Hampel, Keil-Slawik & Ferber, 1999). Thus, a laboratory should allow an explorative learning style and should *encourage self-guided learning* rather than just present concepts. The freedom to set up and combine experiments by themselves trains students to solve problems by themselves rather than adapting given solutions. This also addresses creativity, thus increasing the learners' motivation.

Another aspect of Virtual Laboratories is that they address a broader audience than traditional e-learning solutions; rather than to convey scientific material to students as in a lecture, a Virtual Laboratory is—like its "real" counterpart —a *tool* whose primary purpose is to run experiments. This means that even though the main application of the Virtual Laboratories discussed here is in the training and educational field, applications in research as in a scientific workplace are possible and should be considered.

Due to the larger audience, Virtual Laboratories ought to be able to adapt themselves to the style of the individual users. The necessity to handle multiple application targets with partially diverging goals has several impacts on the software design, which will be discussed in the next section, and is one of the driving forces towards intelligent assistants.

Due to the high degree of specialization we find today, scientific results are more and more accomplishments of cooperations between individuals and the outcome of teamwork; this is due to the high complexity of today's problems that requires the cooperation of experts from various fields. Therefore, *teamwork* has to be actively promoted by Virtual Laboratories as well. By using networked applications, even cooperation across borders should be made available.

Last, but not least, a laboratory should integrate into existing software infrastructure by using standard components from the everyday environment of the working scientist or engineer; this includes products like Maple, Mathematica, or Matlab. In first place these tools provide numerical algorithms to analyze measured data, but using them also allows the students to familiarize themselves with software required for their professional life.

Consequences for the Software Design

The desired pedagogical profile formulated in previous section shows its consequences in the design of a Virtual Laboratory. Since laboratories have to address various targets and interest groups, see the "Virtual Lab Area," a highly granular software design is required which provides laboratory modules that are individually adapted to their target audience. This results in the separation of the laboratory into a kernel and several user interfaces that each fit their respective task and audience best. Furthermore, once the components are equipped with *open* interfaces using *accepted open standards*, the possibilities to combine these components freely to experiments beyond their initial application target and to reuse them outside their initial operational area are gained.

For that reason a three-tiered design for components is promoted in Figure 6.

In the top-middle the kernel which is controlled by the connector layer (rounded boxes) through CORBA interfaces (Scallan, n.d.) (small black boxes). The connectors are linked to various front-ends providing their individual GUIs (light grey, bottom). On the right-hand side, an external component, for example, a CAS, is talking to a connector. Assistant technology observes user behavior and controls the kernel (grey box in the middle) by its own GUI (light grey box within). A user administration (topmost box) controls access to running experiments.

- **Simulation and computation components:** These components implement the number crunchers in Virtual Laboratories; they do not provide any visible user interface, but rather implement the physical modeling of the entities to be measured. The only kind of interface they provide is one that defines the parameters for the experiment they emulate and that allows to extract the experimental results. In Figure 6, this is the kernel.

Figure 6. Software architecture of a Virtual Lab, here VideoEasel

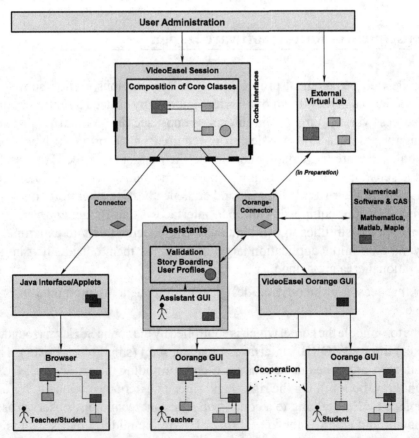

- **Connectors:** Connectors are software components that aid the user to combine and link the components of a laboratory to an experiment. In the simplest case, they could be realized by means of a script that extracts measurements from a laboratory kernel as described in the previous point, and feeds this data back into a numerical algebra program. Ideally, this kind of linkage should be carried out with minimum effort by means of a graphical user interface. The second task of the connectors is to translate and adapt the languages and interfaces between distinct laboratories. Even though we should enforce a unique interface definition for all laboratory components, it seems to be unrealistic to achieve this goal in practice, especially when having to deal with components from various sources. In Figure 6, the rounded boxes in the middle depict these.

- **User interfaces:** User interfaces address the needs and goals of the user group experimenting with a Virtual Laboratory. Depending on the application target, a user interface may present a readily set up experiment for demonstration purposes in a lecture, an applet in an internet browser or an experiment in a GUI showing an experiment for students in practical training. A computer algebra system talking to the laboratory kernel through a connector might also provide a user interface of its own that is better suited to numerical analysis. Thus, in general more than one user interface will be required.

Once the separation into the above classes is understood, it is natural how to address the requirement of supporting cooperative learning scenarios: if we allow data streams between components to cross machine-boundaries, thus allowing the exchange of data in a network, one simulation component running on a server can be observed and investigated by more than one student at once—each experimenting and measuring from a client at a possibly remote location. Side channels would then allow students to communicate and exchange their experiences. A peer-to-peer network would be an alternative architecture for a distributed Virtual Laboratory. Nevertheless, in our understanding *cooperative learning requires networked applications* (Hampel & Keil-Slawik, 2001).

VideoEasel: A Virtual Lab for Statistical Mechanics

An implementation of a Virtual Laboratory prototype in the above sense, demonstrating the impacts of the above demands on pedagogics and software design is the Virtual Laboratory, VideoEasel (Richter, n.d.), developed at the DFG research center Matheon (Matheon) of the Berlin universities. VideoEasel focuses on statistical mechanics, usually lectured in the second semester of the "Mathematical Physics" course. Typically, the audience is a mixture of mathematics and physics students that participate in the course "Mathematical Physics II" which is taught in the sixth semester for mathematicians and physicists.

VideoEasel implements the microscopic rules of physical systems that are of interest in this area, for example, the classical Ising Model or Lattice Gas Models, by using so-called *Cellular Automata* (Toffoli & Margolus, 1987). A cellular automaton defines a time evolution on a matrix, often visualized by colored cells. The next state of a matrix element is hereby computed solely by the so-called microscopic rule from the state of the element and its surrounding neighbours. Cellular automata are simple enough to be described by elementary math while being capable of demonstrating a rich set of complex phenomena. Thus, they invite to experiment without building up barriers when entering the field.

According to the demands mentioned above, VideoEasel is based on a three-tiered software design separated into a computation kernel implementing the microscopic dynamics of a physical system, an interface/connector layer and several GUI front-ends that allow users to observe and manipulate the experiment. The interface between the kernel and the connector is realized by means of the well-established CORBA middleware (Scallan, n.d.), thus making the laboratory a networked application. The kernel is designed to handle several connections at once, even from several users observing the same experiment. VideoEasel, therefore, supports cooperative and remote learning scenarios right away.

The microscopic rules are written in a C-like programming language that is compiled and linked to the kernel at runtime; a set of predefined programs implementing various experiments are available on the server, though the user is always invited to modify and change these rules locally if desired. Similar to the experiments, measurement tools exist as microscopic rules defining the physical entities to be observed and measured. Following the granular design philosophy, they can be plugged into each experiment as long as the objects referred to by the measurement tool exist in the object to be measured on.

Several user front-ends are provided; compare Figure 7: the simplest one is a Java applet which is able to display an experiment along with some of its parameters in a Web browser, thus making it applicable for on-line experiments or quick demonstrations in a lecture. A more complete stand-alone Java GUI

Figure 7a. Java front-end for a Virtual Laboratory

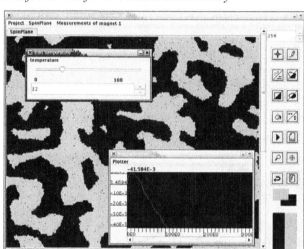

Figure 7b. Oorange interface for a Virtual Laboratory

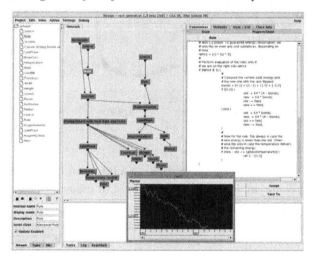

Figure 7c. Oorange interface communicating with Maple

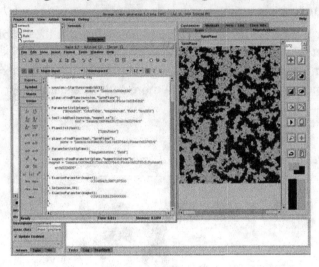

Figure 7d. Applet front-end for a Virtual Laboratory, showing an experiment on the role of reversibility in thermodynamics in lattice gases

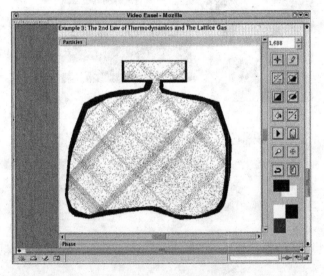

hides most of the complexity while making a large subset of the possibilities available to its users, including the attachment of measurement tools and the editing of the microscopic rules. This interface was mainly designed to be used in practical training since it makes readily set up experiments quickly available for the students.

An interface to the Oorange toolkit, a Java programming tool also developed at the Berlin University of Technology (Oorange, n.d.), is provided to make VIDEOEASEL applicable to research problems. It represents the objects of VIDEOEASEL, that is, algorithms and measurement tools as well as parameters controlling its operation as boxes which can be linked together by means of "drag and drop." Oorange can be used to have VIDEOEASEL talk to external applications, given these applications provide a Java interface themselves. Oorange is therefore a classical connector in the sense of the previous section.

The remaining three all visualize the Ising model, measuring the magnetization over time.

Last but not least, an interface to the computer algebra system "Maple" to analyze the measured data and to control the laboratory from there in order to run even more complex measurement tasks is supplied.

From Microscopic Dynamics to Algorithms

To shed some light on the way VIDEOEASEL works, the classical model of statistical mechanics, the Ising Model (Ising, 1925), is briefly discussed. The automaton operates here on a lattice whose elements are called "spins." Each spin can be in one of only two possible states, classically called "spin up" and "spin down." Within the VIDEOEASEL world, the spin configuration is visualized by a two-dimensional drawing canvas, with spins pointing up shown in white and spins pointing down depicted in black. The offered user front-ends enable the user to manipulate the spin-configuration in a GUI that looks and feels very much like a painting program. The Ising Model and a typical spin configuration for this model is seen in Figure 7a.

The dynamics of the system is launched by a button in the GUI; this dynamics is defined by a "microscopic rule" that computes the next state of a spin —thus the color of a pixel on the screen—by its own state, the states of its neighboring pixels and the set of external parameters that can also be defined in the GUI. For the model at hand, the dynamics is given by the Metropolis Algorithm (Metropolis, Rosenbluth, Teller & Teller, 1953), implemented in the internal language provided by the Lab. Each neighboring pair of spins is assigned a number, called its "energy" where parallel spins contribute low and anti-parallel spins high energy. Leaving some technicalities aside, the Metropolis algorithm computes the energy for all spin pairs and compares this energy with that of a configuration where a randomly picked spin state is replaced by its opposite, that is, with the spin "flipped around." If the energy of the flipped configuration is smaller than that of the current one, the spin is flipped. Otherwise, if the energy difference between new and old configuration is smaller than the energy a "heat bath" contributes, the spin flip is performed as well. In all other cases, the spin remains in its current state. External parameters control the temperature of the heat bath as well as an additional energy source representing an external magnetic field.

Measurement tools operate on the very same spin configuration, carrying out the measurement process by applying their defining algorithm once for each available spin. In the simplest case of measuring the overall magnetization of the Ising Model, this algorithm would simply consist of adding one unit to the magnetization for each spin pointing up and subtracting one for each spin pointing down. Similar, though more complex rules can be formulated for other macroscopic observables, for example, entropy, internal energy, or Helmholtz free energy. Both, parameters as well as measurements can be manipulated by the CORBA interface.

Measurement tools and local dynamics need to match each other to make the measuring process meaningful, though. In the case of VIDEOEASEL, this identification is done in the simplest possible way: an automaton assigns names to its defining elements, and the measurement process identifies the configuration to measure on by their names.

Intelligent Assistants for Virtual Labs

To support users, the laboratory also provides *software assistants* as compiled Java code. Currently two types of assistants are implemented: First, so-called *wizards* provide simplified and streamlined user interfaces; the wizards do not add any functionality to the user interface, they rather bundle existing features and present them in a way that makes the problem at hand more accessible. For example, the configuration wizard of the Ising model allows to set up the interaction energies of all possible spin-neighborhood configurations. The added value lies in the assignment of an interpretation for each of the parameters by the wizard (otherwise only represented by a labelled slider in the regular GUI).

Besides the static adaptation towards users available by selecting an appropriate front-end (see the VIDEOEASEL section) and enriching this front-end by wizards, the second kind of assistants provide user adaptivity through direct feedback from the user input: the so-called *tutors* present a guided tour through a predefined set of experiments to introduce students to a specific matter. That is, their purpose is to lower the entry barrier for students to run experiments on their own. Therefore, the assistants observe user behavior, try to provide intelligent feedback and redirect the user to additional experiments to gain further insight. Figure 8 presents a prototypical tutoring system that demonstrates how matrix convolution operations act as filters on natural images and how to perform some basic image manipulations, here image smoothing.

The tutoring system uses the idea of *storyboards* (Jantke & Knauf, 2005): a storyboard, as it is used here, is a network of assignments similar to the networks presented in "Training Area" section, though the nodes of this graph do not represent complete exercises, but smaller working units; each

Figure 8. A tutoring assistant in a laboratory on matrix convolution

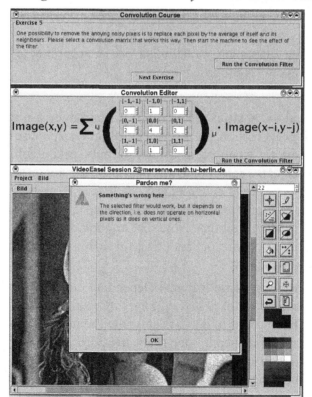

unit leads the user one step further into a possibly complex topic. Navigation on the network is driven by the assistant itself and not under direct control of the user. Figure 9 presents the network for the image convolution filter example introduced above.

The tutoring system observes user behavior, validates and rates the answers and redirects the user to the suitable next step to perform. It is furthermore important to note that this tutoring system only makes suggestions on what the user might want to look at next. A student is always free to leave the tutoring system alone and experiment on his own.

Even though the current implementation uses only the most recent user input to select a path through the storyboard graph, the idea is naturally extended by user profiles, which is the next step to be taken in the development plan: namely, to select custom-tailored exercises by observed usage patterns, and by other side information gained on the user from other sources, for example, the courses a user is participating in.

On top the current assignment to be performed; the middle window shows the configuration wizard for the convolution auto¬maton, the tar-get image is shown below. On top of the target image some feedback given by the assistant.

To perform user adaptation, modelling a learner according to the following "coordinate system" is proposed:

- **Graphical vs. textual orientation:** To introduce a mathematical or physical phenomenon, users might either prefer a precise mathematical description, for example, as textual formula, or a graphical/figurative description of the same content. A possible indicator on which presentation to choose might be the subject the learner is studying: mathematicians might prefer textual definitions whereas engineers might prefer graphical demonstrations. Note that a graphical representation is not necessarily imprecise or less powerful than a textual presentation of the same content.

- **Serialistic vs. holistic learner:** Depending on preference or learning goal, a learner might first want to get a broad overview over a given field, or might want to delve deeply into the matter first, preferring to learn the material step by step (Pangaro, 2001; Scott, 2001). This type of information is in our understanding best gained by observing the learner on navigation through the user interface, and by that selecting

Figure 9. Excerpt from the storyboard on image filtering techniques

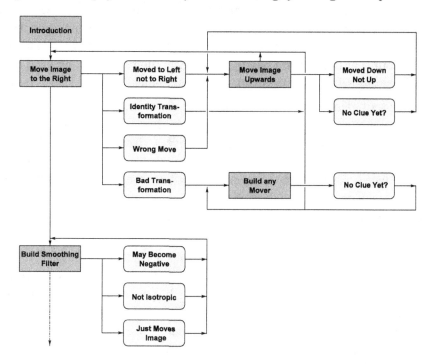

the nodes and learning units that fit best to the navigation style the user preferred so far. Clearly, user interfaces will have to be equipped by software that is capable of collecting this type of information.

Working units in boxes, possible evaluation results in rounded boxes show the conditions for which assistant branches off to related experiments.

Conclusion and Outlook

VIDEOEASEL is currently still in a prototypical state, only limited practical experiences have been gained so far. A school project at the Heinrich Hertz School in Berlin revealed that the technology developed for cooperative learning and teaching is also very useful to help the administrator in providing individual support to students and to demonstrate individual achievements to the class. In contrast, unrestricted access of each student to the workplace of every other student as it was available in a preliminary version causes a lot of turbulence in the classroom. Therefore a minimal user administration was added. A second experiment using VIDEOEASEL as part of the Mathematical Physics course at the Berlin University of Technology is in progress at the time of writing; so far user feedback looks promising.

The process of gaining more experience with the content and training areas is going on, though the focus here is on undergraduate mathematics, specifically on the course on linear algebra for engineers. Besides purely technical aspects, a second problem specific to overcrowded undergraduate courses has to be faced: namely that of properly motivating abstract concepts and explaining their relevance to the audience's field of interest. Concrete exercises showing how abstract mathematics solve concrete problems is a major goal of our system.

To conclude, let us remark that we are not aiming at replacing frontal lectures or training courses by electronic media; we rather impose a *blended learning* approach: electronic media will *enrich* traditional courses by providing learning experiences that have not been possible before and that are more necessary than ever due to the changing demands of education. Intelligent assistants are a valuable concept to reach this goal since they allow tailoring the software to the individual needs of the very broad audience we face at the Berlin University of Technology. The field of mathematics might act as a toy model to drive development of intelligent assistants in other fields further; even though construction of this technology for teaching mathematics might be simpler due to the highly developed internal structure and strongly formalized language hardly found anywhere else, we still believe that concepts and experiences gained here carry over to other fields.

References

Beierle, C., & Kern-Isberner, G. (2000). *Methoden wissensbasierter Systeme.* (*Methods of knowledge based systems.*) Vieweg, Braunschweig, Wiesbaden.

BeLearning (n.d.). *Barrierefreies eLearning in Natur- und Ingenieurwissenschaften.* (*Asscessibility Issues of eLearning Platforms for Natural*

Sciences and Engineering) Retrieved June 3, 2006, from http://www.belearning.de

Caprotti, O., & Carlisle, D. (n.d.). *OpenMath and MathML*: *Semantic mark up for MathematicsOpenMath*. Retrieved June 3, 2006, from http://www.openmath.org

Dahlmann, N., Jeschke, S., Seiler, R., & Sinha, U. (2003). MOSES meets MUMIE: Multimedia-based education in mathematics. In F. Malpica, A. Tremante, & N. Sala (Eds.), *International Conference on Education and Information Systems: Technologies and Applications* (pp. 370–375), Orlando, Florida. International Institute of Informatics and Systemics.

Dahlmann, N., Jeschke, S., Seiler, R., & Wilke, M. (2005). *Semantische Kodierung fachwissenschaftlicher Applets*. (*Semantic coding of field specific applets*.) Lecture Notes in Informatics: Marktplatz Internet: Von e-Learning bis e-Payment (pp. 172–177). Bonn: Köllen Druck+Verlag GmbH.

European Union. (1999). *The Bologna Declaration: Joint declaration of the European Ministers of Education*. Retrieved June 3, 2006, from http://www.bologna-berlin2003.de/pdf/bologna_declaration.pdf

Explorations: *A new form of highly interactive learning materials*. In P. de Bra & J. Leggett (Eds.), *Proceedings of WebNet99: World Conference on the WWW and Internet* (pp. 463–468). Charlottesville: Association for the Advancement of Computing in Education.

Görz, G., Rollinger, C.-R., & Schneeberger, J. (Eds.). (2000). *Handbuch der Künstliche Intelligenz*. (*Handbook of artificial intelligence*.) Oldenbourg, München, Wien.

Hampel, R., & Keil-Slawik, T. (2001, May 1-5). sTeam: Designing an integrative infrastructure for Web-based computer supported cooperative learning. In *Proceedings of the 10th International World Wide Web Conference* (pp. 76-85). Hong Kong, China.

Haun, M. (2002). *Handbuch Wissensmanagement*. (*Handbook of knowledge management*.) Berlin, Heidelberg: Springer.

Ising, E. (1925). Beitrag zur Theorie des Ferromagnetismus. (On the theory of ferromagnetism.) *Zeitschrift für Physik, (Journal of Physics) 31*, 253–258.

Jantke, K.P., & Knauf, R. (2005). Didactic design through storyboarding: Standard concepts for standard tools. In *Proceedings of First International*

Workshop on Dissemination of E-Learning Systems and Applications (DELTA 2005). ACM Press.

Jeschke, S. (2004). *Mathematik in Virtuellen Wissensräumen: IuK-Strukturen und IT-Technologien in Lehre und Forschung.* (Mathematics in virtual knowledge spaces: ICT Structures in Academic Education and Research.)Doctoral thesis, Technische Universität Berlin.

Jeschke, S., & Keil-Slawik, R. (2004). *Next Generation in eLearning Technology: Die Elektrifizierung des Nürnberger Trichters und die Alternativen.* Informationsgesellschaft. Alcatel SEL Stiftung. (Publisher Alcatel, Conference Proceedings GML, 2004)

Jeschke, S., Kohlhase, M., & Seiler, R. (2004). *eLearning-, eTeaching- & eResearch-Technologien : Chancen und Potentiale für die Mathematik. (eLearning-, eTeaching & eRearch technologies: Chances and potentials for mathematics.)* DMV-Nachrichten.

Jeschke, T., Richter, R., & Seiler, S. (2005). VideoEasel: Architecture of virtual laboratories on mathematics and natural sciences. In *Recent research developments in learning technologies: Vol. 2* (pp. 876–880).

Matheon. (n.d.). *DFG Research Center Matheon.* Retrieved June 3, 2006, from http://www.matheon.de

Metropolis, N., Rosenbluth, A., Teller, M., & Teller, E. (1953). Equations of state calculations by fast computing machines. *J. Chem. Phys, 21,* 1087-1091.

Moses. (n.d.). *Mobile services for students at the Berlin University of Technology.* Retrieved June 3, 2006, from http://www.moses.tu-berlin.de

MuLF. (n.d.). *Multimedia Center for eLearning, eTeaching & eResearch at the Berlin University of Technology.* Retrieved June 3, 3006, from http://www.mulf.tu-berlin.de

Mumie Community. (n.d.). Retrieved June 3, 2006, from http:// www.mumie.net

Natho, N. (2005). *mArachna: Eine semantische Analyse der mathematischen Sprache für ein computergestütztes Information Retrieval.* Doctoral thesis, Technische Universität Berlin.

Nemesis. (n.d.). *New media support and infrastructure at the Berlin University of Technology.* Retrieved June 3, 2006, from http:// www.nemesis.tu-berlin.de

Onsager, L. (1944). A two-dimensional model with an order-disorder transformation. *Phys. Rev., 65,* 117–149.

Oorange. (n.d.). *Oorange: The Oorange development environment.* Retrieved June 3, 2006, from http://www.oorange.de

Pangaro, P. (2001). THOUGHTSTICKER 1986: A personal history of conversation theory in software, and its progenitor, Gordon Pask. *Kybernetes, 30*(5/6), 790–806.

Richter, T. (n.d.). *VideoEasel.* Retrieved June 3, 2006, from http://www.math.tu-berlin.de/~thor/videoeasel

Saarland Universität (n.d.). *TU Eindhoven, RISC Linz. OMDoc.* Retrieved June 3, 2006, from http://www.mathWeb.org/omdoc/

Scallan, T. (n.d.). *A corba primer.* Retrieved June 3, 2006, from http://www.omg.org/news/whitepapers/seguecorba.pdf

Scott, B. (2001). Conversational theory: A constructivist, dialogical approach to educational technology. *Cybernetics & Human Knowing, 8*(4), 25–46.

Sun Developer Network. (n.d.). *Enterprise JavaBeans technology.* Retrieved June 3, 2006, from http://java.sun.com/products/ejb/

Toffoli, T., & Margolus, N. (1987). *Cellular automata machines.* Cambridge: MIT Press.

W3C Math Working Group (n.d.). *MathML.* Retrieved June 3, 2006, from http://www.w3.org/Math/

Chapter XII

Building a Virtual Trainer for an Immersive Haptic Virtual Reality Environment

Alexander Krumpholz, CSIRO ICT Centre, Australia

Abstract

This chapter describes the virtual trainer we developed for CSIRO's temporal bone dissection simulator. This simulation software runs on an immersive haptic virtual reality environment. The prototype system uses a task model based on a finite state machine to describe the procedure and interactive landmarks to trace the user's action in relation to vital structures. This gives the user situation related feedback based on user actions. The future virtual trainer would need to be based on research on intelligent tutoring systems to tailor feedback for the students and maximize their knowledge and skill acquisition. Various features for such a system are described.

Introduction

CSIRO is currently developing a temporal bone surgery simulator based on its haptic workbench (Stevenson, Smith, McLaughlin, Gunn, Veldkamp, & Dixon, 1999). The system allows an expert to interactively tutor a surgical trainee in temporal bone surgery. This chapter explores adding intelligent tutoring to the system to allow the student to learn alone. First we will introduce the application context followed by an overview of an initial prototype. After a brief description of the use of artificial intelligence in education, the chapter concludes with the proposed features for a future intelligent trainer system and a comparison to related work.

Temporal Bone Surgery

The temporal bone at the side of the skull houses the organs of the middle and inner ear. The mastoid, a trabeculated part of the temporal bone around the auricle, contains important nerves and blood vessels like the facial nerve and the sigmoid sinus. Several surgical interventions require the surgeon to remove portions of the mastoid (mastoidectomy). Another common procedure is the implantation of a cochlear hearing aid, a small device that stimulates the nerves in the cochlea. Surgeons who carry out a mastoidectomy need a detailed knowledge of the anatomy of the temporal bone and the embedded structures, the surgical anatomy (the anatomy as seen by the surgeon undertaking a specific surgical procedure) and the technique. A high degree of dexterity is also needed for the procedure.

The traditional way for a student to learn about temporal bone dissection is to study all theoretical issues from literature and then to attend bone dissection classes where they watch experts in the field doing a dissection on donated specimens. Every student repeats the intervention on a new bone. After several bone dissection courses and once the expert surgeon attests that the student has reached a high level of confidence in doing the operation, the student begins to take part in real operations. The student initiates the task under close supervision of the expert. If the student becomes uncertain at any stage of the operation, the expert takes over and concludes the operation with the student watching. This teacher-centered apprenticeship model of learning temporal bone dissection is typical for the medical field, but is very time intensive for the expert surgeon and requires a large number of donated temporal bones.

Virtual Environment

The platform for our surgical simulation is the haptic workbench (Stevenson et al., 1999), a system that consists of a monitor showing the 3D scene, which is watched through a mirror using shutter glasses, and a Phantom haptic device from SensAble Technologies (SensAble Technologies, n.d.), which enables the user to touch virtual objects. A Phantom consists of a robotic arm ending in a pen-like device which is hold by the operator. The position and orientation of the pen are permanently sent to the computer. Forces due to collisions between the virtual pen and other virtual object are calculated and fed back into the Phantom haptic device. This allows the user to feel the interaction through the hand-held pen. The setup of the haptic workbench allows the user to watch the 3D object through a mirror; therefore the 3D object appears to hover in front of the user exactly in the same position as the work area of the Phantom haptic device. This has the advantage of allowing the virtual objects to be touched from all sides (even the areas that normally appear inside the monitor) and the physical tool on the Phantom

Figure 1. The architecture of the haptic workbench

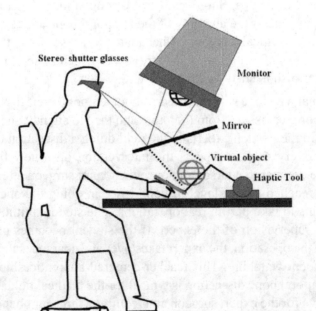

to correlate with the virtual tool seen on the screen. While the user can cope with the offset between the mouse on the table and the cursor on the screen in a standard WIMP (Windows, Icon, Mouse, and Pointing) environment, the correlation in the haptic workbench gives the user a high feeling of immersion and therefore realism. The virtual environment is currently built using the Reachin API (Reachin Technologies AB, n.d.), which uses a VRML-based scene graph with haptic extensions. Additional nodes and other software components can be added using C++ and Python. Further features of the haptic workbench are a Logitech Magellan 3D controller (Logitech Technologies, n.d.) to navigate in the scene, and network capabilities, which allow two haptic workbenches to be linked together and their users to share the same virtual environment. This configuration enables remote training sessions between a student and a trainer even over long distances (Gunn, Hutchins, Adcock & Hawkins, 2003).

To run the temporal bone surgery simulator on the haptic workbench, an additional Phantom has been added to allow two handed operation, as well as a foot pedal to let the user control the speed of the dissection burr.

Temporal Bone Surgery Simulator

The CSIRO temporal bone dissection simulator (Hutchins, O'Leary, Stevenson, Gunn, & Krumpholz, 2005) has been built in close collaboration with surgeons from the University of Melbourne, who introduced us to the problems involved in teaching this surgical procedure. The main motivation for developing the system, from the point of view of the surgeons, is the increasing difficulty in acquiring the number of bone samples necessary and the differences between cadaver samples and live organs. From the developer's point of view, the modelling of solid bones and simulating of the dissection is much easier than implementing physically accurate soft tissue manipulation, particularly if the software is meant to run on off-the-shelf hardware. Using a rapid prototyping, we have collaboratively developed a networked virtual bone dissection simulator, which shows positive subjective feedback from both expert surgeons and students. Formal results for trial tests of our system in real bone dissection courses are still pending. Other research teams have also started to build temporal bone dissection simulators for similar reasons (Sewell, Morris, Blevins, Barbagli, & Salisbury, 2005; Wiet, Stredney, Sessanna, Bryan, Welling, & Schmalbrock, 2002).

Figure 2. The simulator's user interface

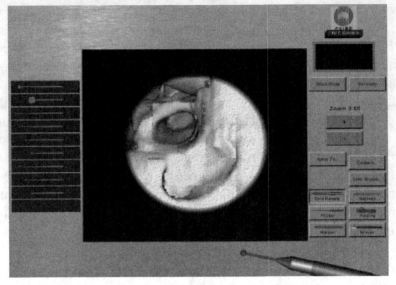

In terms of the interaction model, the temporal bone simulator currently has the following input/output capabilities:

- Input
- SensAble Phantom positional information
- Logitech Magellan 3D Controller for model orientation
- Foot pedal for drill speed
- Output
- 3D Stereo Vision
- Playback of recorded sound and speech
- Haptic Feedback via the SensAble Phantom

The simulator works on a 3D voxel model, built on CT scans of a temporal bone. A visible surface is rendered from the exposed voxel surfaces and an appropriate texture is applied. The tool used for dissection is a spherical burr on a shaft mounted in a virtual hand held power drill. A number of burr sizes and types are available. When the rotating burr touches the surface, the voxels to be removed are calculated and removed. At each graphics cycle, a new surface is calculated and rendered. In the dissection phase, the second hand usually operates the irrigator and sucker tool, which is used to cool the bone under the burr and to remove the bone slurry. This is currently only visualized by bone dust being removed by the sucker.

Virtual Assistant

The collaborative environment of our networked haptic workbenches supports the features needed for the current apprenticeship model of teaching, even if the expert and the student are far away from each other. The ability to share the same virtual environment not only allows cross country bone dissection sessions, it is also beneficial if the two simulators are located right next to each other. Since this setup enables them to see and work in the identical scene it allows a level of interaction, that is, not even possible in a real temporal bone dissection where the narrow spaces do not allow four hands to be in the same place at once.

To ease the workload of the surgical experts and furthermore allow automatic assessment against the curriculum goals, an automatic training and assessment component has been identified as an important feature for our simulator. This will therefore move from an expert centered process to a student centered approach.

Landmarks

Landmarks are distinctive features in an environment that can be used for orientation as well as interaction (Müller-Tomfelde, Paris, & Stevenson, 2004). We built special VRML nodes that can be used as building blocks for interactive landmarks and are able to create events when the user interacts with them. The landmarks can be points, lines of points along the center line of a tube or arrays of points on a surface. Specifying a set of radii around each of those points allows us to generate events of varying importance, depending on the distance between the user's tool and the landmark (see Figure 3). In the case of our bone dissection simulator, one of these structures is the facial nerve which must not be touched with the drilling burr. There are five radii around the facial nerve which are used for:

- **Initially biggest radius:** Dynamically changes to the closest distance the tool had to the landmark. It is used to calculate the mean dissection distance in multipoint landmarks.

- **Approaching distance:** Defined to generate an event that identifies the landmark being approached.

- **Dissection level:** This is the ideal distance the student should dissect to (i.e., drill down to). When the mean dissection distance is less than this value, the landmark is considered "identified."

- **Warning distance:** Installed to warn the user of the proximity to the landmark. It can also be used to recommend the switch from the dissection burr to the nerve probe.

- **Smallest radius:** The landmark itself. Going closer than this distance causes damage to the landmark.

The mean minimum distance between the tool and each point of the structure is measured to calculate the degree of dissection, which is used to trigger an event marking this structure as correctly identified. The coefficient of variation (COV) of those minimal distances can be used as a measure for the current evenness of the dissection. Recording these COV over time allows the homogeneity of the dissection process to be evaluated.

In the real operation, the surgeon has to avoid hitting the vital structures embedded in the mastoid and the recommended, safe procedure is to dissect and thereby positively identify each of the landmarks before progressing to deeper regions in the bone. The usually honeycombed mastoid is solid

Figure 3. The different distances around a landmark

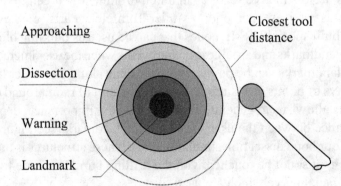

around each organ enabling it to be identified by the surgeon, who should leave a protective layer of bone around each structure. The dissection should be done in long and even strokes along the landmarks, which usually represent either tubular structures like nerves and blood vessels or surfaces like membranes.

Nerve Probe

One of the risks in undertaking temporal bone surgery is damage to the facial nerve, which is located slightly differently in every patient. Damaging the facial nerve permanently paralyzes the associated side of the patient's face which results in a severe disability of the patient. To support surgeons in positively identifying the thin facial nerve, a nerve probe has been developed, which gives the surgeon an audio cue to reveal the facial nerves position. A sensor is placed on the patient's face that traces finest muscle movement. The nerve probe can stimulate the facial nerve by sending impulses through the facial nerve to the cheek. When the nerve probe touches the bone close to the nerve, the sensor picks up the signal and warns the surgeon with an audio signal and a graph on a device monitor. The closer the probe is placed to the facial nerve, the louder the audio signal becomes.

To simulate the nerve probe in the haptic workbench, we modelled the facial nerve as a landmark, which measures the closest distance to the nerve probe. When a threshold is breached, a virtual device monitor shows a graph and an audio signal similar to the real alarm is generated, with the volume representing the distance between the facial nerve and the nerve probe.

Task Model

To model the complex tasks that the user has to perform during the virtual operation, a finite state machine (FSM) is used to describe the order of tasks and the feedback for each state. Events, like those created by the landmark structures embedded in our prototype trigger the playback of recorded audio files and are also used to trigger the transition to a new state in the FSM.

The example in Figure 4 shows three hypothetical tubular structures composed of a series of landmark points. The nested, semi-transparent spheres around each point are only used to visualize the radii while exploring the prototype, but are not meant to be used in a real simulation. Figure 5 shows

Figure 4. Three interactive tubular landmarks

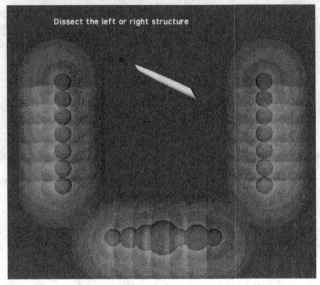

Figure 5. Task model for three landmarks that have to be dissected in a certain order

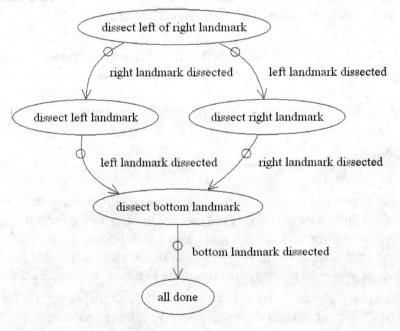

a simple finite state machine that shows the states and transitions involved. In the first state, the user can decide to dissect one of the vertical structures, but not the horizontal one on the bottom.

When students have identified one of the landmarks by dissecting it to the correct degree, the FSM switches to the next stage and asks for identification of the second virtual structure to be identified next. Alternatively, if the users approach the horizontal landmark first, the system asks them to concentrate on the vertical landmark.

Intelligent Tutoring Systems

The first prototype of the virtual assistant tracks which stage of the process the student is currently working on and produces generic feedback according to the student's action at that task. While this is a useful feature, we want to go much further and generate individual user-specific feedback to optimize the learning effect for each student and take the optimal training strategy for that student into account.

Artificial Intelligence in Education

Siemer and Angelides (1998) describe the three models that an intelligent tutoring system (ITS) should comprise: The *domain model*, the *student model* and the *tutoring model*. The *domain model* contains the expertise, that is, knowledge about the subject of the tutoring system. It is used to answer questions of the students, reason about problems and allow the generation of alternative teaching strategies. The *student model* is the diagnostic component and it is being used to build up knowledge about the student like the course history, learning preferences, previous achievements, errors, and so on. For simulations, the *student model* is ideally realized as a *performance model,* that is, it is based on physical measurements of the actions of the students. Movements of the tools, distances and forces can be measured and set in relation to the time needed to perform given tasks. An *error model* can also be useful for student modeling in simulation environments. It contains commonly made errors students tend to make while performing the task. The work of the students is checked against these errors to assess their learning progress. The knowledge gained about the students is used to tailor the course to each of them specifically, for example, to increase the learning affect. The *tutoring model* is used to build training sessions by setting goals and construct sessions by selecting appropriate topics and arranging them in a didactic way. Finally, an overall system component orchestrating the three models and a user interface are seen as major parts of an ITS.

Related Work

Other research groups working on temporal bone dissection also started to develop tutoring components, but none of them appears to implement an intelligent tutoring system as specified by Siemer and Angelides (1998).

The "Intelligent Tutor" described in Wiet et al. (2002) offers an identification mode, which allows the student to ask the system where certain parts of the anatomy are and what a certain structure is; and an expert mode, where the student can replay a recorded surgical session.

Sewell et al. (2005) implemented a system that measures forces and velocities for all areas in the scene and compares them to the forces and velocities that were recorded when expert surgeons undertook the incision. This is used to recognize when students are not yet performing appropriately. They also verify that all voxels removed from the mastoid are in sight of the surgeon, since dissecting below an overhanging piece of bone is not allowed and can result in a landmark getting damaged.

A system to assess a student's skill acquisition for a simulation-based ITS is described by Yacef and Alem (1997). Their efforts to assess operational skills are based on research in cognitive science in skill and knowledge acquisition. When the initial analytical knowledge of students is repeatedly applied in various situations, situational knowledge is being created. Complex tasks always require operational knowledge, which consist of both the controlled processing of analytical knowledge in short-term memory and the fast automatic processed situational knowledge in long-term memory. Therefore, the strategy for their simulation-based ITS for air traffic controllers is to first practice a variety of situations that require certain skills and then to increase the workload and introduce exceptions to automate those skills. For the assessment they distinguish between three levels of skill acquisition: a *beginning stage*, a *second stage* where the student performs accurately in all given situations, and a *third stage* where the student performs well even under a high workload.

Although the skills of an air traffic controller are different to those of temporal bone surgery, in that the situations are more repetitive and the workload can vary significantly, surgical procedures are also skill based and an automation of the operational skills is still applicable. Therefore, the aspects discussed in this chapter are relevant and will be taken as the basis for the work on an intelligent tutor for our simulator.

Virtual Trainer

A future intelligent tutoring system for a temporal bone surgery simulator must be built based on the results of previous studies in the field of Artificial Intelligence in Education like the ones described in the previous chapter, that is, adequate domain, learner, and tutoring models have to be developed to support the assessment of student's skill acquisition.

Goals

Switching from an expert centred process to a *student centred leaning approach* takes workload off the surgeon in early stages off the training, allowing more interaction later in the student's curriculum.

Ideally, an intelligent tutoring system does not only help building the set of skills usually learned in a bone drilling course in the lab, but instead help the student to quickly gain all the knowledge and skills usually being acquired in the various stages of the conventional training. The visualization features in the 3D scene help the students to understand the complex anatomical structures of the region which reduces the time students need to build a mental model of the structures reading textbooks and attending courses. The safe procedure to dissect the temporal bone and to access the inner ear as well as the knowledge of the surgical anatomy involved can be explored repeatedly on different virtual bones. Finally, full operations in the virtual environment can help to decrease the number of cases when students become uncertain at supervised operations on real patients. Using an intelligent tutoring system, all these steps reduce the time the experts have to spend on repetitive trainings sessions. Networked haptic workbenches could be used to support groups of students to explore and dissect a bone together, sharing and discussing the feedback of the intelligent tutoring system.

The features used in an intelligent tutoring system could furthermore be used to *objectively assess the performance* of students and allow regular evaluations of surgeons' performances.

Features

For an intelligent tutor to be accepted and appreciated by the student, the support must not be too disruptive and experienced as helpful in the learner's current situation. Due to the nature of the immersive environment and the fact that the student has to perform a difficult task maybe even within time restrictions, the virtual trainer should initiate a dialog verbally using generated or pre-recorded speech. More intrusive ways of interaction and pausing of the current trainings task might be chosen by the student as a response. The intelligent tutor has to adapt to the students level of experience to avid annoying repetitions. The usefulness of the trainings simulator will also vary according to the quantity and quality of assistant features being implemented. Examples of features with a different level of disruption follow:

- **Nondisruptive feedback:** The feedback should be tailored to all aspects of the learner's model like the student's history. When a student is good in some areas but not others, the system should generate scenarios that increase the skill acquisition for this user, for example, could the system create bone samples with an unconventional layout of the facial nerve, and so forth. A briefing preceding the training session could comment on the quality of previous tasks. Minor changes to the model or the task could be done on the fly to adapt to the student's progress.

- **Verbal feedback:** According to the state of the operation and the tools in use, students in early stages can be reminded to change the magnification on the virtual microscope, to switch to a more appropriate type or size of burr, and so forth. Gestures and the interplay of the two tools (e.g., burr and sucker) could be analyzed and the students reminded of the correct usage to improve their dexterity.

- **Verbally initiated dialog:** When the students dissect close to a landmark too quickly, they could be asked which landmark they expect to show up next, to increase the awareness for the distance.

- **Visual feedback:** Since the simulator is based on an immersive environment, visual output is the major way of providing feedback for the user.

- **Audio feedback:** Around landmarks the density of the bone also changes the burring sound. Simulating this effect might help students to identify critical regions.

- **Haptic feedback:** Once the students become confident with the dissection process, exceptions like blockages of the sucker, empty irrigator or damaged drills could be introduced to get them used to distractions from the primary task. Those problems would be modeled to generate additional cues for the students (e.g., though minor haptic effects like a flaky drill or visual effects like missing suction), who should learn to recognize them and to react appropriately.

- **Possible abort of the simulation:** Surgeons supervising operations have identified that, while students are usually confident in the initial phase of the operation, they sometimes become uncertain in how to proceed. The supervisor can identify this situation because the student stops using the safe technique of using long and straight burr strokes to dissect a single landmark at a time and instead begins to dissect more randomly. In a real operation such behavior would cause the surgeon to take over from the student.

Risks

Potential problems involved in the usage of a virtual trainer are generally errors in the models, which could lead to unwanted behavior of the system. Errors in the *domain model* could result in skills being trained wrongly, that is, the student could be forced to repeat wrong behavior over and over again instead of learning to perform a task in the correct way. A wrong *tutoring model* would effect the selection of tasks and could cause part of the training being missed or repeated instead of being presented in a didactic way. A problem in the *student model* might allow the student to "play the simulator," for example., to acquire credits without actually performing as expected. Since the application domain of the simulator is the medical field, such errors can have fatal impact and effective quality assurance measurements have to be taken when authoring or building the actual models.

Summary

This chapter described our bone dissection simulator which is based on the haptic workbench and the currently implemented prototype of a tutoring component. It shows that a major improvement is needed to turn this virtual assistant into an intelligent tutoring system as described by the Artificial Intelligence for Education community. Potential features for this future system have been outlined in the previous chapter. The suggested system could help to improve the training for surgeons while taking load of the teaching experts.

Acknowledgments

The temporal bone dissection simulator has been jointly developed with my colleagues, Duncan Stevenson, Chris Gunn, and Mathew Hutchins at the CSIRO ICT Center.

We would like to thank the surgeons Prof. Stephen O'Leary and Prof. Brian Pyman from the Department of Otolaryngology, University of Melbourne, Royal Victorian Eye and Ear Hospital for their collaboration.

This work was funded under the CeNTIE project. The CeNTIE project is supported by the Australian Government through the Advanced Networks Program of the Department of Communications, Information Technology and the Arts.

References

Gunn, C., Hutchins, M., Adcock M., & Hawkins, R. (2003). Trans-world haptic collaboration. In *SIGGRAPH '03: Sketches & Applications*, San Diego, California. DOI: 10.1145/965400.965495

Hutchins, M., O'Leary, S., Stevenson, D., Gunn, C., & Krumpholz, A. (2005). A networked haptic virtual environment for teaching temporal bone surgery. In *Proceedings of the Medicine Meets Virtual Reality 13 (MMVR2005)*, 204-207. Long Beach, California.

Logitech Technologies. (n.d.). Retrieved June 3, 2006, from http://www. logitech.com

Müller-Tomfelde, C., Paris, C., & Stevenson, D. (2004). Interactive landmarks: Linking virtual environments with knowledge-based systems. In *Proceedings of OZCHI2004 Conference*, Wollongong, Australia.

Reachin Technologies AB. (n.d.). Retrieved June 3, 2006, from http://www. reachin.se

SensAble Technologies. (n.d.). Retrieved June 3, 2006, from http://www. sensable.com

Sewell, C., Morris, D., Blevins, N., Barbagli, F., & Salisbury, K. (2005). Quantifying risky behaviour in surgical simulation. In *Proceedings of Medicine Meets Virtual Reality 13 (MMVR2005).*451-457. Long Beach, California.

Siemer, J., & Angelides, M.C. (1998). A comprehensive method for the evaluation of complete intelligent tutoring systems. *Journal of Decision Support Systems, 22*, 85–102.

Stevenson, D.R., Smith, K.A., McLaughlin, J.P., Gunn, C.J., Veldkamp, J.P., & Dixon, M.J. (1999). Haptic workbench: A multisensory virtual environment. In *Proceedings of SPIE, the International Society for Optical Engineering, 3639,* 356–366.

Wiet, G.J., Stredney, D., Sessanna, D., Bryan, J.A., Welling D.B., & Schmalbrock, P. (2002). Virtual temporal bone dissection: An interactive surgical simulator. *Otolaryngology – Head and Neck Surgery, 127,* 79–83.

Yacef, K., & Alem, L. (1997). Towards an assessment of skill acquisition in student modelling. In B. du Boulay & R. Mizoguchi (Eds.), *Proceedings of AI-ED '97 (Artificial Intelligence in Education)* (pp. 530–536). Kobe, Japan.

Glossary

Preamble[1]

Several of the terms defined and explained to my knowledge do not enjoy having a commonly agreed understanding neither in the wider communities of "information systems", "artificial intelligence", "informatics", or "computer science" nor in the more narrow community of the contributors of this book. Providing such a glossary on the one hand implies thus quite a risk of getting involved into a fruitless debate of meanings of terms. On the other hand, such a glossary may aid in understanding the chapters in this book. I hope furthermore that this glossary will contribute to the inevitable evolution of term-meanings and will impact higher usability and accuracy. This glossary does not necessarily represent a consensus of all book contributors. I do not believe such a consensus would have been possible. The glossary represents my attempt of providing a unified conceptual base for the enterprise of aiding the genesis of intelligent assistant systems, as I see these systems now. I have, for a couple of entries, included further references. In a few cases, when I was unaware of a suitable English reference, I provided German references. Terms in italics are meant to refer to glossary entries. The latter are bold face. I thank Gunter Grieser, Klaus P. Jantke, Alexander Krumpholz, and Yuzuru Tanaka for suggestions regarding an earlier version of this glossary.

Action

"The process or condition of acting or doing (in the widest sense), the exertion of energy or influence; working, agency, operation" (OEDO). In planning the elementary building block of a plan; action may be seen as a syntactic object that has an operational semantics.

Actor

The one acting in a framework in which *actions* occur.

Agent System

See *intelligent assistance*.

Algorithmic Learning

The capability of a *system* of learning to distinguish between the elements of a predefined set of objects by executing an algorithm or program. Executing the algorithm or program enables the system to obtain data that can be used for confirming or refuting automatically generated hypothesis regarding the elements of the predefined object set. Learning is then accomplished if the gathered data is used for working out a set of hypothesis that is sufficient for distinguishing from each other all the objects in the predefined set.

API

Application programming interface. Interface to a software library for developers who want to use that library in their application.

Automatic Assessment

The automated, objective evaluation of task performance. To allow for automatic assessment to take place the quality of the performance has to be measurable.

Cellular Automaton

A *finite state machine* that is capable of communicating with other automata of the same kind and that usually has a rather simple state-space with only a small number of states. John Conway's "game-of-life" is a well-known example of using cellular automata. At http://www.math.com/students/wonders/life/life.html one can find more information and a nice implementation of the game. In this game the automaton's state-space is particularly simple and has only two states, i.e. alive and dead, with the (more or less) obvious state transitions. Assume that a graph is given, i.e., a pair of nodes and edges between them. Two nodes are called adjacent or neighbors if they are connected by an edge. To each node there is allocated an automaton. A subset of these automata can be defined to be in state alive. The state of the game is defined as the subset of the automata that are alive. For each state of the game a follow-up state is defined. For obtaining that follow-up state for each automaton one computes the number of its living neighbors. Then one applies the following rules: (1) a dead automaton with exactly three neighbors that are alive becomes alive itself; (2) an automaton that is alive stays alive if it has exactly two or three neighbors that are alive; and (3) each automaton either dies or stays dead for which the first two rules don't apply.

The graph on which the game is played usually is defined by a chess-board like structure of tiles in which the tiles are considered as the nodes. Two nodes are said to be adjacent if the respective tiles have a common boundary point. It is not difficult to understand this game in terms of finite state machines. Cellular automata can be used for simulating the evolution of large collections of interacting actors with limited individual behavior capacity. Obviously one could play the game on graphs that are inspired by three-dimensional structures such as Rubick's Cube or similar. One could furthermore label the edges of the graph and modify the above rules accordingly such as to break up the symmetry and introduce field effects. For an overview of the history of cellular automata, see e.g., Sankar (2000). A brief history of cellular automata. *ACM Computing Surveys, 32*(1), 80-107.

Choreography

see *coordination*.

Computer

A self-acting device that implements an active *medium* in which a control *process* manages the conditions of *actors* to meet. These conditions include parameters such as the accuracy of representing the utterances they perform, the period of time within which these representations can be accessed, the actors' senses appealed to by the utterances, and the resources the actors have access to. The control process, however, (1) has a representation within the implemented medium that in principle can be accessed and manipulated by the actors and the computer itself, and (2) can be modified by manipulations of that representation. Computers are similar to amplifiers in so far, as they create a process with an imposed structure. They are different from amplifiers in so far as amplifiers take that imposed structure from a dynamic and emerging pattern (i.e., a process) while computers take it from a static pattern (i.e., the control process representation). The currently dominating implementation technology is based on electronics. Patterns of magnetization or voltage are frequently used as the material substrate on top of which the medium is implemented. Mathematical models of the control process include Turing machines, finite automata, the λ-calculus, while-programs, Petri nets and similar. A good source regarding many respective issues is Kozen, D. (1997). *Automata and computability*. New York: Springer Verlag. Computers can be distinguished with respect to whether their basic physical level is conceptualized as discrete (such as binary) or continuous. Computers furthermore can be distinguished with respect to the expressiveness of the language in which the control process representation can be encoded. A computer is usually called general purpose computer if its control process encoding language is as expressive as the language of while-programs. The control-process representation language usually has sub-languages that are tailored towards being highly usable for computer users, i.e., actors who interact with the medium. By incorporating expressions of one of the mentioned sub-languages into the control process representation computer users can modify the control process. The respective activity is called programming (or software development) and the mentioned expressions are called program (or software system). The basic physical level of current general purpose computers is usually conceptualized as discrete. Most recently there are several attempts of employing quantum theory for the conceptualization of the basic physical level of computers, as one believes that significant performance increases can be achieved that way.

Computerized System

A *system* having a component that contains a *computer* or is executed by a computer.

Conditional Judgment

A *judgment* that depends on a logical condition such as judgment U has been made. The concept of conditional judgment enables to in a simple way to deal with aspects of the contextually of human verdictive speech.

Confidence[2]

An *actor's* mental attitude of trusting in or relying on a judgment as well as the degree to which A trusts or relies on the judgment.

Connector

A software component aiding the user of a virtual lab in combining and linking the components of that lab for setting up an experiment.

Constraint

A logical formula or condition, or more general a linguistic expression that is used for restricting the structure, appearance, variability, number, lifetime, etc., of a given class of entities. In data modeling constraints such as multiplicities, cardinalities, functional dependencies etc. are used. In object modeling constraints are put on objects such that their object identity cannot be changed, or that they cannot enter (i.e., become an instance) or leave (i.e., cease being an instance of) certain classes. Languages dedicated to constraint specification have been defined. The currently most well-known of these is perhaps the object constraint language OCL that is a sub-language of the UML. For an accessible outline of the UML and its OCL (that unfortunately is no more up-to-date) see, for example, Bennet S., Skelton J., & Lunn K. (2001). *UML*. New York: McGraw Hill.

Constraint Monitoring

The *activity* of observing and controlling the constraints as applying to an executing process.

Conversational Agent

An *embodied interface agent* of a system Σ that is capable of communicating verbally with the users of Σ.

Cooperative Learning

A *process* of acquiring knowledge or skill that involves several *learners* who contribute to the process, each in their way with their individual capabilities, so that their constrained egoisms contribute to a fruitful learning context.

Coordination

"The action of co-ordinating" (OEDO). This in turn means "to place or arrange (things) in proper position relatively to each other and to the system of which they form parts; to bring into proper combined order as parts of a whole." (OEDO)

CORBA

Common object request broker architecture. An architecture standard for distributed system's architecture that is maintained by the OMG.

Course Creator

The human defining the details of a course in a learning institution such as a university or a school. The term in particular is used to refer to the creator of those courses that employ as a key component an e-learning system.

CT

Computer Tomography (or CAT scan), a technique of using x-rays from various angles to generate a three dimensional image of internal structures like the skull.

Declarative Programming

See *logic programming*.

Deduction

A particular mode of reasoning that is based on axioms and rules. See *induction*.

Deontic Logic

A modal logic for reasoning about permissions (*rights*) and *obligations*.

Didactics

The discipline of to how best deliver the content and organize the *learning process* of a particular group of learners such as a class of pupils or students.

E-Learning

Learning processes that may be driven by a particular didactic goal and that are aided by information and communication technology.

E-Learning System

A *computerized system* that is supposed to aid a learner in practicing a form of technology enhanced learning.

Edit Distance

The distance d(A, s, t) which, for an alphabet A and finite strings s and t over this alphabet (i.e., s, t ∈ A* with A* being the set of all sequences of elements of A) denotes the minimum number of insertion, deletion, or replacement operations needed for transforming s into t. The edit distance is obviously symmetric, i.e., d(A, s, t) = d(A, t, s), for all s, t ∈ A*.

Embodied Interface Agent

An *agent* that is integrated into the user *interface* of a *system* and the representation of which is guided by the *metaphor* COMPUTER IS A LIVING BEING. This being or character is represented to the computer user as a lifelike "body".

Computer output appears then as utterance of that character which even may be anthropomorphized. Introducing this metaphor to agents has the potential of increasing effectiveness and efficiency of human-computer interaction, as metaphors drawn from the area of communication in everyday life can be exploited. The metaphor in particular involves the various modes of human communication, such as speech, facial expressions, and body gestures.

Executability

The quality of being capable of execution or enactment that applies to a specification. While also structure specifications, such as database schemas, may be executable the predicate is mainly applied to programs or algorithms the execution of which means the instantiation of a *process* inside a *computer* that performs activities as specified by the programs or algorithms.

Execution Time

The time at which an instance of a *process model* is executed.

Explorative Learning

A mode of a learning process in which the learner aims at obtaining an overview of the available content or parts of it rather than at understanding the details.

Federation

The definition and/or execution of selection, interoperation, and coordination of intelligent resources that do not have *interfaces* designed for these tasks.

Feedback

The response of a *system* to an event or trigger in its environment. Feedback is understood as particularly important for human learning in so far as it helps the learner to understand his / her current achievements and deficits. It is one of the big challenges in creating e-learning systems to generate and provide to the learner effective and efficient feedback. The impact of feedback on *learning* performance obviously in part is a consequence of the authority that is accredited by the learner to the feedback provider.

Finite State Machine

F is a tuple F = (S, E, A, C, α, ω, t) where S is a finite set of so-called states with subsets α, $\omega \subseteq$ S, the elements of which are called initial and final states respectively. Furthermore, E, A, C are finite sets of events, activities, and conditions. Finally, t is a mapping with the signature t: E$\times$S$\times$C $\rightarrow$ S$\times$C$\times$A. With finite state machines the behavior of a system Σ can be discussed if Σ can be attributed a state and if it responds to external stimuli, the so-called events. Such a discussion is based on the assumptions that (1) Σ initially is in one of the states in α, and that (2) a behavior thread under scrutiny is finished when Σ enters one of the states in ω. The behavior of Σ within a thread of behavior is defined by mapping t which specifies that if Σ is in state s, event e occurs and condition c holds then Σ transitions into state s' and while doing so performs activity a and is in condition c' after that if t(s, e, c) = (s', c', a) holds. The concept of finite state machine can be considered as a *semantic model*, i.e. a model that enables one to create behavior models by providing the basic terms and an overall framework for behavior modeling. In this semantic model the basic terms (i.e., the modeling notions) are "state", "event", "condition", "activity", and "state transition". These modeling notions can be instantiated such as to define individual finite state machines. Creation and representation of finite state machines can be simplified by introduction of abstraction concepts. Abstraction concepts introduce ways of relating to each other domain concepts. Harel has pioneered the use of abstraction concepts with respect to finite state machines. His work was then reused in the object modeling technique OMT of Rumbaugh, et al. A second edition of the book introducing OMT is now available as Blaha, M., & Rumbaugh, J. (2005). *Object-oriented modeling and design with UML*. Upper Saddle River, NJ: Pearson Prentice Hall.

Finite State Transducer

a *finite state machine* that is capable of translating a sub-language S (i.e., a part of a language L) into a sub-language T (of a language M). Often it is assumed that the inputs and outputs of a finite state transducer are represented on an input and an output tape respectively.

Fuzzy Logic

A logic in which the classical assumption is not made that an assertion is either *true* or false. Rather, degrees of truth are considered. Truth values of variables in fuzzy logic may therefore be represented by elements of the unit interval [0, 1]. An assertion in fuzzy logic may therefore be considered as truer than another assertion.

Haptic

The word means related to the sense of touch.

Haptic Device

A computer input/output device which generates three-dimensional force output for the user to feel.

Haptic Workbench

A *computerized system* that has (1) a graphical output device (a monitor), which is visible via a mirror and therefore causes a spatial visual perception in its human user, and (2) one or more *haptic devices* that simulate for the workbench user the capability of carrying out physical operations in the perceived space. The haptic workbench is designed for its users to experience a *haptic virtual environment* in a natural way.

Incomplete Information

True information that is not sufficient for a given *actor* to solve a given *problem*. Take for example a postman in a large city such as New York. If he has to deliver a letter that shows only the name of the receiver and street in which he / she lives but not the house number and apartment number then the information though true might not be sufficient for the letter being delivered and would then considered as incomplete. If one admits problems the solution of which requires infinitely many chunks of information then each finite set of information chunks would have to be considered as incomplete.

Induction

A particular mode of reasoning, i.e., generating a hypothesis H from a pre-supposition P. In this mode the amount of available *semantic information* is increased, i.e., $\sigma(H) > \sigma(P)$. In contrast to induction the term deduction is used for a reasoning mode in which the amount of available semantic information is not increased. Because of this, deductive reasoning if carried out properly, i.e., if following an axiom system that applies, to a *problem* solving context, does not need to be verified, i.e., it comes to true conclusions if starting from true premises. Inductive reasoning, however, requires verification, as it increases the amount of available semantic information and thus excludes more states or situations.

Inductive Inference

The process of reasoning on information that usually (but not always) is incomplete. The term is in particular used to refer to the process of *learning* from incomplete information such as synthesizing a grammar from expressions belonging to a given formal language, see also *induction*.

Information

See *semantic information*.

Information Extraction

The task of identifying and retrieving structured or semi-structured information (e.g., text chunks) in a document that fit a search condition. In particular in use with respect to processing semi-structured documents that is aided by wrappers. Furthermore, the creation of *information* in response to and for processing documents which are stored in a repository. Information extraction thus not necessarily limited to copying chunks of text found in the documents in the repository.

Information System

A *medium* that was implemented with technical means such as a printing press or a *computer* and that serves the purpose of recording, storing, and disseminating linguistic expressions as well as drawing inferences from such expressions (Langefors).

Intelligent Assistance

A mode of aid in human *problem* solving that is realized by a *computerized system* that has machine intelligence incorporated and that can be distinguished from the mode of aid that is provided by a tool or an agent respectively. Assisted problem solving differs from tool-based problem solving in the following respects. Firstly, a tool leaves the burden of working out a plan for solving the problem to its user. An assistant, however, can be actively involved in finding such a plan. Secondly, an assistant can start aiding its user based on goals of this user while a tool responds only to instructions. Assisted problem solving differs from agent-based problem solving in that an assistant maintains a dialog to its user during creation of a plan for problem solution and while executing the plan. An agent rather only reports details regarding the problem solution (if the problem could be solved).

Intelligentpad

A two-dimensional representation of a *meme-media architecture*. It employs the *metaphor* "sheet of paper" for noting the available *meme media*. Its application to the Web provides a framework for reusing functionality of Web application.

Intelligent Tutoring System

A *computerized system* that uses a set of internal *models* for aiding students in improving their *learning* outcomes by adapting the course to the student. Traditionally this set of models includes a domain model, a student model and a tutoring model.

Intelligent User Interface

An intelligent user *interface* of a *system* Σ, i.e., an interface of Σ that has a reasoning capability incorporated. This reasoning capability often is used for *user adaptation* or for combining basic system services in a way that makes it easier for the user to benefit from using Σ.

Interaction Scenario

Patterns for sequences of exchange acts, as they occur in communication such as human conversation, human-computer interaction, or computer communication.

Interface

The set of operations of a system Σ that is accessible at the boundary of Σ, i.e., the set of components of Σ that directly interact with a system Σ' that does not belong to Σ. Each operation in the interface specifies a kind of stimulus to which Σ responds to as well as the way it responds to in case a particular stimulus of that kind occurs.

Interoperation[3]

A *process* in which several independent *systems* operate in conjunction. This is obviously addressing a form of high-level software-reuse. Making this reuse work is by no means a simple task, as not only functionality of the individual systems needs to be looked at. Rather the used communication protocols, data types, and software architectures and presupposed usage *models* need to be considered, as well as the different versioning policies that are applied to the individual systems.

Judgment

The most elementary kind of verdictive utterance. By means of a judgment an actor A, such as a human, accredits a predicate notion P to the instances s of a subject notion S in a way specified by a copula notion C. A judgment thus can be represented as a predicate U(S, P, C, A). The judgment U(Swan, is white, accredits, John) means thus that John to each instance s of "Swan" accredits the predicate notion "is white". Rather than being a universal notion, as in the example discussed right now, the subject notion in a judgment may be an individual notion, as is the case in the following example. U(US, invades Iraq, accredits, John), which means that John accredits to the United States of America the predicate notion "invades Iraq". The concept of judgment is the primitive unit of verdictive speech, as omitting one of the components of the predicate makes the resulting rest not having the quality of a verdict. For a source on the theory of judgment see Pfänder, A. (1921). *Logic*, (In German). Halle an der Saale: Max Niemeyer Verlag.

Knowledge Acquisition

A process in which an *actor* aims at identifying, accessing, and making operational representations of the knowledge that according to the actor's assumption is helpful for executing a task at hand.

Knowledge Atom

A logically simple description of a fact, i.e., a description of a true assertion that is not composed of other fact descriptions.

Knowledge Base

a set of data items representing facts, i.e., true assertions about some system. Usually one considers a knowledge base as being maintained by a knowledge management system.

Landmark

A point of orientation. Knowing the position of an object relative to a landmark helps to find that object once the landmark is identified.

Learner Model

A particular *user model* that takes into account that the user is a learner; therefore particular aspects are included into the model such as 'achievements in learning', 'time spent with learning objects' and the like.

Learning

A *process* of adaptation of a *system* Σ to its environment such that Σ changes its stimulus-response behavior until further adaptation takes place due to learning or forgetting. One typically would accredit having an internal state and in particular goals to a system that one considers as learning. Learning would then be considered as a process of change such as to more effectively or efficiently achieve the goals. That process of change would be considered as mainly affecting the internal state of Σ. Learning thus can be understood as a process of preparation, of becoming more capable of solving given problems or of acquiring world knowledge. Therefore learning often would be exercised in an artificial environment or context (which is not the problem solution environment or context) such as the ones provided by a learning institution, or a learning session respectively. Application of advanced technology has transformed many of these artificial contexts into virtual ones, as is the case with a flight-simulator (for acquiring or perfecting the piloting skills) or an e-learning system (for acquiring or perfecting theoretical knowledge of some kind). As far as humans are concerned this creation of artificial environments for learning even has a genetic base, as the young individuals for a quite long time and by their nature are not fit for the problem solving environment or context and need care and protection.

Learning Algorithm

An algorithm that creates hypothetical knowledge based on examples or observations, see *algorithmic learning*.

Learning Object

An entity consisting of content and functionality that is maintained by an *e-learning system* and is supposed to be delivered to learners while learning with that system.

Learning Theory

(a) the discipline that theorizes about, investigates empirically and aims at optimizing cases of human *learning*; (b) more specific in the sense of computational learning theory: Mathematical theories of *algorithmic learning*. Its main models are *inductive inference*, PAC learning, and Bayesian inference.

Legacy Application

A *computerized* or software *system* that is operative in the context of a software project such as a development or a maintenance project.

Linguistic Analysis

An analysis of something (such as a text, a situation, a process, etc.) in terms of the language means occurring in that something or that are used to deal with it.

Location-Based Federation

A *federation* of a number of systems that depends on the physical location at which the federation is taking place.

Logic Programming

Programming paradigm the languages of which enable writing programs that are based on (1) declaring facts and (2) providing rules for deriving true assertions from facts and already derived *true* assertions. Paradigmatically the programs written in a logic programming language, such as Prolog, do not contain directions regarding how to in detail obtain the desired true assertions. In so far logic programming differs from imperative programming. Programming languages complying with the latter paradigm are for example C, C++, C# or Java. In these languages programs need to explicitly specify the algorithms for obtaining the values of program variables. Programming languages that do not explicitly specify the algorithms for obtaining variable values are also called declarative. The query languages (such as SQL) that come with modern database management systems are typically declarative or at least have expressive declarative sub-languages. While declarative programming languages often are considered as easier to learn and use than imperative languages the latter often are more expressive than the former ones.

Lookup Service

A service that provides the *information* in a repository that best matches a search expression.

Machine Intelligence

The capability of a machine such as a *computer* to solve *problems* the archetypical solution of which, as executed by humans, involves human experts exercising their cognitive capacities. These capacities are often understood as being a consequence of (1) proper use of stored data that is adequate for the problem to solve; (2) sophisticated ways of deriving hypothesis from facts and already derived hypothesis; and (3) the experience based capability of accepting generated hypothesis for later use or of ruling hypothesis out from further use. Machine intelligence often is realized by programs the execution of which creates processes that are similar or resemble real or potential human reasoning processes. Such programs often are implemented with neural networks or logical programming languages such as Prolog.

Medium

"A person or thing which acts as an intermediary", i.e., as "one who acts between others; an intermediate agent; a go-between middleman, mediator." Also "something acting between persons or things ..." (OEDO).

Meme Media

Are *media* for representing and disseminating knowledge that provide direct manipulation operations to humans for editing and disseminating the represented knowledge. A medium is a means enabling agents to meet each other in a way typical to the medium. For example, a book is a medium in which readers can meet authors in the sense that they can perceive their written utterances. The Internet is a medium, as it enables humans to exchange e-mails or to phone each other, etc.

Meme Media Architecture

A software architecture that enables the implementation of *meme media* objects.

Meme Pool

A publishing reservoir of *meme media* objects.

Metadata

Data that is related to other data in the sense that it specifies some of the other data's characteristics or conditions of its use etc. Many different characteristics of data may be important for the users of that data. Therefore many different sets of meta data may be defined and used for each set of data. A frequently used kind of meta data focuses on the structure of that data.

Metaphor

A partial mapping from a cognitive source domain into a cognitive target domain. The mapped concepts in the source domain thus are put into a new context in the target domain. Knowledge regarding the target domain thus can be reused with respect to the mapped source domain concepts. According to Lakoff & Johnson human thinking is essentially metaphorical. Well-known metaphors that were discussed by Lakoff are LIFE IS A JOURNEY and LOVE IS A JOURNEY. In these terms in small caps the term prefixing the infix "is a" is the source domain and the term postfixing that infix the target domain. For more information regarding metaphor see for example Lakoff's chapter in Ortony A. (Ed.). (1993). *Metaphor and thought*. Cambridge University Press (2002 digital printing of the 2nd ed. of 1993). Furthermore the book Lakoff, G., Johnson, M. (1980). *Metaphors we live by*. Chicago: The University of Chicago Press. A number of computer related metaphors was briefly discussed in the preface of this book.

Model

An entity that is used by an actor as a substitute or proxy for another entity (following Stachowiak, see below). The modeler, i.e., *actor* A refers with a model M to a model original O. This reference can be made in a number of different ways, which are denoted as reference modes. Typically this reference is such that (1) A denies some of the characteristics to M that it accredits to O (truncation property); and (2) A recommends using M as a proxy for O only to specified model users, period of time, purposes, location and context of investigation as well as methods and means of such investigation (pragmatic property). Since modeling is not limited to abstracting the model-original reference typically is furthermore such that (3) A accredits to M characteristics he / she does not accredit to O (extension propery). Frequently used reference modes are for example 'descriptive' (A describes O as M, as is the case with the analysis model), 'prescriptive' (A prescribes O as M, as is the case with the design model), 'idealizing' (A idealizes O as M, as is the case with the software process model), and 'constitutive' (A constitutes O as M, as is the case with an ontology for a domain). Models are similar to *metaphors* in that they relate a source entity to a target entity.[4] In Stachowiak's conceptualization models, however, differ significantly from metaphors in that they not-only involve a source-to-target mapping but additionally also involve a target-to-source mapping. The first of these mappings is used to translate the *problem* in terms of the original (that one in a modeling case actually wants to solve) into a problem in terms of the model. Provided the model is chosen suitably then one more likely can solve this proxy problem than one could have solved the original problem. The target-to-source mapping is then used to translate the solution of the proxy problem into a solution candidate of the original problem. The modeler is considered as successful if this candidate solution is an admissible solution of the original problem. For more in depth information regarding models and modeling see, for example:

Stachowiak, H. (1973). *General model theory* (In German). Vienna, New York: Springer Verlag.

Lloyd, E. (1998) Models. In E. Craig (Ed.), *Routledge encyclopedia of philosophy* (pp. 443–447). London; New York: Routledge.

The terminology used in parts of artificial intelligence for talking about models and modeling is quite different and more targeted at modeling processes conducted by *computerized systems*. It technically is quite advanced. Respective references are:

Holte, R. C., & Choueiry, B. C. (n.d.). Abstraction and reformulation in artificial intelligence. *Philosophical transactions of The Royal Society: Biological Sciences, 358*(1435), 1197–1204.

Zucker, J.-D. (n.d.). A grounded theory of abstraction in artificial intelligence. *Philosophical transactions of The Royal Society: Biological Sciences, 358*(1435), 1293–1309.

Monotonicity

A quality of reasoning *processes* of a particular kind, i.e., the knowledge obtained throughout the reasoning process will not be invalidated by the very process and thus the amount of knowledge as obtained during the reasoning process is not decreasing.

Multimodal Presentation Markup Language

A markup language for defining multimodal presentations.

Natural Language Processing

An automated *process* that has an input parameter, which is a chunk of text in natural language and the syntactical or semantic characteristics of which control the execution of the process.

Navigation

A *metaphorical* denotation of a particular activity in human-computer interaction. The metaphor COMPUTER USE IS NAVIGATION presupposes another metaphor, the metaphor of COMPUTER IS AN INFORMATION SPACE or COMPUTER IS A KNOWLEDGE SPACE. The metaphor COMPUTER USE IS NAVIGATION is supposed to exploit human knowledge regarding the ways of effectively and efficiently move from ones current location (i.e., the source location) in a given part of the world to a target location in that part of world. The set of parts of the real world with respect to which navigation is/was of particular importance includes "ocean", "space", "city", "complex of buildings", etc. Navigation within these parts of the world usually works such that with a set of dedicated tools firstly the source location is identified, as the relative position of the current location to a point of reference is identified. Secondly, the target location is determined. This involves the purpose of the journey or trip that is made through the affected part of the world. Thirdly, a path is determined that leads from the source location to the target location. Fourthly, that path is actually traversed. Obviously, a number of navigations from a source to a target may be combined. For choosing the path from source to target location as well as for traversing that path a number of models of the part of the world (i.e., maps) is used. To make computer use resemble more navigation first of all a user location in the virtual knowledge space is defined. The user is permanently notified of his / her current location. Furthermore, locations in the information space are named and signs are introduced that (similar to traffic signs) point towards these locations. Additionally there is help functionality available for identifying and explaining the information and functionality that is accessible at the named locations in information space. Last but not least there is transfer functionality (so-called links) accessible for changing the current user location into certain target locations. If for a given target location such transfer functionality is not available then usually an immediate transfer to that target location is still possible if the user knows the name of the target location. For the wider audience the navigation metaphor became a topic only after the invention of the Web. It is, however, worth noting that it is actually in use for quite some time. For legacy computerized systems with complex interface navigation can be used for explaining how to use these legacy systems. A change, however, is that now navigation mainly refers to the content while it in the past referred to the user interface. In more abstract terms can navigation be understood as a process of successive creation of filters for the elements of a predefined set of items out of the meta data regarding these items.

Neural Network

" ... is first and foremost a graph, with patterns represented in terms of numerical values attached to the nodes of the graph and transformations between patterns achieved via simple message-passing algorithms. Many neural network architectures, however, are also statistical processes, characterized by making particular probabilistic assumptions about data. ... Neural networks have found a wide range of applications, the majority of which are associated with problems in pattern recognition and control theory. In this context neural networks can best be viewed as a class of algorithms for statistical modeling and prediction. Based on a source of training data, the aim is to produce a statistical model of the process from which the data are generated, so as to allow the best prediction to be made for new data." Jordan, M. I., & Bishop C. M. (2004). Neural networks. In A. B. Tucker (Ed.), *Computer science handbook*. Chapman & Hall / CRC and ACM.

Notion

A set of terms that within a given context can be used interchangeably (adapted from Kamlah & Lorenzen, see below). Each of these terms can be used to represent the notion. A term is a word or phrase that for use in a specified context has been given a meaning. While, certainly, for terms and notions a mental correlate exists the definition here avoids using that correlate in an attempt to focus on what makes a notion capable of being intellectual property of a community of humans. For more detail on notions, one may refer to Kamlah, W., & Lorenzen, P. (1996). *Logical propaedeutics: Preschool of sensible discourse* (In German). Stuttgart, et al.: Metzler.

Obligation

A legally, contractually, morally, or otherwise motivated duty to comply with regulations such as to perform or desist certain activities under stated conditions.

Orchestration,

See *coordination*.

Persistence

The quality of enduring temporally. The predicate is, for example, applied to variables that survive the termination of certain programs. That survival may be guaranteed by storing the value of the variable in a database. That database may or may not be maintained by a database management system. For example, the environment variables of an application system such as the standard printer, the location of recently processed files, or user profiles are typically not maintained by a database management system.

Pervasive Computing

An open system of intelligent resources in which users can dynamically select, interoperate, and coordinate some of these intelligent resources to perform their jobs satisfying their dynamically changing demands.

Phantom

A *haptic device* from Sensable Technologies.

Plan

A *model* in the prescriptive or idealizing mode of reference to the *process* of solving a problem. Models of the structure of a building, etc. often are called plan as well.

Plan Execution

The activity of firstly creating and secondly enacting an instance of a plan.

Plan Monitoring

The activity of observing and controlling the enactment of an instance of a plan.

Plan Revision

The subprocess in planning in which a plan has to be corrected according to recently acquired information from other subprocesses such as monitoring.

Planning

The activity of creating a plan.

Planning Assistant

An assistant dedicated for humans to use for working out plans.

Planning Time

The time at which a plan is produced.

Planning Tool

A tool dedicated for humans to use for working out plans.

Presentation Agent

An *embodied interface agent* for delivering presentations that are attractive for humans.

Presentation Style

A term for addressing the particular way in which an e-learning system presents its content to the learner. Usually the learner can choose the style. Examples of presentation styles are example-oriented (a style in which the contents is presented in an example-oriented manner) and theory-oriented (a style in which the contents presentation is oriented at the Mathematical triad of definition, theorem, and proof).

Probability

The likelihood of an event in terms of a formal Mathematical approach. Nowadays the most frequently used Mathematical approach to probability is the axiomatic system of Kolmogorov.

Problem

A negatively assessed difference between a current and a potential state of a *system*.

Process

A coherent real or mental entity that endures temporally and achieves something. Often processes are understood as emergent entities to which several actors or entities contribute their capability to carry out actions. Accordingly processes are defined as partially ordered sets of actions. Due to being emergent processes have characteristics that are not inherited of any of the contributing actors or entities. The set of kinds of process that have been found interesting for computer science includes "business process", "workflow", "software process", "usage", and in particular "learning process". For managing and enacting process specifications a specific kind of infrastructure software system has been invented, i.e., workflow management (and similar) *systems*. The specifications that are maintained by a workflow management system often are called process as well. In that case the actual processes that comply with a given process specification are often called process instance. That is actually a view of the notion process that is consistent with the view of process concept in operating systems or computer architecture. Formal models of process were invented for in particular discussing software specification and program properties. Among the more well-known of these formal models are Petri nets, CSP (communicating sequential processes), CCS (calculus of communicating systems), and ACP (algebra of communicating processes). For much more information on formal approaches to processes and in particular CCS see, for example, Milner's chapter in Van Leeuwen, J. (1990). *Handbook of theoretical computer science, Vol. B: Formal models and semantics*. Amsterdam, et al.: Elsevier & The MIT Press.

Prolog

See *logic programming*.

Proxy Object

An entity that functions as a substitute of a given entity.

Repository Service

A service that enables managing a defined type of structured entities in a database that is called repository.

Right

A legally, contractually, morally, or otherwise motivated permission to comply with regulations such as to perform or desist certain activities under stated conditions.

Ripple Down Rule

An if-then-else-exception rule, i.e. a predicate R(C, X, T, F, E) that includes logical condition C and X, and predicates T, F, and E. The semantics of the predicate is that if (1) $C \wedge \neg X$ is true then T is evaluated, (2) if $\neg C \wedge \neg X$ is true then F is evaluated, and (3) if X is true then E is evaluated. If one interprets X as an exception condition then exception handling is performed in case that X is true. Otherwise T and F are performed in case condition C is true or false respectively. As T, F, and E are predicates they may be ripple down rules and thus ripple down rules may be nested. Nesting these rules, however, should be constrained such that the graph is a tree that results from representing rules as nodes and representing the nesting relationship as directed edges. A set of nested ripple down rules can be understood as representing knowledge if one considers that the predicates T, F, and E may also represent an activity to be carried out by some actor. Nesting ripple down rules thus can be seen as a specific way of specifying preconditions of activities.

Role

The potential behavior of a user of a computerized system. Specifying *obligations* and *rights* of a user is a way of specifying the role of that user.

Search Engine

A *computerized system* that can be used for defining filters and for identifying and retrieving documents stored in a respective infrastructure system (such as the Web, a computer or a document repository) that match the defined filter.

Self-Controlled Learning

A mode of a learning process in which the learner defines the learning outcomes himself / herself.

Semantic Analysis

An analysis of something (such as a text, a situation, or a process, etc.) in terms of what the entities mean that are part of or related to the analyzed something.

Semantic Information

The quality of a constraint to function as a filter and to eliminate states of affairs out of a set of eligible such states. Compare, for example p. 435 of Johnson-Laird P. N. (1988). A taxonomy of thinking. In R. J. Sternberg & E. E. Smith (Eds.), *The psychology of human thought* (pp. 429–457). Cambridge, et al.: Cambridge University Press. The amount $\sigma(C)$ of semantic information contained in a constraint C is proportional to the cardinality of the set of states of affairs eliminated by that constraint. Filters in application system are a good example of how semantic information works. Take for example the Apple "song" management system "iTunes". It provides the capability of defining a filter (i.e., a constraint) by typing a search string into a window. iTunes filters then those mp3-files out of a play list that match the search string. The more semantic information this string contains, the smaller the number of files that is displayed to the user. If the user wants to listen to a particular "song" then the amount of information contained in the search string S needs to be increased such that out of the play list only a few songs are displayed and a choice can be made out of these based on the meta information available for theses "songs". Note, that the amount $\sigma(S)$ of information contained in the string S depends on the play list L with which the search string is matched. If too much semantic information is contained in the search string (i.e., this information is inconsistent with the play list) then no "song" at all is displayed to the user. If no information at all or incomplete information is contained in the search string then too many "songs" are displayed to the user for him or her to choose the wanted one. Please note finally that there are many publications about "information". In a recent one Claude Shannon, the inventor of the mathematical theory of communication (that often is referred to as information theory), is quoted "The word 'information' has been given different meanings by various writers in the general field of information theory. It is likely that at least a number of these will prove sufficiently useful in certain applications to deserve further study and permanent recognition. It is hardly to be expected that a single concept of information would satisfactorily account for the numerous possible applications of this general field." Compare, Floridi, L. (Ed.). (2004). Information.

The Blackwell Guide to the philosophy of computing and information (pp. 40–61). Blackwell Publishing. An interesting recent publication is also Lyre H. (2002). *Information theory* (In German). München: Wilhelm Fink Verlag GmbH & Co. KG.

Semantic Model

A *model* that is used in the constitutive reference mode and the original of which is a class of models. It is also known as "modeling grammar" (Ron Weber). It defines what a model (of a particular kind) is and in that sense is supposed to aid in the creation of models. A semantic model provides a number of modeling notions and a number of abstraction concepts. The modeling notions are going to be instantiated by modelers when these cognitively constitute the domain they want to model. Well-known modeling notions are "entity type" (entity relationship-model), "class" (object models), "table" (relational model), or "state" (finite state machines) and similar. The modeling notions of a semantic model function as an ontology, as they enable a modeler to cognitively constitute a domain of interest (also known as universe of discourse). The domain concepts, i.e., the instantiated modeling notions may or may not be type-like. In a finite state machine each of its states typically would be understood as an individual notion. In a class diagram, however, the classes typically would be considered as universals. A class "employee" for example would typically serve as a framework for managing several "employee"—objects, i.e., instances of that class. The abstraction concepts of a semantic model serve as a framework for conveniently relating to each other the domain concepts. The perhaps most frequently used abstraction concepts often are referred to by the terms "specialization", "aggregation", "classification", "refinement", and "abstraction layering". Specialization is often used for deriving new domain concepts by adding detail to already defined domain concepts. Its inverse "generalization" accordingly is often used for deriving new domain concepts by omitting detail from already defined domain concepts. Aggregation is often used for creating new domain concepts out of already defined ones in the sense of a "part-whole-relationship". Its inverse decomposition accordingly is used for breaking up a concept into part-concepts. Classification is often used for defining relationships between domain concepts that are similar to the one between a container and the things it can contain. Refinement is often used for replacing a concept by a model and fit that model into the model that contained that concept. The opposite operation is often called clustering. Abstraction layering often is used for grouping model parts according to the conceptual distance to an actor such as a user.

Semantic Retrieval

A mode of retrieving entities of a given kind, such as documents, that involves a filter that focuses on the meaning of contents of the entities that are searched for.

Semantic Web

A future version of the Web in which parts of documents stored in the Web are annotated with predefined labels such as to enable *computerized systems* to adequately process the stored documents. The semantics achieved by these annotations might be considered as quite limited. Labeling document parts, however, establishes a partially mapping out of a syntactic domain (i.e., the stored documents) without meaning into a semantic domain (i.e., the definitions of the terms used as labels) in which things have an agreed meaning. If more or more rigorous semantics would be needed then more terms might be defined and used as labels or the definitions can be formalized respectively. Finally, the semantics introduced by the defined terms can be used as a *semantic model* (i.e., the labels can be considered as modeling notions) and abstraction concepts can be introduced for creating relationships between the domain concepts.

Semi-Structured Document

A document that does not necessarily fit, or for which there does not exist, a predefined schema, that, however, more or less fits a non-trivial obvious pattern of variable and variable value association. Examples of semi-structured documents are HTML files, XML files, and this glossary.

Shallow Parser

A parser that parses linguistic expressions such as natural language sentences "… to a point where a rudimentary level of grammatical structure and meaning can be realized; this is often used in order to identify passages of text which can then be analyzed in further depth to fulfill the particular objective."

Quotation retrieved February 12, 2006, from http://portal.bibliotekivest.
no/terminology.htm.

Similarity Measure

A function s that for each two elements a, b of a set S obtains a quantitative
expression s(a, b) that measures the degree of similarity of a and b.

Storyboard

A conceptual specification of the *navigation* scenarios available to the users
of a *computerized system*. Storyboards thus can be used in representing a
learner community's experiences with a particular e-learning system. Storyboards have been formalized as story algebras and in particular as Kleene
algebras with test. Formalized as Kleene algebras (see for a discussion of this
type of algebra for example, Kozen, D. (1997). *Automata and computability*.
New York, et al.: Springer Verlag) with test equational reasoning becomes
applicable to storyboards and can be used for adapting the functionality to
the users who have access to it. While this adaptation initially is a design-
time adaptation it can be combined with data mining methods and machine
learning procedures for identifying changes in the behaviour of users and
thus in principle can also be used for run-time adaptation, i.e., after system
implementation. It is, however, clear that far reaching changes should be
carried out only on respective decision of the user.

Surgical Landmark

A part of the anatomy which helps locating other anatomical structures in
surgical anatomy.

System

"… a set of interdependent components (…) that create a whole entity. The
components are dynamically linked. That is to say, each one affects and is affected by other components." see p. 73 of Ahituv, N., & Neumann, S. (1990).
Principles of information systems for management. Dubuque, IA: Wm. C.
Brown Publishers. The point that makes the system concept important is its
extreme generality, which results in a common terminology being provided
for talking about such diverse things as software, organizations, individual
living beings, and inanimate entities such as atoms, planets, or solar systems.

For a book dedicated to systems theory, see Baecker, D. (Ed.). (2002). *Introduction into systems theory: Niklas Luhmann* (In German). Heidelberg: Carl-Auer-Systeme Verlag. A couple of mathematical papers contributing to system theory are included in Albrecht, R. (Ed.). (1998). *Systems: Theory and practice.* Vienna: Springer-Verlag Wien New York. Systems are usually studied in their interaction with their environment, i.e., with something they interact with and that does not belong to them. Systems are then supposed to show a stimulus-response behavior, i.e., when certain events happen in their environment then they issue a response. This is what makes the system concept suitable for modeling computerized systems, as it may serve as a framework for implementing stimulus-response relationships as input-output relationships. Each of these relationships that is implemented by a system can be considered as an operation. The mentioned response to a stimulus, i.e., the output to an input, is generated by an event-depending interaction of the system's components. This interaction often is conceptualized as an exchange of matter, energy, or information. The exchange of information can be conceptualized as a communication, i.e., a message exchange. Obviously, for applications of the system concept in computer science the information exchange is of particular importance. The system concept is assumed to be of general applicability. Thus the system components can be considered as systems. This enables a divide-and-conquer approach to systems design being used that is known as method of Langefors. It consists in the adaptation of the ancient Greek method of analysis and synthesis as applied to systems, see Kaschek, R., Schewe, K.-D., Wallace, C., & Matthews, C. (2004). Story boarding for Web-based information systems. In D. Taniar & J.W. Rahayu (Eds.), *Web information systems* (pp. 1–33). Hershey, PA: Idea Group Publishing.

System Adaptivity

The capability and enactment thereof of a system Σ to change its interface such that it better fits the needs, capabilities, or disabilities of its users. The adaptivity of Σ thus not only requires a model of each of its user types incorporated into Σ. Rather, also means are required for deciding which change to carry out under what conditions.

Technology Enhanced Learning

A form of learning that is supported by advanced technology such as *computers*, agents, assistants, and the Internet. One of the driving factors of technology enhanced learning is the high speed with which new products or new versions of new products are created. Traditional learning and teaching is often assumed to be incapable of meeting the current demands. Another driver of technology enhanced learning is the demand to exploit expert knowledge and skill more effective and efficient than possible with current technology.

Temporal Bone

The part of the human skull that surrounds the middle ear and the inner ear.

Temporal Bone Surgery

The surgical procedure of dissecting parts of the *Temporal Bone*. This operation is done for a mastoidectomy, i.e., removal of infected part of the mastoid, or to gain access to deeper structures like the inner ear and a necessary step of a cochlear hearing aid implantation.

Temporal Bone Surgery Simulator

A hardware and software supported simulation of *temporal bone surgery* for use in a training scenario.

Therapy Planning

The process of designing a therapy of a patient's disease.

Truth

The quality aspect of asserting speech that makes a sensible person in an adequate context assent to the assertion (Peter Janich). Note that this is a definition inspired by pragmatism. Other definitions exist. For example definitions that are more in line with a traditional understanding of the philosophy of the natural sciences such as Physics or Chemistry and according to which truth could be understood as coincidence with objective reality. These ways of understanding truth, however, are threatened from suffering either of the following difficulty. As far as is known that has changed significantly over time what was held for true and this includes even the natural sciences and mathematics. This seems to suggest that many beliefs that were held in the past, contrary to what was believed at that time, actually were not true. There is only little reason to believe that this ongoing process ever will stop that results in the things being changed that are held for true. While the truth definition inspired from pragmatism seems to admit an easy to deal with truth criteria (just check it empirically) and has no problem with the historic evolution of knowledge it seems that truth criteria for the alternative approach to defining truth are hard to come up with or to use. For a more in-depth-discussion of truth see, for example, Janich, P. (1996). *What is truth?* (In German). Munich: C. H. Beck.

Two-Level Learning Algorithm

A *learning algorithm* that first learns to distinguish between the types of object and then learns to distinguish between the instances of these object types.

User Adaptation

The process (and its outcome) of changing the user interface of a comput-erized system or the functionality of that system such that the users of that system can be expected to more effectively and efficiently achieve the goals for which they interact with that computerized system.

User Model

A model of a user of a *computerized system* such as an *e-learning system*. Such a model needs to be incorporated in some way into the e-learning system if that system is supposed to behave in a learner-specific way. If moreover maintainability and exchangeability of learner models are an important design goal then the model needs to be explicitly represented in the *system* architecture as a component. Obviously any *computerized system* has a user model incorporated. This model corresponds to a presupposition regarding what system's functionality and quality makes sense. The user model in general, however, needs not to be explicitly represented.

Virtual Assistant

The first version of an assistant system incorporated in the *temporal bone surgery simulator* as a component.

Virtual Environment

A *system* that creates physical stimuli for the user's senses. For the user this creates the illusion of being in an environment which does not physically exist. The more stimuli are being created and the better their synchronization is, the easier it is for the user to feel emerged in that virtual environment.

Virtual Knowledge Space

The *metaphor* of space applied to a set of representations of knowledge. Venues in space correspond to individual representations and streets or paths between spatial venues correspond to relationships between the knowledge chunks that are represented in the respective venues. Decal information corresponds to links. See also *navigation*.

Virtual Lab

A software *system* that enables a *learner* to practice self-controlled learning by providing the capability of setting up and conducting the experiments that appear reasonable to the learner. The term experiment is here understood as "defining a scenario that can be simulated by the software system and that allows obtaining qualitative and quantitative insight into the scenario." The scenario will, as a key component, contain a model of a structure, a process, or similar regarding which the learner needs to acquire knowledge or the capability of dealing with it appropriately.

Virtual Trainer

The name for a future simulator component, implementing all aspects of an *intelligent tutoring system*. Since it should not only assist the student, but replace the need for permanent feedback by a supervising expert, the name *virtual trainer* was chosen.

Voxel

A cubical data point in a 3D dataset (compares to a pixel in a 2D dataset).

VRML

Virtual reality modeling language. A declarative language to describe a hyperlinked 3D scene.

Web Application

A computer program integrated into the Web and potentially using the Web as a source of content or functionality. Access to these is usually via Web browsers. An HTML-based front-end utilizes resources provided by a remote HTTP server.

Web Information System

An *information system* that is integrated into the Web, i.e., that enables Web users accessing it and that may also enable its users to access the Web.

Web Service

"A Web Service is a software component that is described via WSDL and is capable of being accessed via standard network protocols such as but not limited to SOAP over HTTP." Definition accessed February 12, 2006 from http://www.oasis-open.org/committees/wsia/glossary/wsia-draft-glossary-03.htm.

Wicked Problem

A *problem* that is such that attempts to solve the problem lead to the problem being redefined. Related to Lehman's SPE classification of software that is discussed in software evolution and in which S-type programs (specifyable or static), E-type programs (evolving programs that provide functionality for controlling real world processes), and P-type programms (all programms that are not S-type or E-type) are distinguished. Obviously wicked problems correspond to E-type programms. For more information on software evolution see, e.g., Lehman, M. M., & Ramil, J. F. (2002). Software evolution and software evolution processes. *Annals of Software Engineering, 14,* 275–309.

Wrapper

A program dedicated to extracting information out of documents.

Endnotes

[1]   In the sequel a number of quotations is used from the Oxford English Dictionary Online. These quotations are identified with the acronym OEDO appearing as an embraced postfix.

[2]   This definition is derived from the one in the Oxford English Dictionary Online.

[3]   The definition is derived from the OEDO definition of "interoperable".

[4]   Both of them are similar to simile and analog, as they are reference concepts and the purpose of referencing is information transfer.

About the Authors

Roland H. Kaschek (MSc, mathematics; PhD, mathematics; DSc, applied informatics) is an associate professor with the Department of Information Systems at Massey University, New Zealand. His research interest is in conceptual modeling including its philosophical, linguistic, and mathematical foundations and its application.

* * *

Gunter Grieser is working in the fields of learning theory, machine learning, and data mining, as well as e-learning. He studied artificial intelligence at the Technical University Leipzig and worked in the research groups of Professors K.P. Jantke, W. Bibel, and J. Fürnkranz. He earned his PhD in 2001 and is now working as a research assistant with the Computer Science Department at the Technical University, Darmstadt.

Achim Hoffmann studied computer science and philosophy at the Technische University at Berlin (TU Berlin), Germany. In 1985, he earned a Master of Science in computer science (Diplom-Informatiker); in 1992, he earned a PhD in computer science, and in 1993 a PhD in philosophy with a thesis on the philosophical foundations of artificial intelligence from TU Berlin. In 1997, he earned a Habilitation in computer science from the same institution. He has been lecturer, senior lecturer, and since 2001, an associate professor at the University of New South Wales, Sydney, Australia. His current research interests are in the area of NLP and knowledge acquisition.

Christoph Igel studied sports science, history, political science, and education at Saarland University (1989-1996), and worked on a doctorate in sports science, education, and modern history at Saarland University (1997-2000). Since 2001, he has worked as the scientific assistant of Dr. Reinhard Daugs, chair of sport science. Since 1998, he has been part of the joint coordination of the Information Technologies in European Sport and Sport Science (ITES) project (http://ites.uni-saarland.de), which was backed by the European Commission. Since 1999, he has cooperated in the Virtual Saar University (VISU) (http://visu.uni-saarland.de), which was backed by the Saarland Ministry for Education, Culture, and Science and Saarland University. Since 2001, he has worked on the joint coordination of the e-Learning in Movement and Training Science (eBuT) project, which was backed by the Federal Ministry for Education and Research. Since 2002, he has served as deputy manager of the Competence Center at the "Virtual Saar University" of Saarland University.

Kimihito Ito is an associate professor at Hokkaido University. He earned a PhD in electrical engineering from Hokkaido University in 1999. His research interests are in the areas of bioinformatics, artificial intelligence, and Web engineering. In particular, he has developed an IntelligentPad system called CHIP, with which users can wrap existing Web application with pads to be combined with other Web applications to compose new tools. He also developed an ILP system called BORDA.

Klaus Jantke engaged in studies of mathematics at Humboldt University Berlin (1970-1975), and in 1975, received a diploma in mathematics at Humboldt. In 1979, he earned a PhD in computer science; in 1984, he earned a Facultas Docendi and Habilitation (DrSc) in computer science, winning awards such as the Karl Weierstrass Prize in 1977 and the Humboldt Prize in 1981. He has held professorships at Kuwait University, Leipzig University of Technology, and Hokkaido University Sapporo, heading several research and development projects sponsored by DFG, by several German Federal Ministries such as for Research and Technology (BMFT), for Education and Research (BMBF), for Economics (BMWi), for Economics and Labor (BMWA), and by NATO and other institutions. He has done additional teaching at Ilmenau University of Technology, Saarland University Saarbrücken, Darmstadt University of Technology, and Darmstadt University of Applied Sciences. He has been a visiting researcher at ICSI, Berkeley (USA), and the Fujitsu Research Labs, Numazu, Japan. His main research and development interests are in algorithmic learning theory, meme media technology, and technology enhanced learning. Since 2005, he has been the chief executive officer of FIT Leipzig, the Research Institute for Information Technologies Leipzig, Germany.

Since 1999, **Sabina Jeschke** has initiated and headed numerous e-learning, e-teaching and e-research projects. She worked as an assistant teacher with the Department of Math and earned her doctorate in 2004. Holding a scholarship from the German National Academic Foundation, she spent several months of research at NASA at Moffet Field, CA. In 2000-2001, she worked as an instructor at Georgia Tech in Atlanta. She is one of the principal forces behind the modernization of the mathematical education at the TU Berlin. Since 2005, she has been the head of MuLF Multimedia Center for e-Learning, e-Teaching, & e-Research (MuLF) at the TU Berlin. Her research is aimed at developing new concepts for cooperative virtual knowledge spaces, in particular their application in e-learning, e-teaching, e-research, and e-science in mathematics, natural sciences, and engineering.

Alexander Krumpholz received a Diplom-Ingenieur (equivalent master's degree) in applied informatics from the University of Klagenfurt, Austria (2000). In 1997, he spent six months in Maryland (USA), developing a high performing database application for a successful Web service provider. Since 2001, he has lived in Australia and holds a position as a research engineer for the Commonwealth Scientific and Industrial Research Organization (CSIRO). During this period, he has been a member of various groups within CSIRO, working on a knowledge portal, a search engine, and CSIRO's Haptic Workbench, a platform for Immersive Haptic Virtual Environments.

His research interests are in data and knowledge engineering, information retrieval, visualization, and virtual environments.

Steffen Lange has scientific interests in the following sub-areas of theoretical computer science and artificial intelligence: recursion theory, formal language theory, algorithmic learning theory, and machine learning. He earned the diploma in mathematics and physics in 1984 and a PhD in computer science in 1984—both from Humboldt University, Berlin. He habilitated in computer science at Leipzig University in 2000. In April 2004, he became a professor for theoretical computer science at Darmstadt University of Applied Sciences.

Nataliya Lamonova was born in Magadan, Russia, in 1974. She received the engineer of computer systems degree in computer science in 1997. She became candidate of technical sciences (equivalent PhD) in 2001 on control systems and processes from Kharkiv National University of Radio Electronics, Kharkiv, Ukraine. For six months she was in the Meme Media Laboratory in Japan as a COE postdoctoral fellow. She is currently a senior researcher at the Control Systems Research Laboratory. She has more then 30 scientific publications. Her current research interests are neuro-, fuzzy- hybrid systems, logic programming, meme media technology, forecasting, emulation, and classification of time series.

Carsten Müller is a software developer at SAP AG in Walldorf, Germany. Born in Karlsruhe and raised in Bruchsal, he graduated from Schoenborn Grammar School, Bruchsal, in 1996. After receiving his Master of Computer Engineering from the University of Mannheim in 2002, he started working at SAP AG in Walldorf. He is a PhD student at the FIT Leipzig and is thereby sponsored by SAP AG. His research interests are in information extraction and learning systems for wrapper induction, and their integration into text retrieval systems and SAP Solutions.

Son Bao Pham is currently a PhD student in the School of Computer Science and Engineering, University of New South Wales, Australia. He obtained a Bachelor of Computer Science with Honor Class 1 and The University Medal in 2001 from UNSW. His research interests are natural language processing, knowledge acquisition, and machine learning.

Thomas Richter earned his PhD in 2000 in physics on Quantum Hall conductance and noncommutative geometry. Between 2000 and 2002, he worked as project leader for still image compression, JPEG2000, at the AlgoVision Technology GmbH. While staying active in the JPEG2000 ISO committee, he moved back to the University of Technology Berlin in 2002, where he holds a position as scientific researcher in the Matheon Research Center for key technologies of the Berlin universities. There, he is the chief developer and designer of the Virtual Laboratories research project, G4 of the Matheon, which provides a cooperative learning environment for statistical mechanics. Dr. Richter taught courses in linear algebra and image compression, coordinates the assessment of the junior teaching staff, and develops image compression software for Pegasus Imaging in the U.S. His main research focus is the development of new teaching concepts in mathematics and physics by the application of new media, and image compression.

Klaus-Dieter Schewe (MSc, PhD, DSc) is a full professor at Massey University in New Zealand and director of Massey's Information Science Research Center. His major research interests are database theory and systems, logic in databases and systems development methodologies, in particular for Web information systems.

Roberta Sturm completed studies of sport science focusing on informatics at the University of Technology Darmstadt (1996-2001). From 2001-2004, she served as scientific assistant on the project eLearning in Movement and Training Science (eBuT) (http://www.ebut.de), which is backed by the Federal Ministry for Education and Research at Saarland University. Since 2003, she has served as scientific assistant at the Competence Center at the "Virtual Saar University" of Saarland University (http://visu.uni-saarland.de).

Yuzuru Tanaka is a professor with the Department of Computer Science, Hokkaido University, director of Meme Media Laboratory, Hokkaido University, and a professor of bioinformatics at the National Institute of Informatics. He earned a BEng in electrical engineering; an MEng in electronics from Kyoto University (1972 and 1974, respectively); and a DrEng in computer science from the University of Tokyo (1985). He joined Hokkaido University in 1977. Since then, he has been studying parallel processor architectures, database theory, database machine, and media architectures.

Bernhard Thalheim (MSc, PhD, DSc) is a full professor at Christian Albrechts University, Germany. His major research interests are database theory, logic in databases, and systems development methodologies, in particular for Web information systems.

Alexei Tretiakov (MSc, PhD) is a senior lecturer with the Department of Information Systems, Massey University (Palmerston North, New Zealand). His research interests range from stochastic cellular automata and object-oriented database management systems to Web-based systems and e-learning.

Index

A

abstract program 135
accepted open standards 249
accuracy 110
Action 16, 281
Actor 123, 115, 281
Agent System 170, 171, 281
algorithmic learning 36
Analysis of Didactic Potentials 225
ANNIE 98
annotation 102
API 281
Approaching distance 270
Artificial Intelligence 146
artificial neural network 23
assessment 274
assistance systems 183
assisted KB 106
Audio feedback 277
Austin's Speech Act Theory 69
Automatic Assessment 282
AV-system component 150

B

base types 131
basic KB 106

behabitives 69
BeLearning 235
blended learning 260
body 135
Boolean query 132
Built-in annotations 93

C

category 93
Cellular Automata 252
Cellular Automaton 252, 282
character agent 148
Chinese Room Argument 214
Choreography 185, 282
co-operative 12
commissives 69
complete 125
Complexity 129
component 152
Computer 283
Computerized System 284
concept 70
condition 135
Conditional Judgment 72, 75, 284
Confidence 65, 71, 284
Connector 249, 251, 284

Consistency Proof Obligations 138
consistent 12, 76
Consolidation of Basis 225
constraint 18, 20, 284
constraint evaluation 21
Constraint Monitoring 20, 284
content schemata 134
Contextuality 73
conversational agent 164, 285
cooperative learning 235, 285
coordination 182, 285
CORBA 249, 285
Course Creator 239, 240, 285
CT 285
Custom annotations 95

D

DaMiT 216, 222
DaMiT project 222
DaMiT system 222
DATALOG 132
DBProxyPad 202
Decidability 129
Declarative Programming 285
Deduction 286
default node 90
Demonstration setup 246
Deontic Logic 286
deontic logic 116
Design of Assistance Functionality 225
DFG Research Center 235
didactics 221, 286
dimensions 125
Dissection level 270
document management 234
domain 125
domain model 273
dynamically 244
dynamic consistency proof obligation 139
dynamic constraint 138

E

E-Learning 212, 216, 219, 235, 286
E-Learning System 216, 286
e-learning system's assistance 219
eBologna 235

eBuT 216
edit distance 102, 286
Embodied Interface Agent 146, 286
encourage self-guided learning 248
equational theory 114
error model 273
Evaluation 226
example-oriented 218
exclusion 127
executability 16, 287
execution time 22, 287
exercitives 69
expert system 89
explorative learning 235, 287
expositives 69
extension 76

F

Federation 185, 287
feedback 219, 267, 287
Finite State Machine 288
Finite State Transducer 288
finite state transducers (FST) 91, 98
fully defined 12
fuzzy logic 169, 288

G

GATE 98
general story space proof obligation 137
granularity & structure 243
graphical user interface (GUI) 174
ground fact 132
GST 189
guarded process 122
guarded program 135
GUI 251

H

Haptic 289
haptic device 266, 289
Haptic feedback 277
Haptic Workbench 289
hasAnno 95
hasString 95
headVerbPos 94
headVerbString 94

HERM 117
hierarchies 135
Holistic Learner 258

I

IAS 67
idea 75
Implementation 225
Implementation in research 247
incomplete information 16, 289
induction 17, 289
inductive inference 38, 290
inflationary fixed point 132
Information 2, 3, 38, 92, 242, 290
information extraction (IE) 2, 3, 38, 92,
   290
information retrieval 242
Information System 290
Initially biggest radius 270
Integration 226
Intelligent Assistance 36, 233, 234, 290
Intelligent assistant systems (IAS) 67
IntelligentPad 145, 149, 170, 291
IntelligentPad architecture 170
Intelligent Tutoring System 264, 291
intelligent user interfaces (IUI) 146, 291
interaction object 135
Interaction Scenario 1, 291
interaction type 134
Interface 291
Interoperation 182, 292
invariance 127
Ising Model 252, 256
iteration 135

J

Judgment 64, 292

K

KAFTIE 86
kiviat 125
Kleene algebra with tests (KAT) 114
Knowledge 89, 99, 111, 237, 238, 242,
   292, 293
Knowledge Acquisition 292
knowledge acquisition 111

Knowledge Atom 238, 293
knowledge base (KB) 99, 111, 237, 242,
   293
knowledge based systems (KBS) 89
knowledge bases (KBs) 91, 105

L

Landmark 269, 293
LATEX 241
learner model 217, 293
Learning 24, 36, 221, 293, 294
Learning Algorithm 24, 294
Learning Object 221, 294
Learning Theory 36, 294
legacy applications 209, 294
Lemmatizer 98
lexicon 104
LExIKON 36
LExIKON system 9
Linguistic Analysis 242, 294
location-based ad hoc federation 183
Location-Based Federation 187, 294
location-based repository and lookup service system 187
location-dependent contexts 183
logic program 132, 154, 170, 295
logic programming 154, 170, 295
lookup service 183, 295

M

machine intelligence 8, 36, 295
machine learning 9
mArachna 241
mastoid 265
mastoidectomy 265
Matheon 235
MATLAB 174
media type 116, 135
Medium 296
Meme Media 149, 170, 183, 296
Meme Media Architecture 296
Meme Pool 21, 296
Metadata 221, 296
Metaphor 296
Metropolis Algorithm 255
Modality 71

model 64, 297
monotonicity 27, 298
Moses 235
MPMLPlayerPad 161
MuLF 235
Multimodal Presentation Markup Language (MPML) 145, 148, 298
Mumie 235, 236

N

naive Bayes 100
natural language processing 111, 298
navigation 218, 298
Nemesis 235
Nerve Probe 271
Neural Network 23, 300
node 193
non-hodgkin-lymphomas (NHL) 173
Nondisruptive feedback 276
notion 70, 300
NP 94, 101
NPList 94

O

OBJ (object) 94
Obligation 114, 123, 300
Oorange 255
operations 134
orchestration 185, 300
overall performance 2
overlay model 217

P

paradigmatic shift 212
parallelism 127
parallel process 122
Part-of-Speech Tagger 98
partitioner 242
performance model 273
Persistence 19, 301
personalization 128
Personalization Proof Obligations 139
Pervasive computing 185, 301
Phantom 301
plan 15, 19, 20, 30, 301, 302
Plan Execution 19, 20, 301

plan generation 15
Plan Monitoring 301
plan monitoring 19, 301
Planning 15, 16, 20, 302
Planning Assistant 16, 302
Planning Time 16, 302
Planning Tool 16, 302
Plan Revision 19, 301
plans 16
plot 121
positive attribution 105
post-guarded process 122
postcondition 127
PP (prepositional phrase) 94
precondition 120, 127
preference rule 126
preferences 127
Presentation Agent 147, 302
Presentation Style 218, 302
probability 65, 75, 302
Problem 302
Process 303
process model 224
Prolog 145, 154, 170, 303
propositional formulae 120
Proxy Object 201, 303

Q

Quality 71

R

RASP-wavelets (RAtional functions with Second-order Poles) 24
RecordPad 202
repository service 205, 303
right 115, 123, 304
Ripple down rules (RDR) 89, 304
role 115, 123, 304
rule formulation phase 108, 109
rule recommendation 101
Rule Suggestion Module (RSM) 101, 110

S

SAP solutions 46
SAP TREX 46
scanners 280

scenes 115, 118
SCRDR 90
script language JavaScript 159
search engine 35, 46, 304
self-controlled learning 232, 304
self-guided learning 247
semantic analysis 241, 242, 305
semantic information 80, 305
Semantic Model 306
semantic retrieval 235, 307
Semantic Tagger 98
Semantic Web 186, 307
Semi-Structured Document 1, 38, 307
Sentence Splitter 98
sentiment 88
Serialistic 258
Shallow Parser module 94, 99, 307
signature 135
Similarity Measure 101, 308
Simulation and computation components
      250
single classification ripple down rule
      (SCRDR) 90
Smallest radius 270
software assistants 256
source-view 193
special story space proof obligation 138
static consistency proof obligation 138
static constraint 138
statistical mechanics 237
stories 115
story algebra 121
storyboard 114, 257, 308
storyboarding 115
storyboards 257
story space 115
string 93
student model 273
SUB 103
SUB (subject) 94
Surgical Landmark 308
System 308
System Adaptivity 309

T

Task Model 271
tasks 115
teamwork 249
Technology Enhanced Learning 212, 309
technology provider 214
Temporal Bone Surgery 275, 310
Temporal Bone Surgery Simulator 275,
      310
Text-to-Speech (TTS) 159
text retrieval 37, 46
Textual Orientation 258
text understanding part 108, 109
theory-oriented 218
therapy plan generation 17, 21
Therapy Planning 17, 173, 310
Token 101
Token annotations 93
Tokenizer 98
tool 248
Training and tutorials 246
Transducer 288
TREX 49
Truth 65, 71, 310
tutoring mode 273
tutors 257
Two-Level Learning Algorithm 39, 311
type 94

U

underAnno 95
user-grid 125
User Adaptation 258, 311
user intention 128
User interfaces 251
User Model 311
user profiles 115, 124
user types 124

V

Verbal feedback 276
Verbally initiated dialog 276
verdictives 69
VG (verb groups) 94
VideoEasel 237

Virtual Assistant 311
Virtual Environment 267, 312
Virtual Knowledge Space 234, 312
Virtual Lab 235, 312
Virtual Laboratories Project 235
Virtual Trainer 275, 312
Visual feedback 277
voice 94
Voxel 312
VRML 313

W

Warning distance 270
wavelet networks 23
wavelet neural network 23
Web Application 146, 313

WebApplicationWrapperPad 153
Web information systems (WISs)
    114, 118, 313
Web Service 185, 313
wicked problem 19, 313
Wiki Piazza 204
Wiki service 188
WIS design 115
WIS personalization 114
wizards 256
World Wide Web 3
Wrapper 3, 38, 152, 313

X

XML format 159
XPath 153